The
Postdivorce
Family

The
Postdivorce
Family

Children,
Parenting,
and
Society

Ross A. Thompson
Paul R. Amato
Editors

SAGE Publications
International Educational and Professional Publisher
Thousand Oaks   London   New Delhi

For information:

SAGE Publications, Inc.
2455 Teller Road
Thousand Oaks, California 91320
E-mail: order@sagepub.com

SAGE Publications Ltd.
6 Bonhill Street
London EC2A 4PU
United Kingdom

SAGE Publications India Pvt. Ltd.
M-32 Market
Greater Kailash I
New Delhi 110 048 India

Printed in the United States of America

Library of Congress Cataloging-in-Publication Data

Main entry under title:

The postdivorce family: Children, parenting, and society / edited
by Ross A. Thompson, Paul R. Amato.
        p.   cm.
    Includes bibliographical references and index.
    ISBN 0-7619-1489-7 (cloth: acid-free paper)
    ISBN 0-7619-1490-0 (pbk.: acid-free paper)
    1. Divorce—United States—Psychological aspects—Congresses.
2. Children of divorced parents—United States—Congresses.
3. Divorced parents—United States—Congresses.   4. Family—United
States—Psychological aspects—Congresses.   5. Parenting
Part-time—United States—Congresses.   I. Thompson, Ross A.
II. Amato, Paul R.
    HQ834.P68   1999
    306.89—dc21   99-6018

        01   02   03   04   05   7   6   5   4   3   2

Acquiring Editor:	Jim Nageotte
Editorial Assistant:	Heidi Van Middlesworth
Production Editor:	Astrid Virding
Editorial Assistant:	Nevair Kabakian
Typesetter/Designer:	Marion Warren
Indexer:	Christina Haley
Cover Designer:	Candice Harman

Contents

Symposium Contributors

Paul R. Amato
Department of Sociology
University of Nebraska-Lincoln

Katharine T. Bartlett
School of Law
Duke University

Alan Booth
Department of Sociology
Pennsylvania State University

Robert E. Emery
Department of Psychology
Institute of Law, Psychiatry, and Public Policy
University of Virginia

Michael E. Lamb
Section on Social and Emotional Development
National Institute of Child Health and Human Development

Eleanor E. Maccoby
Department of Psychology
Stanford University

Daniel R. Meyer
School of Social Work
Institute for Research on Poverty
University of Wisconsin

Ross A. Thompson
Department of Psychology
University of Nebraska-Lincoln

Jennifer Wyatt
Department of Psychology
University of Nebraska-Lincoln

Acknowledgments

This volume, and the symposium on which it is based, had many contributors besides the authors of the papers. We are grateful to Professor Brian Foster, Dean of the College of Arts and Sciences at the University of Nebraska-Lincoln, for his financial support of the Family Research and Policy Initiative, a multidisciplinary consortium of faculty with interests in child and family research and its policy implications. Funding for the consortium provided support for the symposium on which this volume is based. We are also grateful to the faculty and staff of the Center on Children, Families, and the Law, and its Director, Dr. Brian Wilcox, for assistance in planning and organization. Thanks to Lori Anderson, Glenn Cacek, Julia Phillips, Shelly Sorensen, and Laura White for helping us to arrange the many details of the symposium. Our colleagues Lisa Crockett (of the Department of Psychology) and Lynn White (of the Department of Sociology) served as discussants at the symposium, and their comments contributed to the lively exchange of ideas that are reflected in the chapters of this volume.

We have personal debts as well. Paul Amato would like to thank Stacy Rogers for her humor, warmth, and practical assistance with the symposium and the subsequent volume. Ross Thompson owes a debt to Janet Thompson and to his sons, Scott and Brian, for their persistent reminders of life's good purposes.

Ross A. Thompson
Paul R. Amato
Lincoln, Nebraska

The Postdivorce Family

An Introduction to the Issues

Ross A. Thompson

Paul R. Amato

Divorce touches the life of virtually every person. About one half of all marriages currently are projected to end in divorce (Cherlin, 1992), and about 40% of all children will experience the divorce of their parents before they reach adulthood (Bumpass, 1984). But even people who have not directly experienced divorce are likely to know of friends, relatives, or coworkers whose marriages ended in divorce, or who grew up in families where divorce occurred. They are likely to think of their own marriages differently because of the very real possibility that divorce may happen to them. Marital dissolution, once considered to be a rare, unfortunate, and somewhat shameful deviation from normal family life, has become part of mainstream America. And many family scholars, cultural critics, and policymakers believe that the increased acceptance—indeed, expectation—of divorce in American family life has led to fundamental changes in marital commitments and responsibility to children that work to the detriment of society.

Divorce, however, does not bring an end to the family. Most children maintain relationships with both parents after divorce even while their family networks may expand to incorporate stepparents and, sometimes, stepsiblings. Most parents find, sometimes to their surprise, that although they expected to make a clean break with their spouse, they have continuing obligations to their offspring that keep them connected to their children's other parent. These obligations remain even if they become remarried and create a new family. An increasing number of children are, in short, growing up in a new kind of family: the postdivorce family.

The norms and expectations for the traditional American family are institutionalized in custom, tradition, and legal policy, but social norms for the postdivorce family are vague and are continuing to evolve. During the process of divorce, of course, parents must decide about where their children will live, how much contact children will have with each parent, the economic responsibilities of each parent to their offspring, and other obligations and privileges of parenting. But these initial decisions create only the scaffolding for postdivorce family life. In the years that follow, noncustodial fathers may visit regularly or infrequently, and may or may not maintain fidelity to their child support obligations, as their lives become increasingly distant from offspring. Custodial mothers may remarry, move to a new part of the country with the children, or experience other life changes that directly affect other family members. Former spouses may be capable of cooperating congenially, or instead battle adversarily, in ways that profoundly influence the well-being of their offspring. The ways that children adjust to marital separation is both a result of how successfully the family has negotiated the transition to postdivorce life, and an important influence on its future. There are no clear societal guidelines, or expectations, about how parents and offspring should live after divorce. And although many (perhaps most) families experience these profound changes as intensely personal concerns, they occur against a backdrop of public policies that are meant to support family members, especially children, in postdivorce life. But there are increasing questions about how well such policies accomplish this goal. Does divorce policy adequately provide for children's economic well-being after divorce? Does it foster the conditions that enable both parents to maintain meaningful parenting roles in the lives of their offspring? Should policies be changed to better enfranchise fathers in the postdivorce family, support the custodial parent, or discourage divorce altogether when children are part of a marriage? Legal scholars, policymakers, and individual parents are each struggling to determine the rights and responsibilities of both parents after divorce.

Children are the focus of these concerns. An emphasis on the well-being of children reflects their vulnerability to the significant changes in family life that follow divorce and the realization that they are least responsible for, and accepting of, the changes that occur. But concern for children derives also from research evidence that divorce has important costs for them. Americans have rarely been sanguine about the effects of divorce on children, but current research reveals that balanced against the benefits that might derive from the end of their parents' conflicted marriage, children often pay the price of a significantly reduced standard of living, emotional pain, and the loss of important parenting relationships in the immediate aftermath of divorce. These costs may be transient or enduring, but they nevertheless justify the efforts of social researchers and policymakers to discover how the conditions of postdivorce family life can be made more supportive of children's long-term psychological health and happiness.

This volume is based on a symposium on postdivorce family life at the University of Nebraska-Lincoln in the spring of 1997. The symposium was sponsored by the Family Research and Policy Initiative, a multidisciplinary consortium of faculty with interests in child and family research and its policy implications. The purpose of the symposium was to bring together experts from psychology, sociology, law, social welfare, and other fields to address issues related to divorce, children's well-being, and public policy. Our goal was to promote interdisciplinary thinking and crossdisciplinary dialogue on family life after marital separation, with special attention to the mutual influence of social research and public policy. The presentations at the symposium were provocative, the discussions were lively (often continuing long after the conclusion of the formal sessions), and although many questions were addressed, new ones were continuously posed by presenters, discussants, and audience members. Students in a graduate seminar that was conducted concurrently with the symposium provided additional ideas for thought and reflection. After the symposium, each of the contributors prepared chapters for this volume based on their presentations, the discussions of the symposium, our suggestions, and further development of their own ideas.

The themes of this volume, like those of the symposium on which it is based, are the issues that currently inspire some of the most important research, analysis, and debate concerning divorce and its consequences. For each theme, there are contributions from two scholars who approach the topic from different disciplinary perspectives. Each contributor offers perspectives from empirical research as well as policy perspectives.

In Part I, the contributors focus on the consequences of divorce for children, considering the benefits but also the costs to offspring of marital dissolution, and how to best conceptualize the factors that enhance their gains and reduce their pain. This discussion provides an essential foundation to considering how policy reform can enable the postdivorce family to better support the children in its care, because understanding how the consequences of divorce are mediated by the conditions of family life offers potential avenues to improving children's postdivorce well-being. In Part II, the emphasis is on parental responsibility after divorce, with particular concern for policies and practices of child custody and noncustodial visitation that help to shape postdivorce family life. Each of the contributors to this section of the book struggle with how best to define the standards allocating parental care after divorce, and to ensure that each parent can maintain a satisfactory postdivorce relationship with offspring.

Part III focuses on nonresidential parenting, with special emphasis on the experience of fathers and the factors that influence the frequency of their contact with offspring and the reliability of their child support payments after divorce. These are important determinants of postdivorce parenting for nonresidential parents (they define the quality of care for nonresidential mothers and fathers alike; see Thompson & Laible, 1999), and each has also been the topic of considerable public policy debate in recent years. The emphasis of this section on fatherhood is not meant to neglect the experience of mothers who commonly are custodial parents in postdivorce life, but the multifaceted influences on postdivorce mothering are considered in other chapters in this volume and have also been extensively discussed in other forums (e.g., Arendell, 1986; Bartlett, 1984, 1988; Fineman, 1991; Maccoby & Mnookin, 1992; Weitzman, 1985). Finally, in Part IV, the concern is with divorce and society, and how life in a culture with high divorce rates affects marital expectations, kinship ties, and social institutions. This, too, has been the topic of considerable recent public debate, and our chapters in this section attempt to shed light on these important and contentious issues.

As the chapters of this volume indicate, although there is much that we do not understand about postdivorce family life, a coherent body of research findings has emerged with relevance to divorce policy. For nearly three decades, in fact, social scientists have been studying the impact of divorce and its consequences for children's well-being. Our aim in the symposium, and in this volume, is to provide a forum for analysis and reflection on this information and its implications for public policy.

The Creation of Postdivorce Family Life

The postdivorce family has its origins before parents have divorced, even before they have begun to contemplate marital separation. It begins with the quality of marriage that shapes how children experience family life and subsequently cope with divorce. Considerable research shows that children's postdivorce adjustment is significantly influenced by the conditions of predivorce family life, such as the frequency and intensity of marital conflict, that underlie the stresses and pleasures that children experience in the family and the psychological resources that accompany children through the process of divorce (Block, Block, & Gjerde, 1986; Cherlin, Furstenberg, Chase-Lansdale, Kiernan, Robins, Morrison, & Teitler, 1991; Emery, 1982). Many of the problems that children exhibit in the years following marital dissolution may arise, in fact, from family problems preceding divorce—and these problems often continue after divorce. Predivorce marital life may have an equally profound effect on children's adjustment by shaping their expectations for the future. Alan Booth describes in this volume how children from low-conflict and high-conflict families experience marital dissolution much differently, with children from the former group becoming more distressed because divorce forces a jarring reconsideration of their parents' marriage and their expectations for how family life will continue (see also Amato & Booth, 1997). Research studies like these remind us that although our analysis often begins with divorce as the precipitant for children's later adjustment, all children experience divorce in the context of their previous experience of the family.

The same is true of their parents. Because men and women experience marriage differently, they approach divorce with different expectations and concerns (Bernard, 1972; Emery, 1994; Hetherington & Tryon, 1989). Women often report anticipating the end of marriage long before discussing divorce with their spouses, and they are the more frequent initiators of divorce (Goode, 1956; Kitson, 1992; Spanier & Thompson, 1984). This gender difference probably reflects the fact that women tend to monitor the status and quality of their personal relationships more closely than do men (Thompson & Walker, 1990). By the time the process of divorce begins, they are ready to move on with their lives. But worries over their financial condition can keep many women in unhappy marriages. For men, in contrast, divorce more often comes as an unexpected step and is accompanied by worries over losing contact with offspring (Hetherington & Stanley-Hagan, 1986, 1997). They may resist negotiations over divorce and custody until they have accepted the fact that the marriage has, for all intents and purposes, ended. Both adults are likely to experience anger, bitterness, and feelings of loss and regret to varying degrees, but for somewhat different reasons. Men and women therefore enter divorce differently because of the different readiness and expectations that accompany marital dissolution.

Like their children, men and women arrive at divorce with a family history that guides the postdivorce roles they will assume. For most couples, the mother's physical custody of offspring and the father's noncustodial parenting role are the natural consequences of their child rearing responsibilities during marriage (Maccoby, 1995; Thompson, 1994). Because mothers are primary caregivers in the large majority of families, whether they work outside the home or not, it is unsurprising that although an increasing number of couples share legal custody of their offspring after divorce, between 85% and 90% of children live primarily with their mothers (Fox & Kelly, 1995; Kelly, 1994; Meyer & Garasky, 1993). In the vast majority of cases, these represent the consensual decisions of couples as they negotiate the parameters of postdivorce life. In her chapter, Eleanor Maccoby reports interviews from the Stanford Custody Study to illustrate the efforts of parents to craft caregiving arrangements after divorce that will maintain continuity in care for their offspring, a goal that is shared by policymakers who write the legal standards for custody decisions (see also Maccoby & Mnookin, 1992).

Yet these parenting arrangements may be troubling to the children whose future lives they shape. Within the traditional "winner take all" format of custody negotiations, mothers may win the children but rapidly become over-burdened by the demands of juggling full-time employment, child-rearing needs, enhanced domestic responsibilities, and other tasks that were formerly shared with a spouse. The quality of parenting declines during the years immediately following divorce as custodial parents struggle to manage the demands of single parenting (Emery, 1998; Hetherington, Cox, & Cox, 1982). Even more disconcerting for children—the large majority of whom want to maintain continuing relationships with both parents (Hetherington, Stanley-Hagan, & Anderson, 1989; Wallerstein & Kelly, 1980)—is the fact that fathers often gradually disappear from their children's world. Although visitation may be high during the first year after divorce, during each subsequent year noncustodial fathers tend to visit less frequently (Furstenberg & Nord, 1985; Kelly, 1994; Maccoby, Buchanan, Mnookin, & Dornbusch, 1993; Seltzer, 1991). In his chapter, Michael Lamb argues that this decline derives, at least in part, from the artificiality of a visiting relationship that deprives fathers of the opportunity to maintain a meaningful parenting role in the lives of children (see also Thompson & Laible, 1999). Regardless of the reason, the result is that children experience not only the breakup of their families, but also the eventual loss of one parent.

Family scholars are, as a consequence, pondering how the conditions of postdivorce family life can be changed to foster active parenting by both mothers and fathers. Proposals for policy reform include (1) mandatory nego-tiation of parenting plans by which mothers and fathers must agree about their continuing obligations to offspring after divorce, (2) predivorce counseling or classes to encourage parents to focus on the needs of offspring in their plans for postdivorce life, and (3) changing the terms defining postdivorce parenting to reduce perceptions that some parents "win" while other parents "lose" access to offspring (see Chapter 4 by Bartlett in this volume; see also Emery, 1994). To be sure, the formal arrangements for custody and visitation that parents negotiate neglect the extent to which de facto changes occur over time in the child rearing responsibilities of each parent because of changing life circumstances (such as remarriage, job change, or residential relocation), temporary needs, and the developmentally evolving preferences of offspring (Buchanan, Maccoby, & Dornbusch, 1996; Maccoby & Mnookin, 1992). Yet these formal arrangements, limited as they are, are important because they define the initial parameters of postdivorce parenting.

Child custody and visitation are not the only issues of divorce negotiation. Parents remain financially responsible for their offspring, and this is also a shared responsibility. Because men are usually financially advantaged after divorce because of the career assets they have developed during marriage, their fidelity to their child support obligations determines the economic well-being of their children. Society's recognition of the importance of this obligation was one of the themes of policy reform in the 1980s, when media images of the "deadbeat dad" led to passage of the Family Support Act of 1988, which strengthened enforcement procedures for the child support obligations of noncustodial parents. Yet as Dan Meyer notes in Chapter 6 in this volume, an unwillingness to pay child support is only one of several reasons why fathers may fail to comply. In other cases, fathers simply may be unable to pay child support, or their fidelity to child support awards may depend on the strength of their family ties or their perception of the need for child support (such as when the mother remarries). Because each of the causes of nonpayment has different implications for public policy, more diverse and creative policy initiatives may be needed to ensure that children are adequately supported in postdivorce life (see also Garfinkel, McLanahan, Seltzer, & Meyer, in press).

Child support is the most important but not the only means of financially supporting children. Glendon (1981, 1986) has argued that a "children-first principle" should guide the allocation of marital property in divorce, ensuring that no property is divided between former spouses until allocations have been made to ensure that children's needs are met. More broadly, revised concepts of marital property that include the intangible "career assets" of the noncustodial parent have been proposed to further protect the economic well-being of mothers and their children after divorce. Taken together, they indicate that even under the new regime of child support enforcement, defining and ensuring the financial obligations of each parent after divorce can be complicated. Adding complexity to this equation is the fact that public attitudes are changing toward the public support of economically distressed children, such as those from single parent homes, reflected in welfare reform and other measures. As a consequence, the social safety net for children is rapidly eroding.

Beyond defining economic and child rearing responsibilities, perhaps the most difficult (and certainly the most intangible) facet of divorce negotiations concerns establishing a new postdivorce relationship between parents. This often comes as a surprise to divorcing spouses, especially those who are highly motivated to begin a new life independently of a former marital partner. Yet when children are involved, responsible ex-spouses must continue to work with each other when consulting about visitation arrangements during vacations, financial responsibility for special needs (such as medical or dental costs), and events in the child's life that require their cooperation (such as graduation and marriage). Moreover, continuing consultation between ex-spouses is even more necessary when they share legal custody of offspring and must regularly discuss educational decisions, health and medical care, insurance, and many other matters. Consequently, divorce negotiations set the stage for the postdivorce family in the framework they create (or neglect to create) for constructive consultation between two adults who are no longer married, but who remain the parents of their offspring.

When these negotiations are successful, they can result in formal or informal arrangements that clearly define parental expectations, anticipate adjustments that may be needed as children mature and parents' living circumstances change, and clarify means for resolving disputes that occur unexpectedly or are difficult to negotiate (for example see Bruch, 1978, and Kelly, 1993). Even when this occurs, however, constructive postdivorce parenting requires considerable personal effort to overcome the lingering feelings of anger and betrayal that often follow divorce, and cooperate for the sake of the children. Some former spouses abdicate their responsibilities to offspring by avoiding interaction (and potential conflict) with each other as the noncustodial parent gradually becomes an absent figure in the child's life, sometimes with the tacit assistance of the custodial parent. When this occurs, children are the losers. There is some evidence that the initial 2 years following divorce constitute a particularly crucial period for the development of positive patterns of parenting after marital separation (Thompson & Laible, 1999). But social norms and expectations for the postdivorce family have not yet evolved sufficiently to create the incentives necessary for the reliable negotiation of a constructive postdivorce relationship between ex-spouses, perhaps because of the continuing value placed on enabling each adult to make a fresh start after marital dissolution. This remains one of the thorniest dilemmas of postdivorce family life, and this dilemma is deepened by the consistent research findings that parental cooperation or acrimony is one of the most important predictors of children's adjustment (Cummings & Davies, 1994; Emery, 1982; Grych & Fincham, 1990).

In this light, it might be expected that children emerge from divorce with a mixture of psychological bruises and scars. In most circumstances, they adapt to divorce, showing resiliency, not dysfunction, in the face of the emotionally wrenching personal adjustments required of them (Amato, 1993, 1994; Amato & Keith, 1991a, 1991b; Emery, 1998). Yet as Robert Emery notes, children of divorce also show lingering psychological pain that is rarely clinically noteworthy, but personally significant. They often perceive their parents' divorce as an important, and negative, turning point in their lives. Yet even this portrayal of the effects of divorce on children is incomplete, because the individual differences in children's adjustment are notable. While some children emerge from divorce with a strong sense of loss and feelings of anger or despair, others are capable of acknowledging that divorce has pain but also benefits for themselves and other family members. What determines whether children are scathed or strengthened through the process of divorce? Not surprisingly, these circumstances are the central qualities of postdivorce family life: the nature of the child's relationship with the custodial parent (and that parent's psychological health and adjustment), the quality of the child's relationship with the noncustodial parent, the extent of conflict between these adults, the number of additional stressors that accompany and follow marital separation, and the economic circumstances of the child's household (Amato, 1993, 1994; see Chapters 1 and 2 in this volume). To a great extent, children's well-being in the postdivorce family remains intertwined with the psychological and economic conditions of other family members.

Some family scholars believe, however, that this is an unduly narrow view. Divorce has broader consequences not only for children, but also for the society in which they are growing up. For many children, divorce radically changes family life and their understanding of parenting, gender roles, and the marital relationships that will be part of their future. Divorce may be a prelude to a stepfamily and the creation of a new network of family relationships. For society as a whole, as Paul Amato notes in Chapter 7 in this volume, divorce has equally significant implications for gender equity (especially in economic terms), intergenerational relations, and cultural values concerning marital integrity and family relationships. These societal outcomes have the potential of influencing us all. In a sense, the growing frequency and increasing acceptance of the postdivorce family means that Americans are entering into a postdivorce *society* in which the realities of divorce affect broader social institutions and our views of ourselves in relation to others.

Interpreting the meaning of the emerging postdivorce society has become one of the most important policy debates of the 1990s. Although policy reform of the past two decades has predicated efforts to improve the conditions of single mothers and their children on an acceptance of the social realities of the current high rate of divorce, some scholars are asking whether public policy should instead be oriented toward reducing divorce and affirming marriage and fidelity to child rearing (e.g., Council on Families in America, 1995; Popenoe, 1996; Whitehead, 1997). In this emergent view, family law has a powerfully hortatory influence as an enunciation of consensual social values. With respect to marriage and divorce, they argue, law reforms of the past several decades (most notably the universal advent of no-fault divorce in America) have inadvertently contributed to the progressive deinstitutionalization of marriage and the widespread acceptance of marital dissolution. Yet the costs of divorce to children should motivate a reconsideration of whether this is the proper direction for public policy, they argue, and one result of this reassessment—the Covenant Marriage Law recently adopted in Louisiana—is profiled by Ross Thompson and Jennifer Wyatt in Chapter 8 in this volume as an illustration of the current debate over divorce and family values. This debate arises because of how social values concerning the family are institutionalized, explicitly or implicitly, in the policies and procedures governing marital dissolution.

The postdivorce family is created in the conditions of family life before divorce, shaped in the decisions over child custody, visitation, economic support, and other parameters of divorce negotiations, consolidated in the ways that mothers and fathers craft their lives—and their relationships with each other and with offspring—in the years following marital dissolution, and framed by public policies that are designed to achieve broad (sometimes inconsistent) goals for families and children. The most complex and personal conditions of family life are forged by public policies meant to shape society at large. Efforts to ensure that such policies benefit, rather than undermine, postdivorce family life are founded on research and its insights into the experience of children and other family members throughout the process of divorce. The mutual contributions of research and policy to improving the conditions of family life constitute the basis for this collection of papers.

CONCLUSION

As these contributions exemplify, divorce has both immediate consequences for family members and broader outcomes for society. In drawing attention to the importance of the postdivorce family, our goal is to encourage more thoughtful public policy concerning divorce that will contribute to strengthened family functioning and, hopefully, improved well-being for the children whose lives are changed by their parents' divorce. Ultimately, however, the achievement of this goal depends on the emergence of a societal consensus that although divorce may end a marriage, it does not end the family. Parental responsibilities to children survive divorce, and thus the postdivorce family merits the concerned attention of family scholars, policymakers, and the rest of us.

REFERENCES

Amato, P. R. (1993). Children's adjustment to divorce: Theories, hypotheses, and empirical support. *Journal of Marriage and the Family, 55,* 23-38.

Amato, P. R. (1994). Life-span adjustment of children to their parents' divorce. *The Future of Children, 4,* 143-164.

Amato, P. R., & Booth, A. (1997). *A generation at risk: Growing up in an era of family upheaval.* Cambridge, MA: Harvard University Press.

Amato, P. R., & Keith, B. (1991a). Parental divorce and the well-being of children: A meta-analysis. *Psychological Bulletin, 100,* 26-46.

Amato, P. R., & Keith, B. (1991b). Parental divorce and adult well-being: A meta-analysis. *Journal of Marriage and the Family, 53,* 43-58.

Arendell, T. (1986). *Mothers and divorce: Legal, economic, and social dilemmas.* Berkeley, CA: University of California Press.

Bartlett, K. T. (1984). Rethinking parenthood as an exclusive status: The need for legal alternatives when the premise of the nuclear family has failed. *Virginia Law Review, 70,* 879-963.

Bartlett, K. T. (1988). Re-expressing parenthood. *Yale Law Journal, 98,* 293-340.

Bernard, J. (1972). *The future of marriage.* New York: World.

Block, J. H., Block, J., & Gjerde, P. F. (1986). The personality of children prior to divorce: A prospective study. *Child Development, 57,* 827-840.

Bruch, C. S. (1978, Summer). Making visitation work: Dual parenting orders. *Family Advocate,* pp. 22-26, 41-42.

Buchanan, C. M., Maccoby, E. E., & Dornbusch, S. M. (1996). *Adolescents after divorce*. Cambridge, MA: Harvard University Press.

Bumpass, L. L. (1984). Children and marital disruption: A replication and update. *Demography, 21,* 71-82.

Cherlin, A. J. (1992). *Marriage, divorce, remarriage* (Rev. ed.). Cambridge, MA: Harvard University Press.

Cherlin, A. J., Furstenberg, F. F., Jr., Chase-Lansdale, P. L., Kiernan, K. E., Robins, P. K., Morrison, D. R., & Teitler, J. O. (1991). Longitudinal studies of the effects of divorce on children in Great Britain and the United States. *Science, 252,* 299-318.

Council on Families in America (1995). *Marriage in America: A report to the nation.* New York: Instiute for American Values.

Cummings, E. M., & Davies, P. (1994). *Children and marital conflict: The impact of family dispute and resolution.* New York: Guilford.

Emery, R. E. (1982). Interparental conflict and the children of discord and divorce. *Psychological Bulletin, 92,* 310-330.

Emery, R. E. (1994). *Renegotiating family relationships: Divorce, child custody, and mediation.* New York: Guilford.

Emery, R. E. (1998). *Marriage, divorce, and children's adjustment* (Rev. ed.). Thousand Oaks, CA: Sage.

Fineman, M. A. (1991). *The illusion of equality: Rhetoric and the reality of divorce reform.* Chicago: University of Chicago Press.

Fox, G. L., & Kelly, R. F. (1995). Determinants of child custody arrangements at divorce. *Journal of Marriage and the Family, 57,* 693-708.

Furstenberg, F. F., Jr., & Nord, C. W. (1985). Parenting apart: Patterns of childrearing after marital disruption. *Journal of Marriage and the Family, 47,* 898-904.

Garfinkel, I., McLanahan, S., Seltzer, S., & Meyer, D. R. (Eds.). (in press). *Fathers under fire.* New York: Russell Sage Foundation.

Glendon, M. A. (1981). *The new family and the new property.* Toronto, Canada: Butterworth.

Glendon, M. A. (1986). Fixed rules and discretion in contemporary family law and succession law. *Tulane Law Review, 60,* 1165-1205.

Goode, W. J. (1956). *After divorce.* Glencoe, IL: Free Press.

Grych, J. H., & Fincham, F. D. (1990). Marital conflict and children's adjustment: A cognitive-contextual framework. *Psychological Bulletin, 108,* 267-290.

Hetherington, E. M., Cox, M., & Cox, R. (1982). Effects of divorce on parents and children. In M. E. Lamb (Ed.), *Nontraditional families* (pp. 223-288). Hillsdale, NJ: Erlbaum.

Hetherington, E. M., & Stanley-Hagan, M. M. (1986). Divorced fathers: Stress, coping, and adjustment. In M. E. Lamb (Ed.), *The father's role: Applied perspectives* (pp. 103-134). New York: Wiley.

Hetherington, E. M., & Stanley-Hagan, M. M. (1997). The effects of divorce on fathers and their children. In M. E. Lamb (Ed.), *The role of the father in child development* (3rd ed., pp. 191-211). New York: Wiley.

Hetherington, E. M., Stanley-Hagan, M., & Anderson, E. R. (1989). Marital transitions: A child's perspective. *American Psychologist, 44,* 303-312.

Hetherington, E. M., & Tryon, A. S. (1989, November/December). His and her divorces. *The Family Therapy Networker,* pp. 1-16.

Kelly, J. B. (1993). Developing and implementing postdivorce parenting plans. In C. Depner & J. Bray (Eds.), *Nonresidential parenting: New vistas in family living.* Newbury Park, CA: Sage.

Kelly, J. B. (1994). The determination of child custody. *The Future of Children, 4,* 121-142.

Kitson, G. C. (1992). *Portrait of divorce: Adjustment to marital breakdown.* New York: Guilford.

Maccoby, E. E. (1995). Divorce and custody: The rights, needs, and obligations of mothers, fathers, and children. In G. B. Melton (Ed.), *The individual, the family, and social good: Personal fulfillment in times of change.* Nebraska Symposium on Motivation (Vol. 42, pp. 135-172). Lincoln, NE: University of Nebraska Press.

Maccoby, E. E., Buchanan, C. M., Mnookin, R. H., & Dornbusch, S. M. (1993). Postdivorce roles of mothers and fathers in the lives of their children. *Journal of Family Psychology, 7,* 24-38.

Maccoby, E. E., & Mnookin, R. H. (1992). *Dividing the child: Social and legal dilemmas of custody.* Cambridge, MA: Harvard University Press.

Meyer, D. R., & Garasky, S. (1993). Custodial fathers: Myths, realities, and child support policy. *Journal of Marriage and the Family, 55,* 73-89.

Popenoe, D. (1996). *Life without father.* New York: Free Press.

Seltzer, J. A. (1991). Relationships between fathers and children who live apart: The father's role after separation. *Journal of Marriage and the Family, 53,* 79-101.

Spanier, G. B., & Thompson, L. (1984). *Parting: The aftermath of separation and divorce.* Beverly Hills, CA: Sage.

Thompson, L., & Walker, A. J. (1990). Gender in families: Women and men in marriage, work, and parenthood. In A. Booth (Ed.), *Contemporary families: Looking forward, looking back* (pp. 76-102). Minneapolis, MN: National Council on Family Relations.

Thompson, R. A. (1994). The role of the father after divorce. *The Future of Children, 4,* 210-235.

Thompson, R. A., & Laible, D. J. (1999). Noncustodial parents. In M. E. Lamb (Ed.), *Nontraditional families* (pp. 103-123). Hillsdale, NJ: Erlbaum.

Wallerstein, J. S., & Kelly, J. B. (1980). *Surviving the breakup: How children and parents cope with divorce.* New York: Basic Books.

Weitzman, L. J. (1985). *The divorce revolution.* New York: Free Press.

Whitehead, B. D. (1997). *The divorce culture.* New York: Knopf.

PART I

The Consequences of Divorce for Children

Any effort to understand the postdivorce family must begin with the consequences of divorce for family members. Mothers, fathers, and children are each changed by the experience of divorce, but for several reasons greatest concern is devoted to the effects of divorce on children. Children are least responsible for the upheaval they experience when their parents part and are, in most respects, most vulnerable to the emotional pain and other difficulties that accompany the end of marriage. They are likely to be least understanding and accepting of the loss of relationships that divorce can mean for them. Moreover, an accurate and sensitive assessment of the consequences of divorce for children is required for thoughtful policy reform intended to strengthen the postdivorce family. In the past, changes in divorce policy have often been predicated on revised assessments of its impact on children, and the same is true today. However, accurately understanding the impact of divorce on children is not an easy task—nor is discerning its implications for policy reform.

In the opening chapter of this section, Robert Emery discusses the nature of postdivorce family life for children. Understanding the outcomes of divorce for children is a more difficult task than one might expect because of the tendency, in the past, either to dismiss the costs of divorce to children (by those emphasizing the liberating benefits of divorce) or exaggerate its harms (by contemporary critics of no-fault divorce). Instead, Emery offers a more realistic, and nuanced, portrayal of the consequences of divorce by underscoring that (a) children experience multiple stressors associated with marital dissolution but most are impressively resilient in their coping, (b) resiliency does not mean that they are invulnerable to the psychological pain that accompanies divorce, and (c) individual differences in adjustment provide an important perspective on how children's coping is influenced by the quality of the relationships they share with each parent, and the economic hardships that often accompany marital dissolution. His conclusions lead to policy recommendations that emphasize the importance of parents recognizing children's needs and interests in postdivorce life—which is, ironically, the same quality that contributes to children's well-being in maritally intact homes.

In the next chapter, Alan Booth complements this analysis by offering his own assessment of the causes of the changing divorce rate in the current century, and the consequences of these changes, especially for children. Booth emphasizes some surprising findings yielded by recent research, such as the discovery that children from high-conflict and low-conflict marriages differ significantly in their adjustment to divorce. It is unsurprising that children from maritally conflicted homes improve after marital dissolution, but the realization that children from low-conflict homes—which constitute the majority of divorcing couples—suffer more than those from high-conflict families highlight the special difficulties posed by having to cope with the unexpected and unwelcomed news that parents have decided to part. The reasons that divorce can have intergenerational consequences and the influence of multiple (sometimes overlapping) postdivorce family transitions add further complexity to this portrayal of children's adjustment to divorce. This leads Booth to an outline of future research needs, and to reflections on how counseling and other efforts to assist children's coping with the sometimes jarring effects of divorce might promote greater long-term well-being.

Chapter 1

Postdivorce Family Life for Children

An Overview of Research and Some Implications for Policy

Robert E. Emery

This chapter offers an overview of research on postdivorce family life and some implications for policy with an emphasis on children's well-being. In the present context, children's well-being is defined broadly to include not only indices of children's "adjustment" (e.g., mental health, educational attainment), but also measures of children's more subtle psychological distress (e.g., doubts about parental love) as well as of their family relationships and economic standing. Therefore, this chapter includes some evidence on the circumstances of mothers and fathers following divorce, but the presentation is limited to those aspects of mothers' and fathers' individual adjustment, parenting, and coparenting that are of greatest importance to children's well-being.

The chapter makes five main points about children's well-being following divorce. First, divorce creates a number of stressors for children and families, such as separation from and loss of contact with one parent; potentially troubled relationships with each parent; and involvement in conflict between both parents. Divorce also causes considerable financial hardship for children, families, and society, and in fact, the economic consequences of divorce (and nonmarital childbearing) often form the underlying, if unstated, motivation behind various policy reforms or proposals for reform. The financial motivation is to reduce welfare rolls, since, for example, about 90% of children receiving Aid to Families with Dependent Children (AFDC) live with a single parent but have a second living parent (National Instititute for Child Support Enforcement, 1986). Fewer families would qualify for AFDC if child support awards were higher and compliance with payments was better, and especially if there were fewer single-parent families.

Second, the stressors associated with divorce can lead to adjustment problems among children, as evidence makes it clear that divorce is a risk factor for a number of children's social, psychological, and educational or occupational difficulties. Third, despite the increase in risk, *resilience* is the normative outcome of divorce for children, that is, most children from divorced families function as well as children from married families on various commonly used indices of their adjustment. Fourth, there nevertheless appear to be some more subtle costs of coping with divorce for children. Most children are resilient, but they experience and express much subclinical distress or "pain" about their past, present, and future in relation to their parents' divorce.

Fifth and finally, there are important individual differences in the psychological adjustment of children following a parental divorce and many differences are attributable to postdivorce family relationships, especially: (a) the quality of children's relationship with their residential parent, (b) the degree and manner in which conflict is expressed between parents, (c) the family's economic standing, and (d) the children's contact and relationship with the nonresidential parent. These four factors are listed in decreasing order of their importance for children's psychological adjustment, according to the author's reading of the literature. However, it should be noted at the outset that some consequences of divorce that commonly are viewed as stressors (e.g., poverty) are important *outcomes* in their own right, irrespective of their relation with measures of children's psychological adjustment. That is, individual parents, and society as a whole, do not want children to grow up in the poverty that can result from divorce even if poverty is marginally or unrelated to children's psychological adjustment. Furthermore, it is important to note again that "psychological adjustment" is not the same as the absence of "distress" or "pain." Some problems in the postdivorce family (e.g., troubled relationships with fathers) appear to be a considerable source of distress for children despite their relatively weak relations with measures of children's psychological disturbance or academic standing.

Chapter 1 is intended to be a selective overview of research findings. The chapter particularly highlights evidence based on large, often nationally representative, samples of children or families. The author has offered more detailed reviews of the extensive research literature on divorce elsewhere (Emery, 1998), as have a number of other reviewers (Amato & Keith, 1991a; Hetherington, Bridges, & Insabella, 1998). Thus, the studies reviewed in this chapter illustrate rather than summarize this larger body of research and some of the policy implications that can be drawn from the empirical findings.

DIVORCE AND FAMILY STRUCTURE IN THE UNITED STATES

In order to understand research and policy, it is important to gain some perspective on the broader context of divorce. The most concrete evidence on the historical and current context of divorce comes from demographic data. Although there is considerable debate about the moral, cultural, and economic factors that underlie demographic trends, a number of demographic facts are clear. Divorce rates in the United States have been rising steadily since the time of the Civil War with decelerations occuring during the Great Depression and the 1950s and accelerations following World War II (very briefly) and during the 1960s and 1970s. Divorce rates peaked around 1980 and have remained relatively stable (with a slight decline) since that time (Burns & Scott, 1994; Cherlin, 1992; Hernandez, 1993).

There are numerous ways to summarize the current rate of divorce. One valuable and accurate statistic is the projection that, based on historical trends, about 50% of the first marriages of "Baby Boomers" will end in divorce, as will 40% of the first marriages of "Generation X" (U.S. Census Bureau, 1992). In terms of the experience of children, Bumpass (1984) has predicted 38% of all white and 75% of all black children born to married parents will experience a parental divorce before the age of 16.

Nonmarital Childbirth

The qualification, "born to married parents," is an important one as rates of nonmarital childbirth have increased greatly in the United States, particularly from the 1960s through the 1980s (Ventura, Clarke, & Mathews, 1996). The rate of nonmarital childbirth seems to have stabilized during the 1990s, about a decade later than the stabilization of the rate of divorce, but both rates remain on a high plateau. In 1996, 32.4% of all births in the United States occurred outside of marriage, including 25.7% of all births to white mothers, 40.9% of births to Hispanic mothers (of any race), and 69.8% of births to African American mothers (Ventura, Peters, Martin, & Maurer, 1997).

**Contemporary Family Status
and Differences by Ethnicity**

Taken together, divorce and nonmarital childbirth have had dramatic effects on the family living circumstances of children. Of all children who lived with a parent in 1994, 72.1% lived with two parents, 24.5% lived with a mother only, and 3.4% lived with a father only (U.S. Census Bureau, 1996). However, there are major and important subgroups within single- and two-parent families, and there are equal or more important variations between major ethnic groups in all family structures. The best estimates indicate that over 11% of children live with a stepparent, most commonly a stepfather (U.S. Census Bureau, 1992). (Other children in two-parent families live with adoptive parents.) We can estimate based on 1994 census data that although 72.1% of U.S. children resided with two parents, only 58.8% lived with their *biological* mother and father including 66.9% of white children, 23.4% of black children, and 54.0% of Hispanic children (see Emery, 1998).

As for single-parent families, across all major ethnic groups close to 90% of all children live with a single mother following divorce versus somewhat more than 10% who live with a single father. However, the reason for single mother-hood varies considerably by ethnic group. In 1994, 14.4% of white children lived with a single mother who was separated or divorced versus 9% with a never married mother. For black children, 24.7% lived with a separated or divorced mother and 32.9% lived with a never-married mother. For Hispanic children, 15.6% lived with a separated or divorced mother and 12.0% lived with a never-married mother (U.S. Census Bureau, 1996). (About 1% of children lived with a widowed mother across all major ethnic groups.)

Finally, it should be noted that the U.S. Census Bureau does not collect data on the number of children living in joint custody. The National Center for Health Statistics (1995) has documented that in 1990, 16% of divorce decrees specified joint *legal* custody. However, joint *physical* custody is notably less common—likely involving less than 5% of children nationally (see Emery, 1998).

There are any number of potential explanations for the recent increases in divorce and nonmarital childbirth, including among others macroeconomic factors, changing societal values, and increased life expectancy (and marital longevity) (Burns & Scott, 1994; Hernandez, 1993). Briefly, variations on these explanations suggest that the supplementary, rather than complementary, roles of the dual-earner household lead to less stable unions; that the continued rise of individualism has undercut values of family commitment and self-sacrifice for the sake of children; and/or that marriage once was as unstable as it is today, but it was cut short by death not divorce. Such broad explanations can be debated against one another and against more psychological accounts, but a number of facts are clear irrespective of one's theoretical position. First, the "Ozzie and Harriet" family portrayed in the 1950s and 1960s television shows is by no means the prototypical American family. Second, nonmarital childbirth is an important contributor to children's family living circumstances, although this important factor is not the focus of this chapter. Third, remarriage and living in a stepfamily are common and important experiences for children, although, once again, the focus of thisw chapter is on divorce as opposed to remarriage. Fourth, there may be a slight, recent increase in the proportion of single father (and stepmother) families and the absolute number of both is large given the high rates of divorce and nonmarital childbirth (Meyer & Garasky, 1993), but it nevertheless is true that the great majority of children live primarily with their mothers or mothers and stepfathers following a divorce.

Divorce as a Stressor for Children

Divorce is a common experience for families in the United States today, but the stressors that accompany divorce are not ordinary. There are many potential negative events that result from divorce, for example, parental depression, frequent changes in residence, and social stigmatization. This section highlights four stressors of particular relevance to children's well-being and to divorce law and policy: declining family living standards, loss of contact with one parent (usually the father), potentially troubled relationships with both parents, and interparental conflict. It should be noted at the outset that some of these family difficulties (e.g., troubled parenting) likely precede divorce in certain families, and other stressors (e.g., parental conflict) may be relieved rather than exaccer-bated by a separation or divorce. Thus, evidence pertaining to the timing of the onset of various stressors is noted in the following sections. Nevertheless, it also should be made clear that other stressors (e.g., lowered standards of living) are clearly *caused* by separation and divorce, and for many families, divorce increases rather than lessens all family difficulties even including child-related interparental conflict.

Lowered Standards of Living

Family status is a powerful predictor of children's poverty status. According to the U.S. Census Bureau (1996), 21.9% of children in the United States were living below the poverty level in 1994. This figure includes 11.5% of children living with two parents, 24.1% of children living with a single father, and fully 52.2% of children living with a single mother. The reasons for single-parent status also are strongly related to children's poverty rates, as divorced mothers and fathers generally fare better economically than never-married parents. Thus, "only" 37.6% of children living with a divorced mother were living in poverty in 1994, as were 15.0% of children living with a divorced father.

In 1994, 17.4% of white children, 45.4% of black children, and 40.5% of Hispanic children were living below the poverty level (U.S. Census Bureau, 1996). According to census data, the relation between poverty and family status holds across these different ethnic groups, and, in fact, family status is a more powerful predictor of child poverty than race. Among white children, 10.7% who lived with two parents were growing up in poverty, as were 45.4% who lived with a single mother (35.2% for a single, divorced mother) and 21.6% who lived with a single father (11.1% for a single, divorced father). Among black children, 17.2% who lived with two parents were growing up in poverty, as were 63.8% who lived with a single mother (48.0% for a single, divorced mother) and 33.5% who lived with a single father (31.4% for a single, divorced father). Among Hispanic children, 30.8% who lived with two parents were growing up in poverty, as were 64.5% who lived with a single mother (53.2% for a single, divorced mother) and 25.9% who lived with a single father (19.9% for a single, divorced father) (U.S. Census Bureau, 1996).

People with lower incomes are more likely to divorce, therefore some of the poverty associated with family status is due to a selection effect. Still, it is clear that divorce causes a family's living standards to decline, if for no other reason than it simply is cheaper to live in one household than in two. In fact, longitudinal data indicate that the living standards of women and children fall by about 10% in the year after divorce and, if the mother remains single, living standards remain near that same lowered level even five years later. In contrast, the living standards of married families, fathers, and remarried mothers all rise by about 30%, on average, during a comparable five-year period (Duncan & Hoffman,

1985). Other longitudinal evidence has found that during the years 1966 and 1981, the poverty rate increased from 9.9% among married women with children to 28.7% after a divorce for whites and from 33.4% among married women with children to 44.3% after divorce for nonwhites (Nichols-Casebolt, 1986).

The increased expenses and lowered living standards following divorce may create many more specific pressures for children. The family may have to move to a less expensive house or apartment; children may have to change schools; contact with friends in a neighborhood or school may be lost as a result of these changes; the residential parent may have to begin working or work longer hours; children may be need to be placed in child care; older children may be told that college choices must be limited or that they must pay for their own college expenses; and children may have to deal with parents who are preoccupied with and fight over their various financial struggles. Any one of these changes could be a cause for concern about children's emotional well-being, yet all of these stressors can result from the economic struggles brought on by a divorce—and financial hardship is only one of the major areas of postdivorce stress for children.

Lost Contact With One Parent

Another major stressor that divorce clearly causes for children is lowered or lost contact with one parent, typically the father. Several national surveys have shown that, according to mothers' reports, a large proportion of fathers maintain little or no contact with their children following divorce (Furstenberg, et al., 1983; Mott, 1990; Seltzer, 1991; Seltzer & Bianchi, 1988). In one of the more recent surveys, approximately one-third of divorced fathers had seen their children only once or not at all in the past year; approximately 4 out of 10 fathers had seen their children a few times a year up to three times a month; and about one quarter had seen their children once a week or more (Seltzer, 1991).

Contact between children and fathers declines as time passes after a marital separation. In the same survey, 13% of fathers separated for 2 years or less saw their children once a year or less, while 43% saw them once a week or more. In contrast, 50% of fathers separated for 11 years or more saw their children once a year or less, while 12% saw them once a week or more (Seltzer, 1991). Of course, when a father is the residential parent, children spend less time with their mothers. However, survey data indicate that nonresidential mothers maintain more contact with their children than do nonresidential fathers.

There have been and continue to be numerous, vocal debates about why fathers often maintain little contact with their children after divorce, as well as about whether or to what extent more frequent father contact is related to indices of children's psychological adjustment. Some research on father contact and children's adjustment is discussed later in this chapter, although it is worth noting now that argument far outstrips evidence on this topic. Whatever the reasons for the low levels of contact or the relation between father contact and child adjustment, the present point is more simple and basic. Notwithstanding legitimate questions about whether fathers begin to withdraw from their children prior to separation and divorce (Coiro & Emery, 1998), the decline in contact between children and their nonresidential parents following divorce creates a major change in children's lives. Moreover, inconsistent and low levels of contact can be ongoing stressors for children. If we define children's well-being broadly, lost father contact would seem to be an important outcome in its own right, much the same as economic hardship.

Troubled Mother- and Father-Child Relationships

A large number of studies have used a variety of detailed observational, interview, and self-report measures to document that on average parents and children have less positive relationships in divorced than in married families (Amato & Keith, 1991a; Coiro & Emery, 1998; Emery & Tuer, 1993; Fauber, Forehand, McCombs, & Wierson, 1990; Hetherington, 1989, 1991, 1993; Wallerstein & Kelly, 1980). Parent-child relationships often improve over time after divorce, particularly relationships between children and their residential parents, but difficulties commonly remain (Hetherington, 1989, 1991, 1993; Wallerstein & Kelly, 1980).

The prevalence of troubled parent-child relationships is difficult to estimate, because parenting is a multidimensional construct that is defined and operationalized differently by various researchers. Moreover, most investigations of parenting after divorce have used small, convenience samples. In one of the few studies of postdivorce parenting in a national sample of children, however, Zill, Morrison, and Coiro (1993) developed a useful index of troubled relationships between parents and their children who were aged 12 to 16 years at one assessment and 18 to 22 at a second assessment. Of the 1,147 young people who were included in the analysis, 240 experienced their parents divorce before they were interviewed at age 12 to 16. They were an average of 6 years old at the time of divorce. The investigators defined a "poor" parent-child relationship as a positive answer to zero or only one of four items: feeling close to the parent; being satisfied with the amount of affection received from the parent; desiring to be the kind of person the parent is; and doing things with the parent that the child really enjoyed. This last question was replaced with a item measuring how well the child could share ideas or talk with the parent for the follow-up survey when the children were 18-22 years old.

The percentage of "poor" father-child relationships as defined by the investigators was startling in divorced families—32% at age 12 to 16 and 65% at age 18 to 22. Comparable figures were 14% and 29% for father-child relationships in married families. Mother-child relationships were notably better in both family types, and an identical 8% of 12 to 16 year olds reported "poor" mother-child relationships in both divorced and married families. A significant difference emerged as the children became young adults, however, as 25% of 18 to 22 year old children from divorced families reported poor mother-child relationships versus 18% from married families.

Other research has documented that troubled parent-child relationships precede divorce (Block, Block, & Gjerde, 1988; Shaw, Emery, & Tuer, 1993), but the accelerated deterioration of parent-child relationships in divorced versus married families during the transition to adulthood makes it clear that divorce exaccerbates normative struggles in parent-child relationships. Numerous studies and anecdotal reports of the struggles of parenting alone also suggest that divorce challenges parent-child relationships in many ways that married parents rarely face. Thus, it seems clear that another major stressor resulting from divorce is the risk for troubled relationships with both residential and especially nonresidential parents. As is discussed shortly, troubled parent-child relationships are substantially related to various measures of children's psychological adjustment after divorce.

Children's Involvement in Interparental Conflict

An end to conflict is supposed to be one of the *positive* consequences of divorce for parents. The end of conflict also is expected to be positive for children, as a large body of research documents that children have more psychological problems when their parents have a conflicted marriage (for reviews see Cummings & Davies, 1994; Davies & Cummings, 1994; Emery, 1982; Erel & Burman, 1995; Grych & Fincham, 1990). Conflict obviously precedes marital separation and divorce, however, evidence makes it clear that conflict does not end with a separation. In fact, conflict may come to focus more openly and squarely on the children who may have been buffered from parental disputes during the marriage.

It is not known to what extent confict is lessened or worsened from typical levels during the unhappy marriage to the times after marital separation, but it is clear that interparental conflict is prevalent throughout separation and divorce. In a study of over 1,000 California families who had filed for divorce, Maccoby and Mnookin (1992) found that, $1\frac{1}{2}$ years after the marital separation, 34% of couples had a conflicted coparenting relationship, 26% were cooperative coparents, 29% were disengaged, and 11% were mixed, that is their relationship was both cooperative and conflicted. Even 3 1/2 years after the marital separation, 26% of parents in the study had conflicted coparenting relationships, whereas 29% had a cooperative relationships, 41% were disengaged, and 4% were mixed. Coparenting conflict was unrelated to the type of custody arrangement following separation, as no significant differences in conflict were found for children living primarily with mothers, fathers, or in a joint residential arrangement (Maccoby & Mnookin, 1992).

Other research suggests that, while conflict obviously precedes marital separation in most cases, children in some families appear to be protected from conflict during marriage but entrapped in conflict during a divorce. Amato, Loomis, and Booth (1995) found that children from high-conflict married families fared better following a divorce, but children from low-conflict married families were doing *worse* following the divorce. Evidence thus indicates that separation and divorce can bring about a lessening of conflict and be a relief to all family members in these cases. Nevertheless, it also is true that interparental conflict is prevalent even years following a marital separation in many families; children often are the focus of conflict because they form one of the few remaining ties between former partners; and, for some children, postdivorce conflict is notably worse than the conflict they were aware of during their parents' marriage. For these reasons, interparental conflict can be viewed as yet another stressor that typically accompanies divorce.

RISK AND RESILIENCE: CHILDREN'S PSYCHOLOGICAL ADJUSTMENT AFTER DIVORCE

Turning from stressors to outcomes, it can be noted at the outset that evidence on the psychological adjustment of children from divorced families consistently leads to three clear conclusions. First, only small differences are found when comparing the mean ratings of children from married and divorced families on various indices of children's psychological adjustment, behavior problems, or academic functioning. Second, more notable differences are found at the extreme, as opposed to the center, of the two distributions of children. More specifically, divorce is associated with a variety of unwanted social, psychological, and academic outcomes among children, and for many adverse outcomes, for example, high school dropout, the risk associated with parental divorce increases by a factor of about two. Third, the majority of children whose parents are divorced do *not* drop out of high school or experience other obvious psychological problems or academic or social failures. In other words, most children are psychologically resilient in coping with a parental divorce, a conclusion that seems especially poignant given the number of stressors divorce creates for children, as was outlined in the preceding section.

Small Mean Differences Between Children From Married and Divorced Families

Convincing evidence on the modest average differences in the psychological adjustment of children from married and divorced families comes from a meta-analysis of 92 studies comparing the two groups. Amato and Keith's (1991a) meta-analysis found an average effect size of 0.14 standard deviation units across all child outcomes. The significant difference favored the adjustment of children from married versus divorced families, but such an effect size commonly is considered to be "small." The largest effect for a measure of psychological adjustment was for conduct problems, but even this effect (0.23) was not large. Furthermore, the reviewers found that effect sizes decreased as the methodological sophistication of a study increased, thus suggesting that the true effect may be somewhat smaller (Amato & Keith, 1991a). It is of interest to note that larger effects, but still moderate ones, were found in a second meta-analysis comparing adjustment measures for adults who grew up in married or divorced families (Amato & Keith, 1991b).

Divorce as a Risk Factor

A comparison of mean differences, however, fails to capture potential differences found at the extremes of a distribution, and it is differences at the extreme that are of greatest social and clinical significance. In fact, other evidence indicates that divorce increases the risk for a variety of socially and

clinically significant problems among children. For example, studies of nationally representative samples confirm that children from divorced families are
approximately twice as likely to receive psychological help as are children from
married families (Zill et al., 1993; Zill & Schoenborn, 1990). One can question
whether receiving psychological help underestimates or overestimates emotional problems among children. Many children who are deeply troubled by
their parents divorce surely never receive treatment from a mental health
professional; other children surely are brought for treatment only because of a
custody dispute or a parent's own emotional problems, not because of their own
troubles. Despite the criticisms that can be leveled at the measure, the doubling
of the risk for mental health treatment is significant if for no other reason than
from the perspective of service utilization.

Other researchers have found that divorce is associated with an increased
risk for a number of additional, socially significant problems among children.
Some of the most compelling evidence on increased risk comes from McLanahan and Sandefur (1994) who analyzed data from five different national surveys
of children or families. These investigators found that the risk for dropping out
of high school and for teen pregnancy both were about twice as great for
children from divorced as married families. Although some variations emerged
across samples, the two-fold increase in risk was quite consistent across the five
surveys.

Resilience: The Modal Outcome

National survey data document the risk for various psychological problems
among children from divorced families, yet the same data also highlight the
resilience of most children in the face of divorce. That is, most children who
experience their parents divorce and all of the stressors that accompany it, do
not get pregnant, drop out of school, or require treatment from a mental health
professional. For example, Zill et al. (1993) found that twice as many 12- to
16-year-old children from divorced as married families received psychological
help in their national sample of children—21% versus 11%. However, this
means that 79% of 12- to 16-year-old children from divorced families (versus
89% from married families) had coped with their parents' divorce without
receiving psychological help. Similar results emerge when one computes the
inverse of risk in other prominent studies (e.g., McLanahan & Sandefur, 1994).
Such evidence is an important reminder that most children are resilient in
coping with parental divorce, albeit resilient as measured by a series of imper-

fect indicators. Still, it seems clear that the majority of children from divorced families "pass" rather than "fail" the test of healthy child development as measured by key indicators of their academic, social, and psychological adjustment.

Adjustment Problems Prior to Divorce

Not only is resilience the modal outcome of divorce for children, but another line of research suggests that studies of risk, and of mean differences, overestimate the psychological problems that divorce causes for children. All of the evidence on children's psychological adjustment reviewed to this point has been based on studies comparing children from divorced and married families only after the divorce has taken place. However, divorce does not occur at random, therefore such evidence only documents that divorce is correlated with various indices of children's maladjustment. As every social science student learns early in their training, correlation does not mean causation. In fact, several researchers have used existing data sets of normal child development to study children and divorce prospectively, and these investigators have found that many of the psychological problems found among children *after* divorce actually were present *before* divorce (Block, Block, & Gjerde, 1986; Cherlin et al., 1991; Doherty & Needle, 1991; Elliott & Richards, 1991). Emotional problems that predate divorce cannot be "consequences of divorce." Thus, at least some of the increased risk found in comparing children from divorced and married families is not due to divorce. The differences must either be attributable to selection effects or to disruptions in the predivorce family environment. In either case, prospective research lends further weight to the resilience perspective: the modest mean differences and more substantial differences in relative risk found when comparing the psychological adjustment of children from divorced and married families overestimate the effects due to divorce.

Resilient but Not Invulnerable

Evidence on divorce and children's risk for maladaptive outcomes needs to be qualified by the normative focus on resilience, but the resilience perspective also must be qualified. Resilience is not the same as invulnerability; rather resilience implies that children "bounce back" from the stress of divorce, just as children commonly bounce back from the struggles of abuse, poverty, or to cite perhaps the most extreme example, the experience of the Holocaust.

Children's ability to bounce back from all kinds of stressors is heartening, but given an alternative, we would prefer to avoid the need for children to be resilient. Children may be resilient in the face of divorce, abuse, or poverty, but such a conclusion hardly means that such major life experiences are innocuous for them or for society.

DISTRESS OR "PAIN" VERSUS DISORDER

Measurement issues raise another important qualification about the conclusion that most children are resilient in the face of parental divorce. Most parents, including parents who are mental health professionals, worry about more than the 100 or so items on the Achenbach Child Behavior Checklist, for example, when focusing on their own children's psychological well-being. Similarly, most parents and mental health professionals do not equate positive psychological well-being with not being in psychotherapy, not getting pregnant as a teenager, not dropping out of school, and so on. Parents and clinicians—and children and adults who are reflecting back on their own childhooods—often are concerned with much more subtle thoughts, feelings, and experiences, including unhappy memories of the past, worries about ongoing family relationships, or longing for things to be different in the future. Such psychological experiences are examples of distressed, as opposed to disordered, behavior, or what has been termed psychological "pain" (Emery & Coiro, 1997; Laumann-Billings & Emery, 1988). In many respects, particularly from the outside looking in, distressed or painful behavior is of considerably less significance than disordered behavior. Still, distressing memories, emotions, and wishes are important, especially from the inside looking out in terms of the child's inner experience.

Clinical Observations and Empirical Studies

Many clinical accounts of children from divorced families have highlighted their painful psychological experiences. Children's distressing feelings stemming from divorce may include fear of abandonment; grief over the loss of the family or of specific family relationships; diffuse anger at their parents; secret, irrational hopes for reconciliation; social embarrassment about their family; worries about each parent's well-being; anxiety about balancing divided loyalties; uncertainty about their own romantic relationships; and/or worries over the practical problems created by ongoing parental conflict (Emery, 1994; Wallerstein and Blakeslee, 1989; Wallerstein & Kelly, 1980). These and other thoughts, feelings, and ongoing events are poignant, and they are the types of inner experiences that often seem to form a critical part of the texture of children's and adults' psychological life.

By definition, these examples and other forms of inner distress involve subtle and perhaps fleeting experiences. Thus, by its very nature, psychological "pain" is difficult to measure empirically. In fact, the focus on distress in clinical accounts versus disorder in empirical research may explain the apparently conflicting conclusions of the two literatures. Clinical reports tend to highlight children's struggles in coping with parental divorce, while research studies tend to highlight children's strengths (Forehand, 1992). The clinical literature often concludes that divorce is devastating for children, which it is in many ways. Yet the tight focus on children's inner life can cause clinicians to overlook the broader view, that is, children's successfully coping with parental divorce despite their pain. In contrast, empirical research uses a wide-angle lens that portrays an accurate image of the successful adjustment of most children following a parental divorce, but the broad portrait fails to capture the fine texture of pain that is evident in the clinical close-up.

Distress Among Resilient Young People

A few empirical studies have attempted to combine the two lenses for viewing the adjustment of children following divorce, and this research has found that even children who are resilient in the face of their parents' divorce nevertheless report considerable "pain" or distress (e.g, Kurdek, 1988; Kurdek & Berg, 1987; Wolchik, Ramirez, Sandler, Fisher, Organista, & Brown, 1993). In one recent study, 99 well-functioning college students from divorced families reported a number of distressing feelings, beliefs, and experiences. For example, on a standardized measure, 73% reported that they felt like they would have been a different person if their parents had not gotten divorced; 50% said they worried about events like graduation or weddings when both of their parents would be present; 49% said they really missed not having their father around as much after their parents' separation; 48% reported that they had a harder childhood than most people; 40% said they wish they grew up in a never-divorced family; 29% wondered if their father really loved them; and 18% said they felt doomed to repeat their parents problems (Billings & Emery, 1998).

Many of these painful feelings are specific to parental divorce, but some of the responses could be compared with those of 92 college students who grew up in always-married families. Most of these comparisons produced statistically significant differences, including the following: 50% of the divorced group versus 10% of the married group reported that they worried about events like graduation where both parents would be present; 48% of the young people from divorced families versus 14% from married families felt they had a harder childhood than most people; 46% from divorced families versus 19% from married families wished they could have spent more time with their fathers; and 29% from divorced families versus 10% from married families wondered if their father really loved them (Laumann-Billings & Emery, 1998).

Wondering if your father loves you surely is a painful feeling, and it is important to recognize such struggles faced by even resilient children of divorce. Still, it is worth once again calling attention to the strengths of the young adults in this study. All of the participants were functioning well enough to be attending college, and their scores on standardized measures of depression and anxiety were no different from those of their counterparts from married families. By all accounts, these were resilient young people who nevertheless harbored painful feelings about their parents divorce.

In summary, the psychological consequences of divorce for children defy the simplistic characterization, which often seems to appear in the popular media (Forehand, 1992), of "devastated" versus "invulnerable." Divorce is a risk factor for a number of significant problems, but some of these problems were present prior to the marital separation, and in any case, the majority of children from divorced families successfully adjust to their new family and their new life circumstances. However, their successful adjustment does not mean that children have not struggled both directly with the stressors of divorce and less obviously with inner fears, worries, and regrets. To use a familiar metaphor, some children are irreparably wounded by divorce; the wounds of most children heal; but even healed wounds usually leave a scar.

Individual Differences: Risk, Resilience, and Postdivorce Family Life

To this point, this chapter has largely taken a normative perspective on divorce by emphasizing children's mean or modal experiences and outcomes. There are, of course, numerous individual differences both in terms of the number and severity of stressors children encounter before, during, and after divorce and in terms of the range of the psychological well-being of different children. A comprehensive review of how and why various children and families experience and adjust to parent divorce differently is well beyond the scope of the present chapter, and the interested reader is referred elsewhere for detailed reviews (Amato, 1993; Amato & Keith, 1991a; Emery, 1982, 1998; Emery & Forehand, 1994). However, it is possible to offer a brief overview of individual differences related to the four factors discussed earlier from a normative perspective: (1) the quality of children's relationship with their residential parent, (2) the extent of conflict between the coparents, (3) the family's economic standing, and (4) the frequency of contact and the quality of children's relationship with their nonresidential parent. These four factors are central both to children's psychological well-being and to social policy, and as noted at the beginning of the chapter, they are listed in their order of importance to children's psychological adjustment according to the author's interpretation of existing research. It is readily acknowledged, however, that research is far from conclusive in comparing the four factors, and there are important reasons for suspecting that some experiences (e.g., low father contact) are an important source of distress even if they are only weakly related to disorder.

Children's Adjustment and the Residential Parent

As noted earlier, research consistently has documented that divorce is associated with various troubles in the residential parent-child relationship, and while the relationship improves over time, divorced versus married residential parents still have somewhat more difficulties with their children (Hetherington, 1989, 1991, 1993). Moreover, a number of studies using different measures and samples have linked troubled residential parent-child relationships with increased internalizing and externalizing problems among children (e.g., Buchanan et al., 1996; Fauber et al., 1990; Hetherington, 1989, 1991, 1993; Simons et al., 1994). In general, children fare best when their parents are authoritative, a style of parenting that combines warmth with firm but fair discipline (Maccoby & Martin, 1983).

Children's Adjustment and Interparental Conflict

As with troubled residential-parent child relationships, interparental conflict also has been consistently linked with various problems in children's psychological adjustment in divorced families (Amato, 1993; Amato & Keith, 1991a; Emery, 1982, 1988). As with conflict in married families, children from divorced families typically have more difficulties when interparental conflict involves them directly, is focused on child-related topics (e.g., discipline), and is emotionally intense, prolonged, and remains unresolved (Cummings & Davies, 1994; Davies & Cummings, 1994; Emery, 1998; Grych & Fincham, 1990). Some research has compared parenting problems and interparental conflict in accounting for variance in the behavior problems of children after divorce. For example, one study found that troubled parent-child relationships accounted for the effects of conflict (e.g., Fauber et al., 1990). This conclusion is subject to a number of methodological and conceptual criticisms (Emery, Fincham, & Cummings, 1992). Still, it seems likely that troubled residential parent-child relationships are more strongly related to children's mental health following divorce than is interparental conflict, although both are important predictors of individual differences in children's divorce outcome.

Children's Adjustment and Economic Standing

The family's economic standing also has been found to explain considerable variance in the behavior problems of children from divorced families. In one extensive series of analyses, for example, differences due to parents' marital status were reduced by about half when income controls were introduced into statistical comparisons (McLanahan & Sandefur, 1994). Other evidence suggests, however, that lower income is associated with less adequate parenting; and parenting, not income, explains many of children's behavior problems (e.g., Conger, Conger, & Elder, 1997). Similarly, conflict has been found to be a stronger predictor of disturbed child behavior than income in some research (e.g., Shaw & Emery, 1987). Thus, at least some evidence supports the present ordering of these three predictors of individual differences.

Children's Adjustment and the Nonresidential Parent

Relatively little research has focused on the link between nonresidential parenting and children's psychological adjustment following divorce. In one study of a national sample, no consistent relations were found between the amount of contact or children's perceived closeness with the nonresidential parent and various measures of their adjustment (Allison & Furstenberg, 1989). Other researchers have found either no or inconsistent relations between visitation frequency and children's mental health (Kline, Johnston, & Tschann, 1991; Kurdek, 1986; Kurdek, Blisk, & Siesky, 1981; Luepnitz, 1982). Still other investigators have found that more frequent contact with the nonresidential parent is associated with better adjustment among children, but only when interparental conflict is low (Buchanan et al., 1991; Hetherington, Cox, & Cox, 1978; Wallerstein & Kelly, 1980). Further studies suggest that a good relationship with one parent can buffer the ill-effects of a bad relationship with the other (Camara and Resnick, 1987; Peterson & Zill, 1986). This research, as well as the general weak relationship found between measures of children's psychological adjustment and their contact with the nonresidential parent, thus argues for placing this factor fourth on the current, limited list of four.

Of course, the collective weight of existing research suggests that children will adjust best following a parental divorce if they have a good relationship with both their residential *and* their nonresidential parents, if conflict is low, and if the family's economic standing is sound and stable. The problem, and one reason for ordering the variables, is that there may be a need to trade one stressor for another in individual cases and in social policy. For example, should frequent contact with the nonresidential parent be encouraged even in the face of intense, enduring, and unremitting interparental conflict? Probably not, according to the current ordering of these four variables, all of which are key considerations in divorce custody proceedings.

Such an ordering hardly resolves all of the numerous issues that arise when attempting to translate research findings into policy, however. For example, how much conflict is too much—or how long must it last—before children will fare better with less contact and less exposure to conflict as a result? As another example, is it appropriate to rank problems in postdivorce family relationships according to the strength of their relationships with indices of children's psychological adjustment or maladjustment? More specifically, evidence discussed earlier in this chapter suggests that low father contact is a considerable source of distress for children even if it is only weakly related to disorder. In devising policy, should we consider children's internal "pain" to be less relevant than their achievement? Perhaps, but it seems that these are the sort of questions that have not, and perhaps cannot, be answered by empirical research.

THE GOALS OF DIVORCE POLICY—
AND THE GOALS OF MARRIAGE

Notwithstanding the problems in translating research into specific policies or judicial decision rules, evidence on both normative outcomes and individual differences argues for some clear goals for divorce policy. First, divorce policy should support residential parents, usually mothers, who have the most responsibility for and influence over children following divorce. Second, divorce policy should attempt to minimize conflict between parents by treating both of them fairly in determining divorce settlements, and by making them feel empowered through their participation in the decision-making process. Third, divorce policy should encourage parents to take the long view and recognize that, despite their divorce, they have an ongoing and ever-changing relationship both with their children and with each other. Fourth, divorce policy should encourage nonresidential parents, typically fathers, to be at least somewhat involved in rearing their children after divorce, hopefully very involved, and nonresidential parents also should be encouraged to support the residential parent in every way possible. Fifth, divorce policy should encourage nonresidential parents to support their children financially, but income transfers must not be seen as unfair or undermine the nonresidential parent's incentive to earn. Perhaps economic policy could also recognize or perhaps alter the problems created by lost economies of scale, that is, the inevitable added expense following separation of rearing children in two households rather than one.

All of these are important and worthy goals of divorce policy, and various efforts have been designed to achieve them. Some of the more successful innovations have been: (1) the widespread embrace of joint legal custody and much more limited attempts to promote joint physical custody, (2) the use of detailed parenting plans for sharing time with children, (3) the rapid development of divorce mediation associated with courts and in professional practice, (4) the crafting and use of specific criteria for determining child support awards and the implementation of various support enforcement mechanisms, and (5) the increased recognition that both childrearing and financial arrangements change over time and the associated easing of methods for reworking arrangements both informally (e.g., through mediation) and formally (e.g., simplified modification of child support awards) (Emery, 1998).

These changes in divorce law and policy represent worthy and important innovations. Ironically, however, the five goals that they are designed to promote are the same goals of another central family policy—promoting happy, stable marriage. Marriage is not the topic of the present chapter, but divorce research clearly indicates that the promotion of happy, stable marriages could do much to improve the general well-being of children living in the United States today. Much of the public debate about promoting marriage has focused on the back end by making divorce more difficult through requirements for longer waiting periods before granting a no-fault divorce, returning to fault grounds, or simply by stigmatizing divorce. In the author's view, this is not the most productive, adaptive, or accurate focus. Children, parents, and families who are not fortunate enough to achieve the goal of living in happy, stable, two-parent families need not—and should not—be castigated; indeed, most divorced and never married families function well. Still, the evidence reviewed in this chapter makes it clear that, given the option, children certainly fare better in a happily married family than in a divorced family; thus promoting happy marriage surely is an important goal for social policy. If the goal is to increase happy marriages, however, it would seem to be promoted best by encouraging and supporting marriage, as opposed to stigmatizing divorce and nonmarital childbirth.

REFERENCES

Allison, P. D., & Furstenberg, F. F. (1989). How marital dissolution affects children: Variations by age and sex. *Developmental Psychology, 25,* 540-549.

Amato, P. R. (1993). Children's adjustment to divorce: Theories, hypotheses, and empirical support. *Journal of Marriage and the Family, 55,* 23-38.

Amato, P. R., & Keith, B. (1991a). Parental divorce and the well-being of children: A meta-analysis. *Psychological Bulletin, 110,* 26-46.

Amato, P.R. & Keith, B. (1991b). Parental divorce and adult well-being: A Meta-analysis. *Journal of Marriage and the Family, 53,* 43-58.

Amato, P. R., Loomis, L. S., & Booth, A. (1995). Parental divorce, marital conflict, and offspring well-being during early adulthood. *Social Forces, 73,* 895-915.

Block, J. H., Block, J., & Gjerde, P. F. (1986). The personality of children prior to divorce: A prospective study. *Child Development, 57,* 827-840.

Block, J. H., Block, J., & Gjerde, P. F (1988). Parental functioning and the home environment in families of divorce: Prospective and concurrent analyses. *Journal of the American Academy of Child and Adolescent Psychiatry, 27,* 207-213.

Buchanan, C. M., Maccoby, E. E., & Dornbusch, S. M. (1991). Caught between parents: Adolescents' experience in divorced homes. *Child Development, 62,* 1008-1029.

Buchanan, C. M., Maccoby, E. E., & Dornbusch, S. M. (1996). *Adolescents after divorce.* Cambridge, MA: Harvard.

Burns, A., & Scott, C. (1994). *Mother-headed families and why they have increased.* Hillsdale, NJ: Erlbaum.

Camara, K. A., & Resnick, G. (1987). Marital and parental subsystems in mother-custody, father-custody and two-parent households: Effects on children's social development. In J. Vincent (Ed.), *Advances in family assessment, intervention and research* (Vol. 4). Greenwich, CN: JAI.

Cherlin, A. J. (1992). *Marriage, divorce, remarriage* (2nd. ed.). Cambridge, MA: Harvard University Press.

Cherlin, A. J., Furstenberg, F. F., Chase-Lansdale, P. L., Kiernan, K. E., Robins, P. K., Morrison, D. R., & Teitler, J. O. (1991). Longitudinal studies of effects of divorce on children in Great Britain and the United States. *Science, 252,* 1386-1389.

Conger, R. D., Conger, K. J., & Elder, G. H. (1997). Family economic hardship and adolescent adjustment: Mediating and moderating processes. In G. J. Duncan & J. Brooks-Gunn (Eds.), *Consequences of growing up poor* (pp. 288-310). New York: Russell-Sage.

Coiro, M. J., & Emery, R. E. (in press). Do marriage problems affect fathering more than mothering?: A quantitative and qualitative review. *Clinical Child and Family Psychology Review.*

Cummings, E. M., & Davies, P. (1994). *Children and marital conflict.* New York: Guilford.

Davies, P. T., & Cummings, E. M. (1994). Marital conflict and child adjustment: An emotional security hypothesis. *Psychological Bulletin, 116,* 387-411.

Doherty, W. J., & Needle, R. H. (1991). Psychological adjustment and substance use among adolescents before and after a parental divorce. *Child Development, 62,* 328-337.

Duncan, G. J., & Hoffman, S. D. (1985). Economic consequences of marital instability. In M. David & T. Smeeding (Eds.), *Horizontal equity, uncertainty and well-being* (pp. 427-469). Chicago: University of Chicago Press.

Elliott, B. J., & Richards, M. P. M. (1991). Children and divorce: Educational performance and behaviour before and after parental separation. *International Journal of Law and the Family, 5,* 258-276.

Emery, R. E., (1982). Interparental conflict and the children of discord and divorce. *Psychological Bulletin, 92,* 310-330.

Emery, R. E. (1994). *Renegotiating family relationships: Divorce, child custody, and mediation.* New York: Guilford.

Emery, R. (1998). *Marriage, divorce, and children's adjustment* (2nd ed.). Thousand Oaks, CA: Sage.

Emery, R. E., Fincham, F. F., & Cummings, M. (1992). Parenting in context: Systemic thinking about parental conflict and its influence on children. *Journal of Consulting and Clinical Psychology, 60,* 909-912.

Emery, R. E., & Forehand, R. (1994). Parental divorce and children's well-being: A focus on resilience. In R. J. Haggerty, L. Sherrod, N. Garmezy, & M. Rutter (Eds.), *Risk and resilience in children* (pp. 64-99). London: Cambridge University Press.

Emery, R. E., & Tuer, M. (1993). Parenting and the marital relationship. In T. Luster & L. Okagi (Eds.), *Parenting: An ecological perspective* (pp. 121-148). Hillsdale, NJ: Erlbaum.

Erel, E., & Burman, B. (1995). Interrelatedness of marital relations and parent-child relations: A meta-analytic review. *Psychological Bulletin, 118,* 108-132.

Fauber, R. L., Forehand, R., Thomas, A. M., & Wierson, M. (1990). A mediational model of the impact of marital conflict on adolescent adjustment in intact and divorced families: The role of disrupted parenting. *Child Development, 61,* 1112-1123.

Forehand, R. (1992). Parental divorce and adolescent maladjustment: Scientific inquiry versus public information. *Behavioral Research and Therapy, 30,* 319-327.

Furstenberg, F. F., Peterson, J. L., Nord, C. W., & Zill, N., (1983). The life course of children of divorce: Marital disruption and parental contact. *American Sociological Review, 48,* 656-668.

Grych, J. H., & Fincham, F. D. (1990). Marital conflict and children's adjustment: A cognitive-contextual framework. *Psychological Bulletin, 108,* 267-290

Hernandez, D. J. (1993). *America's children: Resources from family, government, and the economy.* New York: Russell Sage Foundation.

Hetherington, E. M. (1989). Coping with family transitions: Winners, losers, and survivors. *Child Development, 60,* 1-14.

Hetherington, E. M. (1991). Presidential address: Families, lies, and videotapes. *Journal of Research on Adolescence, 1,* 323-348.

Hetherington, E. M. (1993). An overview of the Virginia Longitudinal Study of Divorce and Remarriage with a focus on early adolescence. *Journal of Family Psychology, 7,* 39-56.

Hetherington, E. M., Cox, M., & Cox, R., (1978). The aftermath of divorce. In J. H. Stevens & M. Matthews (Eds.), *Mother-child, father-child relations* (pp. 110-155) Washington, DC: National Association for the Education of Young Children.

Hetherington, E. M., Bridges, M., & Insabella, G. M. (1998). What matters? What does not? Five perspectives on the association between marital transitions and children's adjustment. *American Psychologist, 53,* 167-184.

Kline, M., Johnston, J. R., & Tschann, J. M. (1991). The long shadow of marital conflict: A model of children's postdivorce adjustment. *Journal of Marriage and the Family, 53,* 297-309.

Kurdek, L. A. (1986). Children's reasoning about parental divorce. In R. D. Ashmore & D. M. Brodzinsky (Eds.), *Thinking about the family: Views of parents and children* (pp. 233-276). Hillsdale, NJ: Erlbaum.

Kurdek, L. A. (1988). A one-year follow-up study of children's divorce adjustment, custodial mothers' divorce adjustment, and postdivorce parenting. *Journal of Applied Developmental Psychology, 9,* 315-328.

Kurdek, L. A., & Berg, B. (1987). Children's beliefs about parental divorce scale: Psychometric characteristics and concurrent validity. *Journal of Consulting and Clinical Psychology, 55,* 712-718.

Kurdek, L. A., Blisk, D., & Siesky, A. E. (1981). Correlates of children's long-term adjustment to their parents' divorce. *Developmental Psychology, 1976,* 565-579.

Laumann-Billings, L., & Emery, R. E. (1988). *Young adults' painful feelings about parental divorce.* Unpublished manuscript, University of Virginia.

Luepnitz, D. A. (1982). *Child custody: A study of families after divorce.* Lexington, MA: Lexington Books.

Maccoby, E. E., & Mnookin, R. H. (1992). *Dividing the child: Social and legal dilemmas of custody.* Cambridge, MA: Harvard University.

McLanahan, S., & Sandefur, G. (1994). *Growing up with a single parent: What hurts, what helps.* Cambridge, MA: Harvard University.

Mott, F. L. (1990). When is a father really gone? Paternal-child contact in father-absent homes. *Demography, 27,* 499-517.

National Center for Health Statistics (1995). Advance report of final divorce statistics, 1989 and 1990. *Monthly Vital Statisitics Report, 43*(9), Supp. Hyattsville, MD: National Center for Health Statistics.

National Instititue for Child Support Enforcement, (1986). *History and fundamentals of child support enforcement* (2nd. ed.). Washington, D.C.: Government Printing Office.

Nichols-Casebolt, A., (1986). The economic impact of child support reform on the poverty status of custodial and noncustodial families. *Journal of Marriage and the Family, 48,* 875-880.

Peterson, J. L., & Zill, N. (1986). Marital disruption, parent-child relationships, and behavior problems in children. *Journal of Marriage and the Family, 48,* 295-307.

Seltzer, J. A. (1991). Relationships between fathers and children who live apart: The father's role after separation. *Journal of Marriage and the Family, 53,* 79-101.

Seltzer, J. A., & Bianchi, S. M. (1988). Children's contact with absent parents. *Journal of Marriage and the Family, 50,* 663-677.

Shaw, D. S., & Emery, R. E. (1987). Parental confict and other correlates of the adjustment of school age children whose parents have separated. *Journal of Abnormal Child Psychology, 15,* 269-281.

Shaw, D. S., Emery, R. E., & Tuer, M. D. (1993). Parental functioning and children's adjustment in families of divorce: A prospective study. *Journal of Abnormal Child Psychology, 21,* 119-134.

U.S. Bureau of the Census (1992). Marriage, divorce, and remarriage in the 1990s. *Current Population Reports* (P23-180). Washington, DC: Government Printing Office.

U.S. Census Bureau (1996). Marital status and living arrangements: March 1994. *Current Population Reports* (P20-484). Washington, DC: Government Printing Office.

Ventura, S. J., Clarke, S. C., & Mathews, T. J. (1996). Recent declines in teenage birth rates in the United States: Variations by state, 1990-94. *Monthly Vital Statistics Report, 45*(6), supp. Hyattsville, MD: National Center for Health Statistics.

Ventura, S. J., Peters, K. D., Martin, J. A., & Maurer, J. D. (1997). Births and deaths: United States, 1996. *Monthly Vital Statistics Report, 46*(1), supp 2. Hyattsville, MD: National Center for Health Statistics.

Ventura, S. J., Taffel, S. M., Mosher, W. D., Wilson, J. B., & Henshaw, S. (1995). Trends in pregnancy and pregnancy rates: Estimates for the United States, 1980-92. *Monthly Vital Statistics Report, 43*(11), supp. Hyattsville, MD: National Center for Health Statistics.

Wallerstein, J. S. & Blakeslee, S. (1989). *Second chances: Men, women, and children a decade after divorce.* New York: Ticknor & Fields.

Wallerstein, J. S., & Kelly, J. B., (1980). *Surviving the breakup: How children actually cope with divorce.* New York: Basic.

Wolchik, S. A., Ramirez, R., Sandler, I. N., Fisher, J. L., Organista, P. B., & Brown, C. (1993). Inner-city, poor children of divorce: Negative divorce-related events, problematic beliefs, and adjustment problems. *Journal of Divorce and Remarriage, 19,* 1-19.

Zill, N., Morrison, D. R., & Coiro, M. J. (1993). Long-term effects of parental divorce on parent-child relationships, adjustment, and achievement in young adulthood. *Journal of Family Psychology, 7,* 91-103.

Zill, N., & Schoenborn, C. A. (1990). Developmental, learning, and emotional problems: Health of our nation's children, United States, 1988. *Advance data from vital and health statistics* (No 190). Hyattsville, MD: National Center for Health Statistics.

Chapter 2

Causes and Consequences of Divorce

Reflections on Recent Research

Alan Booth

We begin with a review of changes in divorce rates over the last century. Explanations for the changes are evaluated and future trends are projected. We then examine the implications of future trends, especially as they relate to children. Recent research has revealed some unexpected findings regarding the children of divorce. For example, the negative relationship between parental divorce and child well-being appears long before the divorce takes place. Also, children whose parents exhibit low conflict levels before divorce suffer more than those whose parents exhibit moderate to high conflict. These and other recent findings are explored so that we might identify those divorces that entail high long- and short-term risks for children.

Each person's historical perspective spans three generations at most. Of greatest salience is our own experience; next is the often fragmentary information acquired by children from their parents. Even under these circumstances information may be limited by parents' unwillingness to reveal much about their history. Many parents believe that certain types of information (e.g., divorce, separation, adultery) are better left unshared with children. My own personal experience left me with a very distorted view regarding the frequency and meaning of parental divorce. During my teen years, none of my peers in a graduating class of 150 experienced a parental divorce. One person's father moved to another city to work and never came back. None of my relatives or my parents' acquaintances got a divorce. Both my own experience and that of my parents could lead me to conclude that divorce almost never occurred in the 1950s and that if there was a problem it was fathers abandoning families. That perception would cause me to believe that the rise in divorce over the last 30 years was unique and unusual. Yet a careful look (see Figure 2.1) at the last 100 years indicates a continuous increase in the divorce rate (Cherlin, 1992). It did dip slightly during my high school years but that would have nothing to do with my perception about divorce trends. The rate has accelerated over the last 30 years, but has now leveled off. Given the myopic view of all but a few family scholars, it is no wonder that many politicians, clergy, and observers of the family scene are concerned with our moral decline, believe the contemporary high but seemingly stable divorce rate does not reflect our society's true character, and think that something must have gone wrong in recent years to bring us to our current state of affairs. I think the short-term perspective gets us in trouble both in thinking about future trends in divorce and in contemplating the effects of divorce on children. Therefore, I would like to place current divorce rates within a larger context and then speculate about what the future holds.

I believe Goode (1963) was right when he argued that as the relationship between making a living and family organization weakens, the bonds for keeping marriages intact also loosen. In most modern economies there is seldom a link between one's family and making a living. Few people inherit a family farm, business, or land—vital means to make a living. If significant numbers of families did, we would see many more intact marriages. What we inherit is some insurance money and a few pieces of unfashionable furniture. These inheritances are not going to make people stay in a marriage. In the current economy, families do not get paid; individuals do. When families were the unit of production, people were paid or rewarded because they were members of a particular family. Today, few families are in that situation. Rewards are based mostly on individual achievement. Staying in a marriage seldom affects the amount of income earned from work. A graph created by Hernandez (1993), which has become a classic, shows how the family structure experienced by

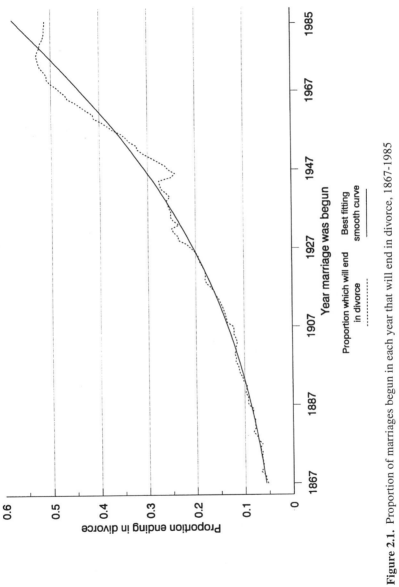

Figure 2.1. Proportion of marriages begun in each year that will end in divorce, 1867-1985

SOURCE: Cherlin, A. J. (1992). *Marriage, divorce, remarriage* (Rev. ed., p. 22). Cambridge, MA: Harvard University Press. Reprinted with permission.

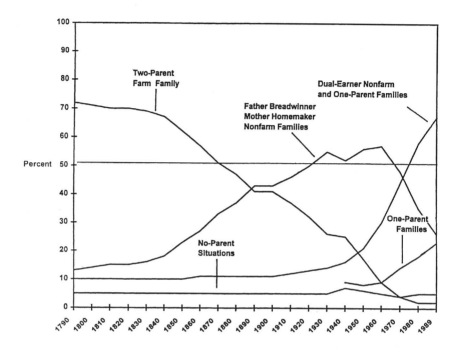

Figure 2.2. Children aged 0 to 17 in farm families, father-as-breadwinner families, and dual-earner families: 1790-1989

SOURCE: Hernandez, D. J. (1993). *America's children: Resources from family, government, and the economy* (p. 103). New York: Russell Sage Foundation. Reprinted with permission.
NOTE: Estimates for 10-year intervals to 1980, and for 1989.

children has changed over the last 200 years (see Figure 2.2). The changes indicate how family structure has separated from the means of making a living, thus weakening the need to remain married. Note the decline in farm families which is an economic production unit, the rise and fall of households where an interdependent division of labor was based on child care and housework and earning an income, and the rise in households where both adults produce income in order to operate the household.

Today, there are few compelling reasons to keep a marriage intact from the standpoint of an interdependence based on generating an income. Women's participation in the paid labor force is a major factor in enabling the dissolution of marriages. Now, either husbands or wives can and do earn money to keep the household viable and provide the necessary child care (although males are less involved in the latter). In short, a single adult can perform all functions needed to keep a household running, especially given the growth in a service sector that prepares our food, cleans our clothes, and tends to our children. Although a single income may not be the preferred lifestyle, it is enough to keep the family going in the majority of households.

Other than child rearing, the primary function of a married couple is to provide each other with socioemotional support and in some cases sexual gratification. Such narrow expectations mean that each member of the couple demands a great deal from the other. In other words, to succeed at marriage partners need to specialize in providing understanding, nurturance, and affection. These few expectations lead to very high performance standards. Given normal differences in the ability to provide support, a great number of marriages are destined to fail. This factor may be significant in keeping the divorce rate high.

While it would appear that people don't put a high premium on marriage, they do value marriage as a source of gratification and happiness. For example, the Massachusetts Mutual American Family Values Study in 1989 showed that "having a happy marriage" was ranked very important by 93% of the respondents (as cited in Glenn, 1996). The Monitoring the Future Survey conducted annually among high school seniors by the University of Michigan Institute for Social Research indicated that respondents ranked "having a good marriage and family life" first; this was rated highest by almost four-fifths of the students (as cited in Glenn, 1996). The importance placed on having a successful marriage as measured by happiness, satisfaction, and other positive feelings, at a time when the legal, moral, and economic constraints on divorce have loosened, contributes to our high divorce rate. As Glenn (1996) points out, such feelings encourage people to move from what they consider to be poorer, but fairly satisfying marriages, to superior ones. Spouses do compare their partner with potential partners and remain open to alternative relationships (South & Lloyd, 1995). When they believe they have a good chance of remarrying should they divorce, they are more likely than others to dissolve their marriage (Udry, 1981).

The act of constantly comparing one's partner with others has its own way of destabilizing relationships. First, as Glenn (1996) notes, individuals are less likely to make the investments and sacrifices needed to ensure that the current marriage works. Second, comparisons are being made with limited knowledge of potential new partners, frequently seen only during work and in other settings where they are at their best. They are only rarely seen first thing in the morning, when many are not at their best, or in stressful situations that arise out of intensive daily contact over a period of months or years. In short, the grass looks greener on the other side of the fence because the brown spots are not visible.

Another reason for the high divorce rate is that marital quality may have actually declined over the last 30 years. General Social Survey data covering a 15-year period revealed a decline in marital quality (Glenn, 1991). The decline in marital happiness may be due to comparisons of spouses with others I mentioned earlier, or to changes in gender role attitudes (Amato & Booth, 1995) and conflict over the division of labor (Rogers & Amato, 1997), or to eroding financial resources and security (Voydanoff, 1990).

What do these factors portend for the future? For the near future the divorce rate will stay high because I don't see any major changes in people's values or new constraints on divorce. I believe attempts at abolishing no fault laws will fail and even if they do not, people will find ways to circumvent the legislation just as they did when, for example, adultery was the only grounds for divorce. One of the reasons the divorce rate has peaked is the delay in marriage (Ahlburg & DeVita, 1992). Those marrying later are not in the midst of changing career or educational objectives or still trying to come to grips with matters of personal identity. They are at a stage in life when most personal attributes are stable, thus eliminating changing identities or status as a source of marital instability.

However, I see some things on the horizon that may decrease the divorce rate. First, many marriage counselors are now aware of the devastating effects of divorce on some children. Recently, the president of the American Association for Marriage and Family Therapy noted that therapists used to believe that adults should leave cold or unfulfilling marriages. While they still agree that children and adults are better off out of verbally or physically abusive marriages, for other couples they now advocate staying together for the children. Therapists are reporting an increasing number of potential divorcees believe that staying in a cold or unfulfilling marriage is worthwhile from the standpoint of financial security, a satisfying relationship with the children, and not having to deal with the breakup of well-established relations with grandparents and other relatives (*New York Times,* 1996).

Another factor on the horizon is the possible increased costliness of leaving a marriage. The regulation and enforcement of child support payments may lead fathers to stay in marriages longer. A study of the effects of public programs designed to establish paternity and enforce child support payments to unmarried mothers showed that such policies were influential (Gaylin & Garfinkel, 1997). In counties with effective programs, the number of nonmarital births decreased.

The effectiveness of policies in this area suggests they may be efficacious in delaying divorce until children reach the age of majority.

The rise in income inequality and the erosion of real income may reach the point where individuals (especially those with children) will need two incomes to survive at a modicum level of comfort. This may act as an incentive to stay in a less than satisfying marriage. The onset of welfare reform legislation may contribute to this pressure in the very near future.

One thing I have not mentioned is the rising rate of pre- and post-marital cohabitation. An increasing proportion of people cohabit before their first marriage. More than 50% of previously married individuals 19 to 44 years of age cohabit (Bumpass & Sweet, 1989). Thirty-four percent of all cohabiting households (3.3 million) have children under the age of 15 (Spain & Bianchi, 1996). Nearly half of the relationships which include children (46%) will dissolve within 10 years (Bumpass et al., 1995). It should be noted, though, that some of the children in these households may have experienced a marriage before dissolution of the relationship. Cohabitation as a family form is increasing, as is the number of children born into such relationships. To date, this family form has largely been ignored. We need to begin to pay attention to the impact of relationship dissolutions on children of cohabiting couples. While some may view such relationships as a phase in their formalization, our own research suggests that at least three-fourths of such relationships are more like marriage in terms of relationship quality and resilience (Brown & Booth, 1996). Dissolution of cohabitation relationships may affect children in ways similar to those who undergo the divorce of married parents.

It is noteworthy that marriages preceded by cohabitation are more likely to end in divorce (Booth & Johnson, 1988). The reason for the higher dissolution rate is that people who cohabit are poor marriage material in that they are more likely to have a drug or alcohol problem, difficulty earning a living, or other problems. Thus, the children of such marriages are at higher risk of experiencing divorce. However, the effects are modest which means a large number of couples who premaritally cohabit have stable marriages.

NEW RESEARCH ON THE CHILDREN OF DIVORCE

There is near universal agreement that children do experience stress around the time of divorce and that it may be manifested in poorer grades, depression, anxiety, precocious sexual activity, and behavior problems, among other things (Demo & Acock, 1988). The elevation in stress prior to divorce appears to decline to near predivorce levels within a year or two. Recent research, however, has revealed a number of unexpected findings that extend and recast this generalization. Recent research alerts us to examine parent-child relations long before parental divorce occurs, to take into account the nature of the parents' marriage before divorce, and to examine the well-being of the children of divorce once they reach adulthood.

Child Well-Being Prior to Divorce

Cherlin and his colleagues (1991), using longitudinal data from large samples of U.S. and English families, showed that child behavior problems and poorer school performance appear years before divorce. Further, parent conflict accounts for part of the observed behavior problems for boys, but not for girls. Further research revealed that the problems continued into adulthood and approximately half of the effect could be accounted for by predivorce factors. Data analysis from our study of marital instability indicates that parental marital quality is linked to problems in parent-child relationships for up to 12 years before parental divorce (Amato & Booth, 1996), a finding that has implications for offspring postdivorce well-being as well as for intervention strategies. The analysis I am going to show you covers the first 8 years of the study. We examined four different measures of marital quality and found the results to be similar. Therefore, I will only show the model for marital happiness. We used a five-item scale of parent-child relations in 1980 and a four-item scale of parent-child affection in 1988, and we know whether the parents obtained a divorce in that period. Because of their potential for confounding our analysis we controlled for respondent's gender, race, age, years of education, family income, number of children in the household, the mean age of the children, and the presence of stepchildren. The model we tested is shown in Figure 2.3. We find parents' marital quality accounts for parent-child relationship problems in families who later experience divorce. We also find that there is no relation between parent-child relationship problems and later divorce, indicating that the child is not implicated as a causal factor in the divorce. Moreover, we find that parental marital happiness affects later parent-child affection as well as divorce. Finally, divorce only has a unique effect on subsequent parent-child affection in the case of fathers, which is consistent with prior research. However, parent-child problems affect subsequent parent-child affection among both mothers and fathers.

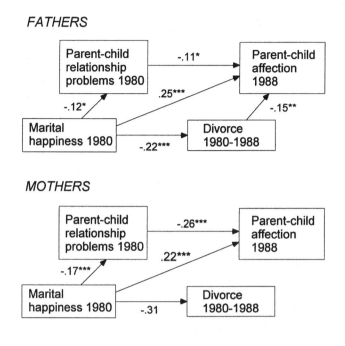

Figure 2.3. Path model showing associations among parental affection for children in 1988, divorce between 1980-1988, parent-child relationship problems in 1980, and parents' marital happiness in 1980

SOURCE: Amato, P., & Booth, A. (1996). A prospective study of divorce and parent-child relationships. *Journal of Marriage and the Family, 58,* 361. Copyright 1996 by the National Council on Family Relations, 3989 Central Ave. NE, Suite 550, Minneapolis, MN 55421 Reprinted by permission.

The link between marital quality, parent-child relationship problems, and later life parent-child affection may be interpreted in two ways. First, marital discord may preoccupy parents, leaving them unable to deal with their off-spring. While this is plausible, some research has shown that mothers intensify their relationship with young offspring by being more supportive when the marriage is threatened (Belsky et al., 1991). Our own research on young adult offspring, however, shows that divorce weakens mother-son relationships (Booth & Amato, 1994). Second, poor relations in both domains may reflect inability to develop and sustain intimate relationships with anyone. I think the second possibility may explain much of the link. Studies on the impact of premarital cohabitation on divorce (Booth & Johnson, 1988) and research on the instability of remarriages suggest that part of the explanation may involve people who are poor marriage material (Booth & Edwards, 1992). Such people are sufficiently skilled to form a relationship in the first place, but unable to sustain it. Either possibility would suggest the need for intensive, comprehensive, and flexible intervention.

There is ample evidence that being ignored by parents and a party to persistent conflict interfere with children's development. For reviews of research showing how parental conflict affects offspring's capability to form intimate relations, ability to maintain family and community ties, socioeconomic achievement, psychological well-being, and relationships with parents, see Amato and Booth (1997). It is clear that children are often directly involved in the parents' marital problems. This suggests that divorce should not be treated as a short-term adjustment problem, but one needing sustained care and perhaps medications. It also may mean that treating the family as a system is not going to achieve much because of the parent's limited ability to deal effectively with any relationship.

Parents' Marriage Prior to Divorce

The evidence suggests that marital quality is often inextricably tied with problems in parent-child relations many years before divorce occurs, and that the event of divorce has additional effects on later parent-child affection in the case of fathers. What is the impact of divorce when marital quality is not particularly bad? We know that many once-happy marriages dissolve and that many divorces occur when overt conflict between the parents is relatively low. Many parents, especially middle-class ones, feel they should not disagree in front of the children. I am afraid the news on divorce's effects on children in low conflict marriages is not good. As part of our study of marital instability we began interviewing a random sample of offspring who had been living in the home in 1980 and who had reached the age of 19 at the time of the 1992 interview. The longitudinal design and two sources of data allowed us to examine the interaction between predivorce parental marital quality and parental divorce for a wide range of offspring well-being indicators (Amato et al., 1995).

We expected children from highly conflictual marriages to often do better after divorce than those who remained in such marriages. However, we were uncertain how the children from low conflict marriages would fare. On the one

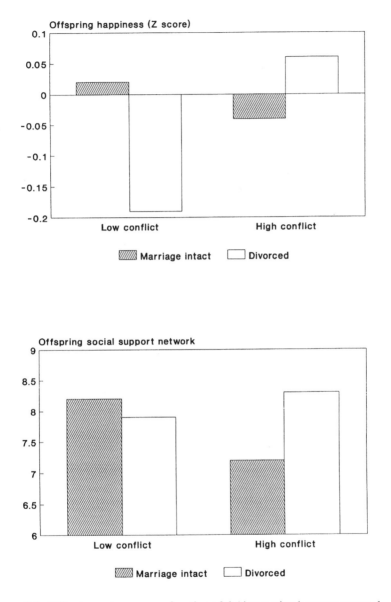

Figure 2.4. Offspring outcomes as a function of the interaction between parental marital conflict and parental divorce on child, controlling for parent's age, sex, race, and education and offspring's sex and age

SOURCE: Amato, P., & Booth, A. (1995). Parental divorce, marital conflict, and offspring well-being during early adulthood. *Social Forces, 73,* 910. Reprinted with permission.

hand, the lack of exposure to predivorce conflict may lessen the effect of divorce. On the other hand, the unexpected absence of a parent and an unpredictable home life may have adverse effects.

Marital conflict was assessed with a scale that tapped the severity and amount of verbal and physical conflict—frequency of disagreements, number of serious quarrels in a 2-month period, and whether spouses ever slapped, hit, pushed, kicked, or threw things at each other. We used the disagreement measure closest to the time of divorce; for those who did not divorce we used the mean conflict score for all interviews. The offspring well-being measures included a widely used scale (Langner, 1962) tapping symptoms of psychological distress, a universally used measure of overall happiness, the number of friends and relatives offspring felt emotionally close to, and, if offspring were married, an eleven-item scale of marital happiness.

As expected, we found that those who escaped a highly conflictual parental marriage did better as adults than those who remained in such marriages (see Figure 2.4). For offspring from low conflict homes, parental divorce was devastating. As can be seen, every aspect of well-being studied was adversely affected. The effect size is not trivial, being .25 of a standard deviation in the case of overall happiness.

We estimated the proportion of divorces that involved severe parental marital conflict prior to divorce and concluded that approximately 30% entailed frequent disagreement, serious quarrels, or physical abuse. Thus, it appears that the majority of offspring who experience parental divorce are from families in which conflict is a minor part of parental interaction.

While offspring from low conflict families do not suffer from the poor parent-child relations that result from low (nonconflict) marital quality, an unexpected and unwelcome divorce can result in suffering. These individuals present a different set of challenges for human service organizations and for the framers of public policy. While ameliorative programs and policies may not need to be as intensive or comprehensive for this group as for those who suffer from years of poor parent-child relationships, the fact that psychological distress and the quality of offspring's marriage are affected well into adulthood would suggest a need for ameliorative programs. Here the focus should be on understanding the unexpected event as well as on coming to terms with the challenges of the events which follow such as parental absence, decline in income, a possible low level of trust in others with whom they are intimate, and possibly having little confidence in their own judgment about forming close relationships.

The most discouraging thing about these findings is the evidence of inter-generational effects. The marriages of children of divorce whose parents did not fight are of lower quality than they would be if their parents had not dissolved their marriage. Not only does this mean that the children of such parents are more likely to divorce themselves, but that their children are apt to experience the same adverse consequences of divorce as their parents. Unless the divorce rate declines, we can expect the same high levels of personal disorganization in generations to come.

One theme emerging from recent research is the role of multiple family transitions in creating social and personal disorganization. In our own research we first noticed multiple divorces affecting offspring outcomes in 1984, but we did give it more than cursory attention. The study's focus was the impact of parental divorce on college students' courtship and dating patterns. In examining both the quantity and quality of heterosexual relations (Booth et al., 1984), we found that offspring of divorced parents were more likely to have sexual intercourse at an earlier age and to be more likely to be going steady, cohabiting, or married. We observed no difference in the quality of heterosexual relations until we examined whether offspring had experienced more than one divorce. Those who had rated their relationships as being of lower quality. Some indicated difficulty dating people who could lead to a serious relationship. A few years later we observed the effect of multiple divorces among the primary respondents in the marital instability study. Those whose parents went through more than one divorce and who reported being less close to one parent were more likely to have psychological distress, more marital problems, and a greater likelihood of divorce (Amato & Booth, 1991).

Recently, using other data sets, researchers have found that offspring who experience multiple transitions such as parental divorce, remarriage, cohabitation, and singlehood show more signs of personal disorganization in their life. For example, Wu (1996), using data from the National Longitudinal Study of Youth, found that multiple parental marital transitions predict premarital births independent of income and after controlling for religion, mother's education, father's occupational status, presence of father at age 14, number of siblings, respondent's mother's age at first birth, and an indicator of the respondent's intelligence. In a study of children born to unmarried women, Aquilino (1996), using data from the National Survey of Families and Households, found that three or more family transitions are related to lower rates of post-secondary educational achievement and faster transitions to adult status. Individuals with more transitions are more likely to live independently from their parents (not counting going to college or serving in the military) and to be in the paid labor force (not counting part-time work while attending school). These findings obtain after controlling for gender, race, age, birth order, number of siblings, mother's education, and whether the family was on welfare while the respondent was growing up. The fact that the majority of divorces are followed by parental remarriage and more than half to people between the ages of 19 and 44 are followed by a period of cohabitation (Bumpass & Sweet, 1989) as well as singlehood indicates that we should begin to separate the effect of multiple transitions from the experience of divorce itself.

There seems to be two questions to answer about multiple transitions. First, what factors predict multiple transitions? Are they mostly individuals with troubled family backgrounds and signs of mental illness (see Forthofer's et al. 1996 study of people who marry early before age 19), persons with antisocial personality traits, or individuals with limited education and occupational achievement which make them marginal participants in the paid labor force? Second, what is it about multiple transitions that accounts for the decline in offspring well-being? Does it have something to do with forming a secure attachment early in life (Belsky & Cassidy, 1995)? Do low levels of parental social support stem from competing loyalties to partners and children as has been found in stepfamilies (White, 1994)? Does it have to do with parents' inability to relate to anybody—children or spouses? What role does the child's temperament play in parental transitions? Do the multiple transitions free the individual from the constraints of the kin group, church, and the community and permit an erratic lifestyle that leads to antisocial behavior? I think these questions need to be part of our research agenda in understanding the impact of divorce on children.

The Children of Divorce as Young Adults

I do not want to suggest that there are no bright spots in recent research. Families are finding ways to adjust to divorce that are beneficial for offspring. For example, in a study of support obtained by the children of divorce from parents, we found that when taking into account help from one or both parents that the total percent of offspring receiving help is not that different from children from intact families. In a nontrivial number of cases (one-fifth) children were receiving support from both parents. While more help comes from mothers than fathers, it is impressive that the portion of the children of divorce receiving help is nearly equal to that of the children from intact families (Amato et al., 1995). This includes help with household chores, advice, child care, small loans, and transportation. It is important to note, however, that this finding does not apply to deep pocket items such as paying college expenses. The study was replicated using National Survey of Families and Household data (Aquilino, 1994) which means we can have some confidence in the results. This suggests that offspring and their parents have developed positive ways to accommodate the high divorce rate.

These accommodations notwithstanding, it is important to realize that divorce affects the lives of young adults much as it does younger children. "Parent divorce is associated with more problematic parent-child relationships (less affection, less consensus, less contact, and less perceived support); an increased probability of divorce among married offspring; and lower socioeconomic attainment (lower education, lower occupational status, and greater economic adversity). Furthermore, these associations are independent of predivorce conflict between parents. In other words, for these outcomes, low parental marital quality lowers offspring well-being, and parental divorce lowers it even further" (Amato & Booth, 1997, p. 219).

Needed Research

Recent studies put a new perspective on needed research. The research showing that problems emerge years before divorce suggests that significant numbers of the children of divorce are living with parents who lack the skills to maintain sustained intimate relations with anyone, including their children. Therefore, divorce may not be the problem, but a history of poor parent-child relationships may be the key to understanding the adverse offspring outcomes often associated with divorce. Relationship problems notwithstanding, one must keep in mind that a nontrivial number of children may suffer from personality disorders which are largely inherited. Personality disorders often create estranged parent-child relations (Sampson & Laub, 1993; Sampson & Laub, 1994) which may be implicated in the decision to divorce and subsequent poor child outcomes. One of the products of divorce are large and increasing numbers of stepfamilies and mother-partner (cohabiting) families. Both have been shown to be poor family environments for children, often because the father has only limited involvement with the children (Thomson et al., 1992), but also because the mother invests less in her children (White, 1994).

Research is needed to separate the unique effects of poor parent-child relations from divorce itself. To do this we need longitudinal studies that monitor the quality of parent-child relations over an extended period prior to parental divorce. Information on whether the parents are capable of developing sustained and intimate relations with their children should rely on indirect measures such as family structure (stepfamily and cohabitation), history of change in marital relations (prior divorce, remarriage, and cohabitation), level of parental and adult-child conflict, amount of parental support (helping children with homework and personal problems, showing affection, talking together), and control (monitoring child behavior as well as giving children age appropriate decision making opportunities). We also need to have detailed information on several indicators of personality disorganization in children which serve both as dependent variables (when estimating the effects of divorce) and independent variables (when estimating the effects of child temperament on parental estrangement). I would recommend three measures of child personality disorganization: (1) inability of the child to form sustained intimate relationships, (2) depression, and (3) antisocial behavior. Following divorce one should continue to track these three outcome variables to see whether divorce and the accompanying drop in family income and rise in residential mobility result in further erosions of these features. The National Survey of Families and Households (NSFH), National Longitudinal Survey of Youth (NLSY), and the Marital Instability Over the Life Course Study (Booth et al., 1994) could be used to make such assessments because they are longitudinal, and include information on parent child-relations, child temperment, and divorce.

The same research strategy could be used to understand why multiple marital transitions on the part of parents are so severe for child well-being. It would be reasonable to expect that such parents are so absorbed in forming intimate relations that they spend little time on relations with their children. It is also probable that such parents are inept at forming sustainable intimate relationships with their children as well as with adults. However, multiple transitions may also indicate other problems such as mental illness or drug abuse which would be destructive for children. The research strategy would be to compare the causes and effects of multiple transitions over and above those of one divorce.

The finding that children residing in low conflict homes who suffer as a result of being confronted with an unexpected parental divorce presents a different research problem. The original study has been replicated once (Jekielek, 1996) which gives us some faith that the finding is probably accurate. The finding that one of the consequences of divorce for children residing with parents in low conflict marriages is lower offspring marital quality and is disturbing because it portends continued high marital instability. More information on the background of the child and the family environment are needed to understand the mechanism at work. Because the divorce-outcome coefficients are relatively low, it suggests that a number of children who experience divorce get through relatively unscathed except for a period of a year or two around the time of the divorce when they may receive lower grades, experience some depression, or disturb parent-child relations. It is clear that significant numbers of children who experience divorce are making successful transitions to adulthood.

The questions needing research are:

1. Are children who are extensively distressed by the dissolution of a low conflict marriage individuals who have exceptionally low tolerance for stress?

2. Are they individuals who are inordinately dependent on both parents as opposed to being primarily dependent on one?

3. Are they offspring who have little autonomy or practice at making decisions for themselves? Do they have low self esteem?

4. Are they people with few social resources other than parents, that is individuals with few friends or relatives with whom they are close?

Perhaps the problem lies with the parents. Perhaps they are not very expressive so that others, including their children, cannot read the cues as to relationship quality. Perhaps the parents are more interested in their own personal welfare (such that they leave a satisfactory relationship for what is potentially a better one) than the welfare of their children. That is, they may be so wrapped up in their own adult world that it takes precedence over the welfare of their children. If that were the case we would expect lower levels of offspring support and control on the part of these parents. Again, longitudinal research would be the best option to explore these questions, but cross sectional information from adults who have recently divorced and from children whose parents have divorce may be sufficient to make significant advances in our knowledge about the severe consequences of divorce among low conflict couples.

One of the products of such research would be to generate fairly precise estimates of the proportion of children who are likely to experience adverse outcomes as a result of parental divorce. Such data would give us a perspective on the numbers of children who will be severely disadvantaged by current family trends. The tendency now is to assume that any negative finding tends to apply to a wide spectrum of children without taking into account those who successfully negotiate family disruption. Not only would the information be useful to researchers, but it would be of value to those planning the need for and distribution of human service. It would also be of use to clinicians who want a known probability that any child of divorce will experience adverse outcomes. The practitioner may use this information for apprising parents of the probable outcomes of divorce as well as for designing a therapeutic course of action for children who have experienced divorce.

REFERENCES

Ahlburgh, D., & De Vita, C. (1992). New realities of the American family. *Population Bulletin, 47,* 1-50.

Amato, P., Loomis, L., & Booth, A. (1995). Parental divorce, marital conflict, and offspring well-being during early adulthood. *Social Forces, 73,* 895-915.

Amato, P., Rezac, S., & Booth, A. (1995). Helping between parents and young adult offspring: The role of parental marital quality, divorce, and remarriage. *Journal of Marriage and the Family, 57,* 363-374.

Amato, P., & Booth, A. (1995). Changes in gender role attitudes and perceived marital quality. *American Sociological Review, 60,* 58-66.

Amato, P., & Booth, A. (1996). A prospective study of divorce and parent-child relationships. *Journal of Marriage and the Family, 58,* 356-365.

Amato, P., & Booth, A. (1991). Consequences of parental divorce and marital unhappiness for adult well-being. *Social Forces, 69,* 895-914.

Amato, P., & Booth, A. (1997). *A generation at risk: Growing up in an era of family upheaval.* Cambridge MA: Harvard University Press.

Aquilino, W. (1994). Impact of childhood family disruption on young adults' relationships with parents. *Journal of Marriage and the Family, 56,* 295-213.

Aquilino, W. (1996). The life course of children born to unmarried mothers: Childhood living arrangements and young adult outcomes. *Journal of Marriage and the Family, 58,* 293-310.

Belsky, J., Youngblade, L., Rovine, M., & Volling, B. (1991). Patterns of marital change and parent-child interaction. *Journal of Marriage and the Family, 53,* 487-498.

Belsky, J., & Cassidy, J. (1995). Attachment: Theory and evidence. In M. Rutter & D. Hay (Eds.), *Development through life* (pp 373-401). London: Blackwell.

Booth, A., Brinkerhoff, D., & White, L. (1984). The impact of parental divorce on courtship. *Journal of Marriage and the Family, 46,* 67-75.

Booth, A., & Johnson, D. (1988). Premarital cohabitation and marital success. *Journal of Family Issues, 9,* 255-272.

Booth, A., & Edwards, J. (1992). Starting over: Why remarriages are more unstable. *Journal of Family Issues, 13,* 179-194.

Booth, A., Johnson, D., White, L., & Edwards, J. (1991). *Marital instability over the life course: Methodology report and code book for Three Wave Panel Study.* Lincoln: University of Nebraska Bureau of Sociological Research.

Booth, A., & Amato, P. (1994). Parental marital quality, parental divorce, and relations with parents. *Journal of Marriage and the Family, 56,* 21-35.

Brown, S., & Booth, A. (1996). Cohabitation versus marriage: A comparison of relationship quality. *Journal of Marriage and the Family, 58,* 668-678.

Bumpass, L., & Sweet, J. 1989. National estimates of cohabitation. *Demography, 26,* 615-625.

Bumpass, L., Raley, K., & Sweet, J. (1995). The changing character of stepfamilies: Implications of cohabitation and nonmarital childbearing. *Demography, 32,* 425-436

Cherlin, A. (1992). *Marriage, divorce, and remarriage.* Cambridge, MA: Harvard University Press.

Cherlin, A., Furstenberg, F., Chase-Lansdale, L., Kiernan, K., Morrison, D., & Teitler, J. (1991). Longitudinal studies of effects of divorce on children in Great Britain and the United States. *Science, 252,* 1386-1389.

Demo, D., & Acock, A. (1988). The impact of divorce on children. *Journal of Marriage and the Family, 50,* 619-648.

Forthofer, M., Kessler, R., Story, A., & Gotlib, I. (1996). The effects of psychiatric disorders on the probability and timing of first marriage. *Journal of Health and Social Behavior, 37,* 121-132.

Gaylin, C., & Garfinkel, I. (1997, March 28). *Will child support enforcement reduce nonmarital childbearing?* Paper presented at Population Association of America meeting

Glenn, N. (1991). The recent trend in marital success in the United States. *Journal of Marriage and the Family, 53,* 261-270.

Glenn, N. (1996). Values, attitudes, and the state of American marriage. In D. Popenoe, J. Elshtain, & D. Blankenhorn (Eds.), *Promises to keep: Decline and renewal of marriage in America* (pp. 15-33). Lanham, MD: Rowman and Littlefield.

Goode, W. (1963). *World Revolution and Family Patterns.* Glencoe: The Free Press.

Jekielek, S. (1996). *The relative and interactive impacts of parental conflict and marital disruption on children's emotional well-being.* Paper presented at the Annual Meeting of the American Sociological Association, New York.

Hernandez, D. (1993). *America's Children: Resources from Family, Government, and the Economy.* New York: Russell Sage Foundation.

Langner, T. (1962). A twenty-two item screening score of psychiatric symptoms indicating impairment. *Journal of Health and Social Behavior, 3,* 269-276.

Rogers, S., & Amato, P. (1997). Is marital quality declining? Evidence from two recent cohorts. *Social Forces, 75,* 1089-1100.

Sampson, R., & Laub, J. (1994). Urban poverty and the family context of delinquency: A new look at structure and process in a classic study. *Child Development, 65,* 523-540.

Sampson, R., & Laub, J. (1993). *Crime in the making: Pathways and turning points through life.* Cambridge, MA: Harvard University Press.

South, S., & Lloyd, K. (1995). Spousal alternatives and marital dissolution. *American Sociological Review, 60,* 21-35.

Spain, D., & Bianchi, S. (1996). *Balancing act: Motherhood, marriage, and employment among American women.* New York: Russell Sage Foundation.

Thomson, E., McLanhan, S., & Curtin, R. (1992). Family structure, gender, and parental socialization. *Journal of Marriage and the Family, 54,* 368-378.

Udry, J. R. (1981). Marital alternatives and marital disruption. *Journal of Marriage and the Family, 43,* 889-898.

Voydanoff, P. (1991). Economic distress and family relations: A review of the eighties. *Journal of Marriage and the Family, 52,* 1099-1115.

White, L. (1994). Stepfamilies over the life course: Social support. In A. Booth & J. Dunn (Eds.), *Stepfamilies: Who benefits? Who does not?* (pp. 109-137). Hillsdale, NJ: Lawrence Erlbaum.

Wu, L. (1996). Effects of family instability, income, and income instability on the risk of a premarital birth. *American Sociological Review, 61,* 386-406.

PART II

Parental Responsibility After Divorce

Arguably the most important decisions inaugurating postdivorce life for children concern the allocation of parental responsibility to offspring. It is not only the legal allocation of custodial responsibilities and the arrangement of visitation that shape postdivorce family life, but also the informal processes by which these arrangements are negotiated, the felt obligation each parent assumes for ensuring that the child maintains a continuing, happy relationship with the other parent, and the emotions associated with marital dissolution that will continue to color postdivorce life. Although formal decisions concerning custody and visitation create only broad parameters governing postdivorce life—as family members' lives change over time, parental caregiving responsibilities evolve also—these decisions create the conditions that make it either easy or difficult for parents and offspring to continue to grow together in a satisfying postdivorce relationship. For this reason, formal and informal policies governing child custody and visitation after divorce have been controversial. In this section, two scholars wrestle with how to define, psychologically and legally, parental responsibility after divorce.

In her chapter, Eleanor Maccoby considers alternative formulations for determining the custody of children and the trade-offs that are entailed in each approach. The costs and benefits of assigning physical custody to the mother, the father, or both jointly are considered in light of factors such as children's age, the parents' work schedules, the predivorce child rearing roles of each parent, the history of interparental conflict, and parents' new relationships. She settles on a preference for the parent who has been the child's "primary caretaker"—that is, the parent who has provided the greatest day-to-day care for the child—as one that best encompasses children's interests and needs, especially when younger children are concerned. Maccoby also considers provisions for the economic support of children and emphasizes the financial obligations of fathers, who are usually the higher wage earners of the family, despite concerns about the perceived unfairness of such obligations absent the shared custody of offspring. In the end, she emphasizes the importance of the obligations of *each* parent to their children in the postdivorce family over traditional (and, all too commonly, typical) views that one parent "owns" the child.

Katharine Bartlett, a legal scholar, shares this view in her discussion of postdivorce parenting arrangements for children. But she frames this goal in the context of the tensions that are inherent in legal decision making concerning custody and the difficulties of current legal formulations (such as "the best interests of the child") for awarding custody of children. She proposes resolving these tensions by allocating responsibility for children in rough proportion to the caregiving responsibilities exercised by parents before the divorce. Reliance on past caregiving patterns, she argues, adds greater certainty and predictability to the decision-making process, without requiring the state to weigh in on one form of custody over another. Determinacy, in short, comes from the prior decisions of the parents themselves, not judges or state legislatures. Her proposal includes a guaranteed minimum amount of responsibility to nonresidential parents to enable parents who were not active caretakers in the past to maintain a meaningful relationship with the child, and deference to the preferences of older children. Central to her proposal are parenting plan requirements, which help structure parental agreement and planning about the child's future and provide for how subsequent disputes will be resolved. Protective provisions in instances of domestic violence and the availability of voluntary, nonadversarial dispute resolution processes are also critical to her scheme. Together, Bartlett argues that these provisions ensure the maximum degree of stability for children, meaningful continued relationships with each parent, and fairness to both parents.

Chapter 3

The Custody of Children of Divorcing Families
Weighing the Alternatives

Eleanor E. Maccoby

When there are children in a family, parental divorce brings with it a cluster of issues that have never arisen in the family before. While children are living with both parents in the same household, there may of course be disagreements between parents concerning how best to deal with the children. Also, there often is some sort of division of labor between the parents concerning which parent is responsible for which child-rearing duties. Still, they share responsibility for the children and both interact with them on a daily basis.

When the parents establish two separate households, decisions must be made concerning which parental household will be the children's primary residence. Decisions about where the child is to live inevitably have much broader implications than simply residence *per se*. Whichever parent the child lives with becomes, almost by necessity, the parent who is responsible for rearing the child: for providing day-to-day care, establishing the rules and values the child is expected to live by, training the child in proper behavior, and making decisions about medical care, education, and religious observance. Until fairly recently, a legal award of custody to a parent carried with it an assignment of the full range of parental rights and obligations to that parent. In this sense, an award of custody to one parent has traditionally meant that the parent who was awarded custody "got" the children and the other parent lost them. One could say that an award of custody signified which parent would "own" the child henceforth.

The changes in divorce law that have taken place in this country over the last several decades have brought about some deep changes with respect to "winning" and "losing" in custody awards. First of all, the changes have allowed for a distinction between physical custody and so-called "legal" custody. Under this distinction, a parent who is awarded physical custody may or may not also be awarded legal custody embodying the exclusive right to make major decisions concerning the child's welfare and future. A second major change has been the recognition of joint physical custody as a legally authorized form of custody. An award of joint physical custody means that the children will spend substantial amounts of residential time with each of the parents. And of course there are lesser degrees of divided residence, in which a child will have a major residence with one parent but make regular overnight visits to the nonresidential parent. Custody law in this country now almost universally embodies the assumption that it is in children's best interests to maintain contact, and as close a relationship as possible, between children and each of the divorced parents. Therefore divorcing parents are expected to accept the viewpoint that neither parent will "own" the children and neither parent will lose them, but that instead, whenever possible, the two parents will continue to have some degree of joint responsibility for the children and must continue to function as coparents at some level even though the other aspects of their marital relationship have been dissolved.

Today, there is a much broader menu of custodial arrangements from which to choose than was formerly the case. Primary physical custody can be awarded to either the mother or the father or to both jointly. In families with more than one child, custody can be split with one or more children living with the mother and other children with the father. Legal custody can be separated from the physical custodial award: For example, today in California, the most common custodial arrangement is an award of physical custody to the mother and legal custody to the mother and father jointly. Given that primary physical custody is to go to one of the parents, there are further choices open concerning visitation with the other parent; how frequently and at what times will visitation take place.

Beyond these modifications of the traditional concept of all-or-none custody, there is a growing interest in a different possibility: a system in which the courts do not make any formal custody award at all. Instead, the parents are required to come up with a "parenting plan," which specifies how the children's residential time is to be divided. This plan is then brought to a court for ratification. Several jurisdictions (e.g., the state of Washington) have adopted this approach. Nevertheless, when arriving at a parenting plan under this new system, the parents must still choose from approximately the same menu of possibilities available under the earlier legal procedures. Negotiating a parenting plan may involve a good deal of conflict between parents when each wants more time with the children than the other wants to give up. Courts must still maintain mediation services and other structures for settling disputes when parents cannot agree on a parenting plan.

Whether or not the courts make a formal custody award, the current reality is that custody decisions are now being left to the parents as much as possible. Parents are not only allowed, but encouraged and sometimes pressured to come up with their own agreement, with or without the involvement of attorneys or mediators. Judges serve mainly to ratify custody arrangements that have been made by the parents alone or at nonjudicial levels of the legal system.

We turn now to the question of how the choices among the alternative custodial arrangements are to be made. In earlier times the choices were easier—or at least, easier for the legal system—because there was a presumption for maternal custody embodied in divorce statutes or case law, and joint custody was seldom considered a viable arrangement. Therefore a mother would almost automatically be awarded custody. A father who wanted full custody or even shared custody faced a difficult burden of proof: he had to show that the mother was unfit or undeserving before he could become the custodial parent. In a rapid state-to-state cascade in the 1970s, divorce laws were rewritten to specify that decisions concerning the custody of children could not be made on the basis of any gender-based preference or presumption. Mothers and fathers were to stand equal before the law, and their respective claims for custody were to be based on how favorable a rearing environment each could provide for the child. Decisions were to be made on a case-by-case basis, considering the best interest of the child, with parental prerogatives or "rights" taking second place.

Criteria for Determining What Is in the Child's Best Interests

How, then, to decide what arrangement would best serve the child's interests and needs? An array of criteria can come into play. Are the parents still engaged in open conflict? If they are, this might affect the viability of a joint custody arrangement, or even of visitation. Which parent will be better able to keep siblings together? Which parent's work schedule fits in better with the children's schedules and the availability of alternative care? Which parent can provide a better physical environment—where children can have their own rooms, or live in a safe neighborhood? Which parent can send the children to better schools? Which parent's new live-in partner is more willing to accept the children? Which parent is more willing to allow unrestricted visitation with the other parent? Which parent is more psychologically stable—in particular, more free of addictions that may impair their functioning, or least subject depressed moods or bouts of impulsive, ill-considered behavior? Does either parent have a history of physical abuse of a spouse, or of the children? Which parent is more competent in providing day-to-day child care? Which parent is more skillful in achieving a workable balance between authority and permissiveness in handling disciplinary issues? And perhaps most important of all: which parent has the closest emotional bond with the children, inspiring their deepest love and trust? And how much weight should be given to a child's own preference (assuming it is deemed not too damaging to ask the child for a preference?)

These questions come up in the offices of attorneys and mediators when custody disputes are being negotiated. But they are also paramount when parents are trying to arrive at their own agreement without the involvement of third parties. As Mnookin and Kornhauser (1979) have noted, parents bargain with each other "in the shadow of the law." In earlier times, when a presumption for maternal custody prevailed, parents made their custody decisions in the light of the knowledge that an award to the mother would be the likely outcome of any court procedure, barring contrary evidence. Today, in their private bargaining, parents know that they must formulate their claims in terms of what will be best for the children. In addition, both parents are expected to remain involved in the lives of their children.

In real-life cases, especially those requiring mediation, it has proved to be extraordinarily difficult to apply and balance the multiple "best interest" criteria. If one parent makes a charge of abuse against the other parent, and the other parent denies it, who is to be believed? How can it be determined which parent has the closest emotional bond with a child, especially when both clearly love the child and both are loved by the child? If one of the parents does not want the divorce, and is depressed over the separation, is this psychological problem likely to persist, or is it only a temporary condition that will not impair the parent's long-term functioning as a parent? In contested cases that reach the level of court hearings, each parent's attorneys will bring in witnesses and experts who will testify to that parent's virtues and the other's faults, the testimony for the two sides often being in direct conflict as to fact.

The "Primary Caretaker" Preference

The agonizing difficulties for parents, mediators, and judges in assessing and weighing the many factors that deserve to be considered have led to a reliance on criteria that are relatively easier to assess. Chief among these is the relative roles of the two parents in the predivorce day-to-day caretaking of the children. Although in some cases this is difficult to determine, in most cases it is not, and it is a criterion that can often be used to resolve disputes in a more objective fashion than is possible when decisions must rest on such issues as which parent has the closer emotional bond with the children, or which parent is more psychologically stable, or which has better parenting skills.

Giving weight to primary caregiving is an attractive choice not only because it can be more reliably assessed than other criteria, but also because it may be seen as a proxy for other criteria. It is reasonable to assume that if one parent has done most of the day-to-day caregiving for a child, that parent has developed greater parenting skills—greater skills in managing the child's daily schedule and being effective in responding to the child's needs—than the parent who has been less involved. In other words, other things being equal, it would appear to be a reasonable assumption that the more experienced parent is likely to be the more effective parent—the one best able to nurture and socialize the child. How strong is the connection between experience and parenting skill? Probably only moderately strong. We know that for some parents, no amount of hands-on practice makes them effective practitioners of the art of parenting. Still, it is likely that the parent who is more effective at dealing with children is the one more likely to have become the primary caregiver in the first place, because both parents recognized that this arrangement as being beneficial to all concerned.

Also, it is reasonable to suppose that a parent—in most cases, a father—who has left the job of daily caregiving to his wife would have a good deal to learn if he were to take over the primary caretaking function following divorce. He might be able to learn fairly quickly if necessary, but his wife would clearly have a head start, in being able to continue her practiced, customary routines with the children. Perhaps more important is the fact that the *children* have become used to her regime. For them, a change of primary caregivers is likely to be disruptive and stressful, at least in the short run. The cumulative stress of divorce is likely to be greater the more changes there are, and most parents, mediators, and judges recognize the importance of providing as much continuity as possible, so as not to compound the stresses that inevitably attend the divorce itself. In the interests of maintaining stability for children, it has usually seemed wisest for all concerned to continue in their accustomed roles unless there are compelling reasons to change.

A longitudinal study of approximately 1,000 divorcing families (hereafter referred to as the Stanford Custody Study) revealed that in mother-custody families, nonresidential fathers usually trusted the quality of the caregiving being done by their ex-wives. And in father-custody families, the mothers expressed few misgivings about the quality of the care he provided for the children. By contrast, mothers' with custody frequently expressed concerns about the father's caregiving skills. This would come up in connection with their worries while the children were visiting their fathers—concerns about the children being neglected or endangered while in his care. Custodial fathers—a much smaller group—for their part, often expressed concerns about the adequacy of the care provided by their ex-wives. We see then that the parents' own knowledge concerning each other's competence in caregiving might well have been involved in the decisions about who was to become the primary custodian at the time of divorce.

It is sometimes assumed that the parent who has been functioning as primary caregiver is likely not only to be the more skillful parent, but also the parent with whom the child has the closer emotional bond. If this inference is valid, primary-caretaker status can serve as a proxy for a close parent-child bond—a bond which everyone recognizes as of paramount importance in making custody decisions, but which is notoriously difficult to assess reliably. It is interesting that in the *Parenting Act*, adopted by the state of Washington 10 years ago, the law specified that the nature of the parent-child bond and the primary caretaker role should be considered jointly (Ellis, 1990; Ellis, 1994). The Act listed seven criteria that should be taken into account in setting up a parenting plan, and rank-ordered them. The list included such factors as the child's preferences, the parents' work schedules, the need to keep siblings together, and so forth, but first priority was to be given to "the strength, nature, and stability of the child's relationship with each parent (including which parent has taken more responsibility for daily care)." Evidently the drafters of this statute recognized the difficulty of assessing the strength, nature, and stability of the child's relationship with each parent independently of who had been the primary caretaker.

In fact, do the two things go together? Clearly, there must be families in which the mother does most of the caretaking but the children nevertheless have a warmer, more trusting relationship with their father. In the usual case, however, the two things probably do go together. We know from Youniss and Smollar's work (1985) that older children, when interviewed, say that they love both parents equally, but that they have a closer, more intimate relationship with their mothers because she knows them better—something that presumably grows out of her long-standing role as primary caretaker in most families.

In the Stanford custody study, also, when parents were asked their reasons for adopting their custodial arrangement for the children, some of their reports pointed to a connection between the primary parent role and bonding with the children. Some examples:

Father of two children ages 5 and 3: "She's the guiding force behind the children. She has more desire to be a mother—more prepared to take on the kids than me. I couldn't give the kids the time they need to bring them up."

Father of a 1-year-old daughter: "I don't know how to be with a baby very well. She's very attached to her mother. She screams a lot and I'm not used to that. She doesn't like being away from her mother—doesn't like being here. It's most sensible (for her to be with her mother)."

Of course there are some fathers— mainly those with older children—who have developed a close bond with their children and feel perfectly willing and competent to take on their primary care, regardless of how involved they were in caregiving prior to the divorce. We know very little about how well the predivorce caregiving roles of the two parents predict the quality of each parent's relationships with the children in the postdivorce situation.

In deciding about the allocation of the child's residential time following divorce, most parents and mediators want to give some consideration to the work schedules of the two parents. There have been several highly publicized cases in which a father has been awarded custody of a young child over the protests of the mother, on the grounds that she is going to school or working full-time and does not have time to care for the child. In these cases, though the father may be working full-time, he has usually been either living with his mother, or remarried to a nonworking wife, so that there has been a woman at his home to be the caregiver while he is at work. The divorced working mother, on the other hand, would have to rely on hired child care, and some judges have deemed this a less favorable environment for the child even though an award of custody to the father and grandmother or stepmother entails separation of the child from the mother. Such custody decisions have understandably generated storms of outrage from working mothers.

Today, however, such a judicial decision would be rare. Most of the cases courts deal with involve families in which both parents are working, and in which either a father or a mother who is awarded primary physical custody will have to rely on relatives or hired day care arrangements to some extent.

In a usual case, not much weight is given in custodial decisions to whether a parent is in the labor force or not. However mediators and courts, and parents themselves, do give some consideration to how well each parent's work schedule can be adapted to the needs of the children. In most cases where both parents are working, the mothers have pre-adapted their work schedules in order to manage their child care responsibilities: they have taken jobs that seldom require out-of-town travel, jobs that do not make unexpected demands for overtime work, jobs that are not too far from home or from the children's school or day care center. As economists say, they have already "discounted" their jobs, foregoing promotions or more attractive work opportunities for the sake of their second-shift duties as mothers and homemakers (Funder, 1986; Hanson & Pratt, 1995; Joshi, 1984). Fathers have much less often done so—a fact which no doubt helps to account for the fact that in families with young children, the fathers are able to earn so much more than the mothers when both are working. The discrepancy in pre-adapting jobs for parenting duties means that at the time of divorce, most mothers' jobs allow them to take on the primary physical custody of children more readily than do most fathers' jobs.

We have now seen several reasons why a prior history of being the primary caretaker of the children figures so strongly in the custodial decisions at the time of divorce. We should note that the primary caretaker criterion appears to have at least as much weight when parents arrive at their own decisions as they do when the legal system is involved in resolving custody disputes, so the use of this criterion is not something being imposed by the legal system. In either case, parents and professionals have to rely to some extent on generally accepted or legally specified guidelines to arrive at their decisions. Of course, however, one size does not fit all, and we might expect that couples who are able to arrive at their own agreement without recourse to the legal system might fall more in the range of cases who fit the general norms. The cases that go into court-ordered mediation or litigation, on the other hand, might have a higher proportion of cases in which the primary caretaker criterion is not as appropriate a basis for decisions as it is in the general case. However a recent review of court-ordered mediation cases in California (Depner, Cannata, & Ricci, 1991) found that in the cases where there was a dispute over custody, mothers were awarded physical custody in 57% of the cases, fathers in only 7% (27% were awarded joint custody, and the remainder "other"). I take these figures to mean that the strong tilt toward mothers as physical custodians reflects a heavy weight being given to the value of continuity in caregiving, whether by the legal system or by parents themselves.

In summary, I believe that the primary caretaker role is given weight largely because it is easier to determine than the "softer" criteria, and also because it is generally believed that it is good for children undergoing the stress of parental divorce to have continuity in as many facets of their lives as possible. But I have argued that the primary caretaker role is probably also given weight because it is presumed to embody a repertoire of caretaking skills, a close emotional tie with the children, and a demonstrated willingness to subordinate at least some of the demands of work to the needs of the children. These things in their turn imply a strong motivation to take care of the children—a strong commitment to their welfare. But we should note that beliefs concerning the associated benefits that primary caregiving is presumed to carry with it are based on assumptions that are not well grounded empirically. We do not know how strong the connections are, although it makes intuitive sense that they are present to some degree.

A Return to a Sex-of-Parent Presumption?

It seems that relying on the primary caretaker criterion amounts to a creeping return of a gendered presumption in custody determinations: a thinly disguised preference for mothers, since mothers have been the primary caretaker in the large majority of families. Although fathers in two-parent families where both parents work have undoubtedly been assuming an increasing share of child care duties (Furstenberg, 1988), mothers still clearly predominate as caregivers. Despite social pressures to change this imbalance, change has been very slow. And the fact is that physical custody is much more often awarded to mothers than fathers. Among the approximately 1,000 families enrolled in the Stanford Custody Study, almost 8 times as many mothers as fathers were awarded physical custody, and this is in a state where any preference based on the gender of the parent has been explicitly excluded as a legitimate basis for choice under the law. Clearly, to the extent that the gender imbalance in custody awards is due to a reliance on the primary caretaker criterion; it has indeed tilted large numbers of custody awards to mothers.

I believe there is a substantial difference between the presumption for maternal custody that previously prevailed and the way custody awards are currently being made. Current practice is more flexible and allows for cases in which the father has been the primary caretaker, or cases in which the two parents have been equally involved in caring for the children. For the sake of discussion, let us consider two hypothetical families:

> Family 1 is a traditional family in which the mother has not worked since the children were born, and has done almost all the child care and household management functions; the father has been the exclusive wage earner. The father regards the care of children to be his wife's sphere and tends to leave decisions about the children to her. When he is at home he plays with them when he is not too tired, and may take a child with him on an errand or outing. Often he reads them a story at bedtime. Sometimes he, too, is involved in discipline. He loves his children, and considers himself intensely committed to their welfare, but is not closely involved in the details of their daily lives.

> Family 2 is a modern egalitarian family, in which both parents work outside the home, working similar hours, and receiving equal pay at their jobs. The children are in day care when both parents are at work. At home, the parents share all the child care and household duties equally. Both parents take turns in taking the child to the doctor or phoning baby sitters when they want to go out of an evening. Either parent may stay with the children while the other does errands or engages in adult out-of-home activities. They each feel free to direct and discipline the children.

If the parents in Family 1 divorce, the primary caretaker criterion obviously dictates that the mother will have physical custody of the children. If the situation were reversed, so that it was the mother who had been the primary wage earner and the father had remained out of the labor force, staying at home to care for the children and to do the housework, then just as obviously he would get physical custody. However, families with mother wage earners and father house-husbands are extremely rare. In Family 2, neither parent has the advantage, in terms of the primary caretaker criterion, and there would be a strong likelihood of an award of joint custody. In this case, any other decision would have to be based on other criteria.

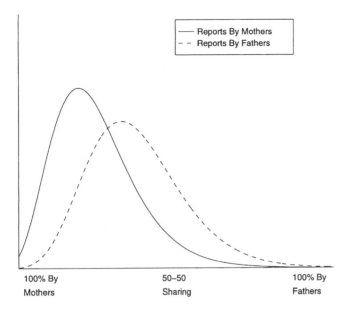

——— Reports By Mothers
– – Reports By Fathers

100% By   50–50   100% By
Mothers   Sharing   Fathers

Figure 3.1. Balance of predivorce caregiving by mothers and fathers

NOTE: Estimated frequency distributions, based on data from Maccoby and Mnookin (1992, Chapter 3).

Neither Family 1 nor Family 2 represents the usual case today. Figure 3.1 illustrates roughly what studies find to be the more usual balance between mother and father caregiving in the predivorce situation:

This differentiation in caregiving by the two parents is usually accompanied by a compensating differentiation of wage earning, with the fathers earning more and the mothers participating in the wage earning function but to a lesser degree. Figure 1 shows two curves,[1] one representing what fathers claim to have been their level of predivorce involvement in providing hands-on care for the children, and the other representing what mothers say was the case. I have claimed that it is easier to determine who has been the primary caretaker than to determine the more subtle aspects of parenting quality, and I believe that it is indeed easier. Still, there are difficulties in coming to a reliable assessment. Both parents usually agree that the mother was more involved in caregiving prior to the divorce, but fathers frequently claim greater involvement than mothers are willing to allow. I suspect that the mothers are more often right. A father may rate himself as quite highly involved because he does more than his own father did, or more than is done by other fathers he knows, rather than by comparison with his wife, and he may not have a clear picture of how much his wife does when he is not present. Still, if we split the difference and assume that the truth lies somewhere between what the two parents tell us, it is clear enough that the primary caretaker criterion would tilt strongly toward mothers as primary custodians in divorcing families.

This picture is clearly not the same as our hypothetical example in Family 1, where the mother did 100% of the caregiving. Many fathers do have quite substantial involvement, though less than mothers. And many mothers work, hiring substitute care and reducing the hours that they themselves spend in caregiving, though they usually still do more of it than fathers. How can these facts be taken into account in custody decisions? One way is to make graded custody decisions, where the amount of the child's residential time each parent gets is proportional to the amount of each parent's predivorce involvement. If, as Michael Lamb and colleagues (1987) have said, fathers spend about one third as much time in interaction with children as mothers do, then out of 30 overnights a month, mothers would get 22 or 23, fathers would get 7 or 8. In other words, mothers would get primary physical custody, but fathers would get liberal overnight visitation. Or, mothers would get primary physical custody and fathers would get joint legal custody. Both of these solutions appear to be widely utilized in present day custody decisions.

Obviously, apportioning the child's residential time exactly according to the balance of predivorce caretaking responsibilities between the two parents is too mechanical. It would have to be fine tuned to the circumstances of the individual family, but according to what has been stated so far, it seems like a good starting point for negotiations.

The Financial Side of the Divorce Decisions

Two years ago, California modified its divorce laws to increase the amount of child support to be awarded to parents with primary physical custody, but at the same time it provided for taking specific account of the amount of residential time awarded to each parent. Under the new law, child-support payments were linked to the amount of residential time. If each parent has at least one third of the child's residential time, the parents are said to have joint physical custody. In families so designated, fathers have to pay less in child support than they would be required to pay if they had liberal visitation but less than one third of the child's residential time. Not surprisingly, when the new law came into effect there was a sudden increase in the number of petitions for modification of custody and child-support awards. Fathers were claiming that their children needed to be with them more, and that they themselves wanted and needed to have more time with their children. They were asking for additional vacation time in the summer, additional time during Christmas or Easter holidays, additional mid-week overnights—any combination that would add up to the 129 overnights a year that would allow them to be designated as joint physical custodians and hence to pay less child support. California court staffers have rather cynically come to call these petitioning fathers "born-again dads," on the understandable assumption that at least some of them were mainly motivated by the desire to save money. It is quite possible, however, that if their petitions are granted and they actually do have more overnight visits from their children, their relationships with the children strengthen. We do not know whether this happens, nor what the effect of increasing father-child time is on the mother-child household.

This story brings front and center the whole other side of divorce negotiations, namely the financial side. Let us remind ourselves that the care and upbringing of children involves much more than day-to-day hands-on caretaking. Someone has to earn the money to pay for the family's food, clothing, shelter, education, recreation costs, and so forth. Considering that in families with young children fathers usually earn considerably more than mothers, it has fallen to fathers to be the major financial providers. In fact, with the birth of children fathers often increase their hours of work so as to compensate for the mother's lost income if she reduces her work hours, or stays out of the workforce altogether, in order to care for the children. Fathers may stick to a job they do not enjoy, work very long hours, and forego opportunities to do more interesting things, in order not to put the family's economic security at risk. Therefore they may reasonably feel that their daily work implies no less commitment to the welfare of the children than the mother's commitment through her daily caregiving.

The upshot of the pattern of greater wage-earning by fathers has been that at the time of divorce, mothers are expected to continue in their customary primary caregiving role, and fathers are expected to continue in *their* customary role of providing economic support for the rearing of the children. Mothers, of course, need to be physically present in the same household with the children in order to provide continuity in caregiving. Hence, the usual grant of primary physical custody to them. Fathers, however, can continue to provide financial support while living elsewhere. Of course, most fathers cannot afford to support two households at the level the family previously maintained, but they are expected to provide a reasonable share of the costs of their former households. In the case of divorce in Family 1, the usual arrangement would be for the father to be required to pay child support and perhaps also some form of alimony— such as support for the mother while she gets schooling or job training that qualifies her to become a wage earner. In Family 2, neither parent would be obligated to pay child support to the other, assuming that they do get joint physical custody and that their earnings are equivalent.

In the more usual case depicted in Figure 1, where both parents work, but the father earns more and the mother has done most of the child care and has been awarded primary physical custody, the father would be obligated to pay child support to the mother. These outcomes rest on a legal doctrine that under- lies custody law that decisions about custody and decisions about money should not be linked. Custody decisions should be made first, and then financial ar- rangements should be set in place that will support the custodial arrangement that has been arrived at. This doctrine has emerged from a consensus that it would be grossly unfair to mothers—and perhaps to children too—if the custody of children were routinely awarded to fathers on the grounds that they have more economic resources.

In practice, then, the relative economic situation of the two parents is seldom given much weight in making awards for physical custody, only in decisions concerning child support. There are exceptions, however, in which the possibil- ity of a mother's supporting an independent household—even with child-sup- port payments from the father—becomes a paramount issue. An example from the Stanford Custody Study comes from an interview with a father who had been awarded custody of a very young child:

> "We felt it would be better for me to have custody, because she didn't have time to be with him or money to support him. She's working two jobs and rides buses."

In this case, and the two or three others like it, the fathers had much higher education levels and financial resources than the mothers. In the large majority of cases, however, the mothers were in a position to maintain a household that would be at least marginally viable, relying on their own earnings plus support payments from the father, or contributions from relatives, or on support from public assistance.

Fairness

Is the usual resolution of the custody and financial settlements equally fair to both parents? No, probably not. In a previous paper (Maccoby, 1995), I tried to argue the case from the perspective of each parent, and concluded that many divorced fathers have reason to consider themselves more unfairly treated than mothers, on the average. Mothers, at least, get to keep primary physical custody of their children, who have been so central to their lives and for whom they have made so many sacrifices. The down side for mothers is mainly financial. Even with some child-support payments from their former spouses, they are usually considerably worse off, unless or until they remarry, and most usually take on more out-of-home work. Fathers find themselves alone; they have lost their homes and their daily contact with their children, and must pay to help support a household to which they no longer have access. In some cases, these things are balanced for both parents by the felt gains that come from no longer having to live with and negotiate with an incompatible spouse. But in the cases in which the father was not the one who most wanted to leave the marriage, he feels trapped. Through no fault of his own, a portion of his income is entailed away by court order to the household where his children are but which is no longer his home.

Of course, out of love for their children, many fathers do accept the require-ment to pay child support even if they feel personally wronged by the divorce. And, a good many fathers realize that they are not in a position to take on the job of raising the children on their own, even if they feel that in a sense they deserve to have the children because they want to be with them and are not at fault for breaking up the family. But, regardless of who was at fault in breaking up the marriage, some fathers do want custody, feeling that they would be perfectly adequate parents even though they did not do the bulk of day-to-day caregiving during the marriage. Indeed, some may say, the very reason that they have been less involved in giving hands-on care to the children is that they have had to be away from the household earning as much as they could. They may well ask, why is a mother's history of caring for the children given so much more weight in the custody decision than a father's history of working to support them?

The material covered so far in this paper is meant to provide a rationale for giving considerable weight to a history of primary caregiving. And I have argued elsewhere (Maccoby, 1995) that to shift the criteria to giving more weight to income-earning capacity and less to a proven capacity for caregiving would be even more unfair to mothers than the present situation is to fathers. Clearly, it is extremely difficult to be fair to both parents. The situation is an inherently intractable one, in that it is no longer possible for the children to live with both parents at the same time, and any kind of division is going to involve a loss of valued residential time with the children, on the part of one or both parents. It may be that we can not do much better than the present patchwork system where parents are encouraged to make their own decisions wherever possible, and where mediators and courts in contested cases give considerable weight to providing continuity of day-to-day care for the children, while maintaining flexibility for recognizing other criteria as well.

More importantly, in both private and court-related decision making, parents are now being led to turn away from a focus on their own rights, or on the question of what is fair to each individual parent. There is reason to believe that some progress is being made in bringing parents to the recognition that neither one of them is going to "own" the children, and that they both will continue to be involved in the children's lives. Given this recognition, parents can more easily see that what is needed is to devise a practical plan based on what role is feasible for each in terms of their respective postdivorce situations: for example each parent's job situation, household composition and location, child-rearing skills, and financial and social resources. With this focus, mothers who were militantly insistent that their husbands were not going to "get" the children or "take them away" from her, and who were so concerned about these matters that they were ready to sabotage visitation, may come to see the advantages of having some time off from child care responsibilities. In many cases, the children's fathers may be the most reliable and committed source of child care assistance available to divorced mothers. However the reality is that the process of devising a practicable postdivorce parenting plan will still almost certainly lead, for a majority of families, to mothers ending up with more of the children's residential time than the fathers, and with fathers paying child support. It is difficult indeed to think of any means of redressing whatever unfairness there may be in these outcomes.

Arriving at a workable plan for combining the contributions of the two sepa-rated parents often takes time and experimentation. At the time of separation, many parents are not in a position to make good decisions concerning residence, visitation, and financial support for their children. Parents make many changes in their arrangements during the years after parents have separated and a divorce decree has been awarded (Maccoby & Mnookin, 1992, pp. 198-199). The language of the formal agreement concerning custody and visitation begins to fade into the background as parents remarry, or move to new locations, or change their work situations and their earnings. The changes that families make in the residential and visitation arrangements for their children, or even in the amounts of child support mutually agreed upon, are usually made informally, without going back to court for formal modification of the terms of the divorce.

The fact that the terms of a decree often do not prove viable in the long run raises the question of whether the legal system should embody some systematic arrangement for periodic review of the provisions of the divorce decree. My own view is: probably not. The legal system is already overburdened, and simply does not have the resources to monitor the postdivorce changes that parents make in their custody and visitation arrangements, to see whether they are in "compliance" with the legal decree. Furthermore, a requirement for all couples to renegotiate their arrangements periodically could reopen old wounds, and by making existing agreements seem temporary, create more instability for families than already exists. It seems wiser to leave families free to make their own modifications at their own pace, if and when their changing family circumstances require it. Of course, some of the changes families make informally may not suit all parties equally. There certainly are cases in which one parent coercively forces changes the other parent does not want—as when a mother unilaterally cuts off the children's visitation to the father. In any case, where a parent is dissatisfied with a new situation and feels coerced, that parent currently has the right to seek redress by coming back to the courts for a restraining order or for modification of the original decree. This protective resource may not be utilized by parents who want to avoid the costs in money and time that level procedures entail, but it does stand as a barrier against the worst abuses.

A Possible Modification of a
"Primary Caretaker" Preference

I have argued that the predominance of mothers in custody awards does, and should, rest largely on their track record as primary caregivers prior to the divorce. I want to suggest, very tentatively, a modification in the weight given to this factor. The suggestion is that this factor should be given more weight the younger the child, and less weight the older the child. In other words, I am suggesting that we revive what used to be called the "tender years presumption."

My hypothesis is that there is a connection between primary caregiving and emotional bonding, but that this connection is stronger the younger the child.

At least in the first three years of life, a child's relationship with others is built on frequent face-to-face interaction, involving closely timed reciprocation of actions, as well as on the sharing of positive emotional states. For a variety of reasons, mothers are usually better equipped and more willing than fathers to take on the demanding function of being an infant or toddler's intimate inter-active partner. Later on, as children gradually become more self-regulating and more cognitively mature, they can span longer periods of time between one person's action and the other's response. Intimacy with older children incorpo-rates more symbolic elements. That is, it involves a child's knowing cognitively about the other person's preferences and interests and probable reactions to the child's own activities, without so great a reliance on immediate inter-personal cues. Thus the close face-to-face interaction that is involved in caring for a young child is more important in developing and maintaining close ties with that child than would be the case for an older child, though it is never unimportant.

It is a common pattern in families with more than one child that when a new baby is born, the father takes on more of the care of the older child or children, while the mother cares for the infant. Fathers come into their own with older children, bringing to bear interactive qualities that are important for children to experience but that are often somewhat different from those provided by the mother. Another bit of evidence in the Stanford Custody Study, is that only 8% of the very young children were living with their fathers; the proportion rose gradually with increasing age of the children, so that by the teenage years nearly 20% were living with their fathers. At every age, far more children were living with their mothers, but nevertheless this increase in father residence would appear to reflect some kind of folk wisdom—or perhaps recognition by the parents themselves—that fathers are better able to take care of older children than younger ones. It is important not to overgeneralize about the parenting styles of mothers as compared with fathers, given how much variation there is among parents of each sex. All that can legitimately be claimed is that most mothers make special adaptations in their caregiving with infants and young children—adaptations that these very young children need and that seem to come less readily to most fathers (Maccoby, 1998). If this maternal ability is to be one of the bases for giving her preference in custody decisions, it follows that those uncommon fathers who have shown themselves able and willing to adapt to infants and toddlers in these needed ways should have an equal claim to custody even of very young children.

My opinion is that the optimal situation is for children to be raised by a cooperating team of two parents, each bringing special and mutually supportive qualities to their dealings with the children. However, in the divorce situation, this parental alliance, however effective it was before the divorce, is disrupted. One parent almost inevitably takes on the major residential-parent role, and there is wide agreement that the choice as to which parent should have this role should be one that is least disruptive to the child's emotional ties with the two parents. With older children, the nature of the bond with their fathers may be just as important for their development, and in their own eyes, as their bond with their mothers, even though their bond with their fathers will not usually have emerged out of the kind of intimate day-to-day caregiving that their mothers have provided. I hasten to say that older children certainly continue to need their mothers, and in our Stanford Custody Study we have found it to be especially important for children who live with their fathers to maintain a relationship with their nonresidential mothers.

If we want to give especially great weight to primary caregiving for younger children, but less for older children, what ages are we talking about? What do we mean by "tender years"? Legal precedent certainly gives us no clear answer to this question, nor can developmental psychologists offer one. There is no clear cut-off point. The developmental changes in what children need from each parent are gradual and all children do not change at the same rate. Even though the law likes discrete categories, and it would be convenient for decision-makers if we were to say, "after the age of six primary caregiving should be given less weight," I see no alternative to relying on a probabilistic, continuously age-graded criterion.

Custody decisions, as we know, involve highly emotional issues, and weighing the alternatives is always a controversial matter. What I have suggested is certainly controversial as well. My hope is that controversy will lead to constructive efforts to improve the way in which decisions are made concerning the postdivorce arrangements for the lives of children and families.

NOTE

1. These are hypothetical curves, based on data from the Stanford Custody Study (Maccoby & Mnookin, 1992, p. 67).

REFERENCES

Buchanan, C. M., Maccoby, E. E., & Dornbusch, S. M. (1996). *Adolescents after divorce.* Cambridge, MA: Harvard University Press

Buehler, C. A., Hogan, M. J., Robinson, B. E., & Levy, R. J. (1985-86). The parental divorce transition: Divorce-related stressors and well-being. *Journal of Divorce, 9,* 61-81.

Depner, C. E., Cannata, K., & Ricci, I. (1991). *Mediated agreements on child custody and visitation, Report 4.* San Francisco: California Family Court Services Snapshot Study, Judicial Council of California

Ellis, J. (1990). Plans, protections and professional interventions in divorce custody reform and the role of legal professionals. *University of Michigan Journal of Law Reform, 24,* 67-188.

Ellis, J. (1994, July) The Washington State Parenting Act in the courts: Reconciling discretion and justice in reconciling parenting plan disputes. *Washington Law Review.*

Furstenberg, F. F., Jr. (1988). Good dads—bad dads: Two faces of fatherhood. In A. Cherlin (Ed.), *The changing American family and public policy.* Washington, DC: Urban Institute

Funder, K. (1986). Work and the marriage partnership. In P. McDonald (Ed.), *Settling up: Property and income distribution on divorce in Australia,* Australian Institute of Family Studies. Sydney: Prentice Hall.

Hanson, S., & Pratt, G. (1995). *Gender, work, and space.* New York: Routledge.

Joshi, H. (1984). *Women's participation in paid work: Further analysis of the women and employment survey* (Research Paper No. 45). London: HMSO, Department of Employment.

Lamb, M. E., Pleck, J. H., Charnov, E. L., & Levine, J. A. (1987). A biosocial perspective on paternal behavior and involvement. In J. B. Lancaster, J. Altmann, A. S. Rossi, & L. R. Sherrod (Eds.), *Parenting across the lifespan: Biosocial dimensions.* New York: de Gruyter

Maccoby, E. E. (1995) Divorce and custody: The rights, needs, and obligations of mothers, fathers, and children. In G. B. Melton (Ed.), *The individual, the family, and social good: Personal fulfillment in times of change.* Lincoln: University of Nebraska Press.

Maccoby, E. E. (1998). *The two sexes: Growing up apart, coming together.* Cambridge, MA: Harvard University Press.

Maccoby, E. E., & Mnookin, R. H. (1992). *Dividing the child: Social and legal dilemmas of custody.* Cambridge, MA: Harvard University Press.

Maccoby, E. E., Depner, C. E., & Mnookin, R. H. (1990). Coparenting in the second year after divorce. *Journal of Marriage and the Family, 52,* 141-155.

Mnookin, R. H., & Kornhauser, L. (1979). Bargaining in the shadow of the law: The case of divorce. *Yale Law Journal, 88,* 950-997

Youniss, J., & Smollar, J. (1985). *Adolescent relations with mothers, fathers and friends.* Chicago: University of Chicago Press.

Chapter 4

Improving the Law Relating to Postdivorce Arrangements for Children

Katharine T. Bartlett

Drafting rules for resolving disputes over children at divorce is a daunting task. The circumstances to which any rule must be applied are numbingly diverse, the stakes are high, and the objectives ambitious and conflicting.

It is the job of the law, of course, to solve complex and important matters, and difficulties abound in all areas: laws of criminal procedure must balance interests of potential victims of crime against the interests of the accused; contract law designed to govern agreements between multinational corporations must apply impartially and fairly to unsophisticated buyers as well.

Disputes over children between divorcing parents raise tensions, however, that make rule-making in this area especially difficult. The first part of this chapter outlines these tensions; the second part describes how the law currently addresses them, and proposes principles on which improvements in that law could be based. The proposed principles emphasize past caretaking patterns as the optimal benchmark for determining a child's best interests and for stimulating parental agreement about the child without the necessity for court intervention.

THE TENSIONS

Determinacy Versus Individualized Decision-Making

Perhaps the most significant conundrum in child custody rule-making is how to achieve results that are both *predictable* across a wide variety of circumstances and *individualized* to those circumstances. We want to know in advance how cases will come out, and we want each one of them to come out right. Unfortunately, these two goals are not fully compatible. Predictable results require rules that constrain judges, but the more constraining the rules, the more difficult it is for judges to reach a good outcome in particular cases that the rule-makers did not have in mind (Schneider, 1991, pp. 2259-2260; *Seymour v. Seymour,* 1980). For example, the rule that biological parents should have custody and control of their children unless shown to be unfit is a good rule, designed to prevent the state from interfering in parent-child relationships. But when a 2-year-old child, such as Baby Jessica (*In re Baby Girl Clausen,* 1993), is raised from birth by another family, the parental preference rule seems unduly formal and unresponsive to the realities of some children's lives (Hollinger, 1995, p. 22).

Conversely, the greater discretion rules give to judges to respond to the individual facts of a situation and reach the "right result," the less predictable the results (Elster, 1987, pp. 28-29; Glendon, 1986, pp. 1190-1191; Mnookin, 1975, pp. 246-247; Mnookin & Kornhauser, 1979, p. 993). The best-interests-of-the-child test, applied almost universally in custody disputes in this country, illustrates the point. Consider a typical hypothetical case of Sandra and Walter, who have 10-year old twin sons. Throughout their twelve-year marriage, Sandra worked part-time outside the home and assumed primary, day-to-day caretaking responsibility for the twins, while Walter worked full-time and provided most of the economic support of the family. Nine months ago Sandra had an affair, for which Walter was never able to forgive her. Their relationship deteriorated into constant bickering over disciplining the twins, financial budgets, who was to drive the newer family car, with whose relatives the family should spend Christmas, and other matters big and small. When Sandra and Walter finally separated, Walter stated that he wanted equal residential responsibility of the twins. He threatened Sandra that if she opposed his request, he would use her affair against her and get primary custody himself. Sandra believed that the twins would suffer unnecessarily if they had to adjust not only to the divorce, but to a substantial realignment of caretaking from her to Walter.

Under the best-interests test, a court will have to decide whether the twin's best interests are served best by having one primary residential parent, or by having Sandra and Walter share equal residential time. If there is to be one primary residential parent, it will have to chose between them, taking into account further information brought before it. Let us assume, for example, that Sandra has been the primary parent in the past, but will have to expand her work hours to full-time after the divorce, when there are two households to support. Walter goes to church; Sandra does not. Walter believes in firm discipline, daily routines, a regular bedtime, and daily chores. Sandra's approach to parenting is more flexible. She stresses spontaneity and fun over routine and discipline; if she is enjoying "quality time" with her kids, she doesn't see the point in breaking up the fun in the service of some "artificial" bedtime. She favors creativity over direction-following, open communication over obedience, emotional security over good manners, and resistance to authority over patriotism and conformism. The children have more fun when they are with Sandra, but they are better behaved when with Walter. Sandra's idea of sex education is to encourage the kids to ask questions, to which she gives honest answers; when they are teenagers and show interest, she will teach them about birth control. Walter thinks knowing about sex only encourages unhealthy experimentation; he favors distraction through sports and, when the time comes, a "just say no" approach.

These facts have significance in the custody dispute between Sandra and Walter only to the extent that the court is prepared to pass judgment about what makes a good parent, a successful childhood, and a healthy, well-adjusted child. These are matters we generally leave up to parents themselves, out of a commitment both to parental autonomy and to family diversity and social pluralism. Judges have little basis for making these judgments, except their *own* views about what is best for children. They can turn to experts for guidance, but paid experts also differ, since such questions have more to do with values than with science. Moreover, the presence of experts may cause Sandra and Walter to engage in strategic behavior to get the expert on his or her side.

To the extent judges may evaluate the facts differently and thus reach different results, Sandra and Walter cannot predict the result of their case, and thus are more likely to fight about it in court (Brinig & Alexeev, 1993, p. 294). If they can afford it, they will each hire their own experts who are paid to disagree with one another and to highlight the shortcomings of the other parent. The resulting adversarial battle often serves to undermine the cooperation required for successful postdivorce custody arrangements. It may also create special unfairness toward the parent most involved in the child's upbringing, who tends to be the most risk-averse, and thus most vulnerable to manipulation by the parent seeking economic concessions in exchange for dropping unreasonable demands related to the child. (Mnookin & Kornhauser, 1979, p. 964).

The unpredictability of outcomes is not the only problem with the open-ended best-interests standard; predictable bias is also an issue. Judges and experts are likely to bring conventional views to bear on what is best for children. Walter will probably be favored as the the churchgoer, especially if he is a member of a mainstream church, although he may suffer if his religious faith leads him to engage in parenting practices that are unpopular or considered off-beat (*Bienenfeld v. Bennett-White,* 1992; *Burnham v. Burnham,* 1981). As the mother, Sandra will probably be *favored* in many courts (Henry, 1994, p. 53); *In re Marriage of Bukacek,* 1995), although her extramarital affair will be a strike against her in some jurisdictions, even more so than an affair by Walter would have been against him (*Lacaze v. Lacaze,* 1993); *In re Marriage of Diehl,* 1991; *Linda R. v. Richard E.,* 1990). If her affair was with another woman, Sandra is even more likely to be penalized (*Tucker v. Tucker,* 1996). If she puts the twins in day care in order to return to full-time employment, the court may well assume that she is willing to put her career above the welfare of their children (*Prost v. Greene,* 1995), even as Walter is viewed favorably for his working long hours to be a responsible provider for the family. And if Walter "helps" Sandra with the kids more than fathers are expected to do so, he is likely also to receive extra bonus points not available to Sandra, whose care of the children is more likely to be taken for granted (*Patricia Ann S. v. James Daniel S.,* 1993; *In re Fennell,* 1992).

In an attempt to make results under the best-interests test more predictable and controlled, a number of states detail a long "laundry list" of factors courts should consider in deciding what is in a child's best interests. These factors include the child's preferences, the strength and quality of emotional connection between the child and each parent, the special needs of the child, and parental abilities (Alaska Stat. 25.24.159(c), 1995; D.C. Code Ann. 16-911(a)(5), 1996). Factors such as parental abilities and the quality of an emotional relationship can be as indeterminate as the best interests test itself. Even when the factor does not provide some direction, the failure of such statutes to weigh or prioritize the factors means that, except in very clear cases, outcomes remain difficult to predict. Sandra may score high on emotional connection to the twins and perhaps on parental abilities if the judge happens to share her values; her extramarital affair, however, may demonstrate moral weakness to some judges, who are likely to see Walter as the more stable parent.

Another approach to making the best-interests test more definite is to use presumptions that favor one particular form of custody over others. Many advocates, for example, urge adoption of a primary caretaker presumption, which would favor giving primary custody to the parent who had spent the greatest amount of time caring for the child (Sack, 1992, pp. 320-328; Fineman, 1988, pp. 770-774; Chambers, 1985, p. 561; Neely, 1984, pp. 185-186). Only the state of West Virginia currently has such a presumption (*Garska v. McCoy,* 1981). The primary caretaker presumption is criticized because it is too favorable to women (Henry, 1994). Ironically, the experience in both West Virginia and in Minnesota, which experimented with the presumption for 4 years, has been that gender bias *against* mothers (especially those who do not conform to gender stereotypes) is the more serious problem (Crippen, 1990; Becker, 1992, p. 201).

Applied without gender bias, a primary caretaker presumption would add some determinacy in resolving the dispute between Sandra and Walter. As the primary caretaker during the marriage, Sandra should obtain primary custody at divorce unless Walter shows that she is unfit. The presumption is not useful, however, when there has been no primary caretaker (*Dempsey v. Dempsey,* 1983). Moreover, a primary caretaker presumption is indifferent to matters of degree; it would produce the same result whether Sandra was performing all of the caretaking responsibilities or only slightly more than Walter.

Joint custody presumptions or preferences are another way to standardize postdivorce arrangements and thus make them more predictable and bias-free. Approximately 13 states now have some form of statutory presumption in favor of joint custody. The enactment of such statutes over the past decade has contributed to the sense that joint custody is a favored trend. In fact, however, most joint custody preferences are quite limited in effect. For example, in five states, the presumption in favor of joint custody operates only when the parents agree to joint custody (Cal. Fam. Code 3080, 1994; Conn. Gen. Stat. Ann. 46b-56a(b), 1995; Me. Rev. Stat. Ann., tit. 19 752(6), 1994; Miss. Code Ann. 93-5-24(4), 1994; Nev. Rev. Stat. Ann. 125.490(1), 1993); such rules have little impact, since they simply ratify what most courts would order even in the absence of such a presumption (Melli et al., 1988, p. 1145). In six of the remaining states, the statutory preference for joint custody operates only as a burden-shifting device, favoring joint custody only when the party opposing it is not able to show, by a mere preponderance of the evidence, that the child's interests would be better served by a different arrangement (D.C. Code Ann. 16-911(a)(5), 1996; Idaho Code 32-717B(1), (4), 1996; Iowa Code Ann. 598.41(2), 1996; Kan. Stat. Ann. 60-1610(a)(4)(A), 1993; Mich. Comp. Laws Ann. 722.26a(1), 1995; Mont. Code Ann. 40-4-224(1), 1995; N.M. Stat. Ann. 40-4-9.1(A), (B), 1994).

Florida and Louisiana have stronger presumptions in favor of joint custody, but the law surrounding these presumptions serves to undermine much of their impact. For example, the Florida presumption requires that shared parental responsibility be ordered even when the parents do not agree to it, unless shown to be detrimental to the child; a provision of the same statute in which the presumption appears, however, provides for an award of sole parental responsibility when in the best interests of the child (Fla. Stat. Ann. 61.13(2)(b)(2) & (2)(b), 1997). Moreover, a number of Florida court decisions imposed a presumption against rotating or divided custody (*Garvie v. Garvie,* 1995; *Caraballo v. Hernandez,* 1993, *Sullivan v. Sullivan,* 1992); the Florida legislature recently rejected these cases with a statutory amendment providing that a court may order rotating custody if in the best interest of the child (Fla. Stat. Ann. 61.121, 1997), but it remains to be seen whether Florida courts which have resisted joint custody are prepared to give in to the legislature's will.

Louisiana presumes that joint custody is in the child's best interests, unless shown to the contrary by clear and convincing evidence (La. Civ. Code art. 132, 1997). Louisiana law also requires, however, that a decree of joint custody designate a domiciliary parent, with whom the child shall primarily reside (La. Civ. Code art. 335(B), 1997), thus undermining some of the practical significance of the presumption.

Iowa also has a strong pro-joint custody rule, requiring courts to consider joint custody if either party requests it and to order joint custody unless the court cites clear and convincing evidence that it is unreasonable or not in the child's best interests; at the same time, however, it permits courts, in implementing joint custody, to give physical care "to one joint custodial parent and not to the other" (Iowa Code Ann. 598.41(5), 1996). Similarly, Idaho law presumes that joint custody is in a child's best interests, but specifies that joint physical custody "does not necessarily mean the child's time with each parent should be exactly the same in length nor does it necessarily mean the child should be alternating back and forth over certain periods of time between each parent" (Idaho Code 32-717B(2), 1996). In all of these states, it appears that states with rules making it most likely that joint custody be awarded counterbalance those rules with others that dilute what it means to have joint custody.

Conversely, states that are the most explicit in providing that joint custody means an equal or near-equal amount of residential time tend to take a very cautionary approach to awarding it. In Arizona, for example, joint physical custody means that the child spends substantially equal time with both parents (Ariz. Rev. Stat. Ann. 25-331.01(3), 1995), but a court may not award joint custody over the objection of a parent unless it makes specific written findings in support of the award, after considering a list of prescribed factors considered adverse to joint custody arrangements (Ariz. Rev. Stat. Ann. 25-332(E), 1995).

It is far from clear how much predictability joint custody presumptions add to custody decision-making. What is more clear is that both the primary caretaker presumption and joint custody presumptions gain whatever predictability they do contribute by assuming that there is a particular custody arrangement that is most beneficial to children. Both kinds of presumptions assume a norm, or standard, based on what the state deems the average family, or the welfare of the greatest number of children, to require. A primary caretaker presumption assumes and reinforces the single-caretaker norm regardless of past caretaking patterns. A joint custody presumption assumes and reinforces the norm that equally shared custodial arrangements are best for children no matter what the prior arrangements.

When the assumptions of the presumption are accurate, the presumption may work reasonably well to protect the child's interests. If not, however, custody outcomes reflect legislative ideals rather than family realities. Private settlement negotiations are skewed accordingly (Brinig & Alexeev, 1993, p. 290). Predictability is achieved, but it is a predictability based on conformity, and at the cost of family diversity and attention to individual circumstances. If the problem with the best-interests test is that its sensitivity to individualized factors produces unpredictable results, the problem with primary caretaker and joint custody presumptions is that their predictability produces outcomes that are not sensitive to individualized factors, and thus are incorrect .

Finality Versus Flexibility

Another tension to be reckoned with in framing custody rules is created by the desire for both finality of results and flexibility in the face of the changing needs of the child. Finality is desirable because it forces the parents to accept and live with the results of judicial decision-making and leads to greater stability for the child. Let us say Sandra is awarded primary residential responsibility for the twins. If the legal standards allow relitigation of this issue, Walter is less likely to learn to live with it and more likely to engage in strategic, disruptive behavior. If the standards make relitigation pointless, Walter is more likely to adjust to the existing circumstances and make them work.

On the other hand, flexibility is desirable because children's needs and the parental circumstances change over time, in ways that cannot always be predicted. Strict no-modification rules can stimulate strategic behavior just as lax rules do. If the status quo is too difficult to change and Sandra and Walter remain on bad terms, Sandra will have less reason to voluntarily accede to Walter's good faith efforts when the children are 12 and 13 and want to see more of their father. But in the same way, if equal residential time for both parents is ordered but Walter does not exercise his share, the difficulty of modification may hinder the ability of Sandra to obtain an order that reflects the reality on which an adequate child support award may depend.

Current law officially favors finality by treating a custody decision as a fixed event, at which the court decides what "rights" each party has to the child for the remainder of the child's minority. Since so much is at stake, if Sandra and Walter can not come to an agreement on their own, much time and resources will be put into which one of them should have his or her own way. In contrast, little or no attention is given to how future conflicts should be resolved, or how to help the child and the parents adjust to their new circumstances. Relitigation of the custody ordered is discouraged or precluded by rules imposing a moratorium on modifications and, increasingly, rules requiring that the child be in actual danger before a modification may be ordered. Under the Uniform Marriage and Divorce Act, for example, a custody decree may not be modified earlier than 2 years after its date, unless the court determines that "the child's present environment may endanger seriously his physical, mental, moral, or emotional health" (Uniform Marriage and Divorce Act 409(a), 1970; see also Colo. Rev. Stat. 14-10-131(1), 1987; Del. Code Ann. tit. 13, 729(c), 1993; Ill. Ann. Stat. ch 750, para.5/610(a), 1996; Ky. Rev. Stat. Ann. 403.340(1), 1995; Wis. Stat. Ann. 767.325(1), 1993). Other states prohibit changes, except under a heightened standard, within one year of the decree (Ariz. Rev. Stat. Ann. 25-332(L), 1995; Minn. Stat. 518.18(1), (b), 1996). Even after the waiting period is over, in some jurisdictions the court may not change the custodian of a child unless present endangerment to the child is shown (Uniform Marriage and Divorce Act 409(b)(3), 1970; Colo. Rev. Stat. 14-10-131(2), 1987; Ky. Rev. Stat. Ann. 403.340(1), 1995; Ohio Rev. Code 3109.04(E)(1)(a), 1995).

Despite the law's assumption of finality, changes frequently occur after the original order, many leading to demands on the court for modifications of the original order. Faced with these concrete circumstances, courts hesitate to leave children in residential arrangements that are not working, and thus entertain requests for modification on standards looser than the applicable statutes would appear to allow (*Peterson v. Peterson,* 1991). The result is the worst of both worlds: there is neither finality, nor is there real planning or mechanisms put in place to settle disputes that may arise when circumstances change.

Judicial Supervision Versus Private Ordering

Responsibility for children in this society is allocated to a child's biological or adoptive parents. That responsibility is broad and near absolute (Bartlett, 1984, pp. 883-885). Allocating responsibility to parents builds on the impulses parents seem to have to do right by their "own," impulses that in turn are strengthened by the degree of power vested in parents by the state (Bartlett, 1988, pp. 299-302). It also decentralizes decision-making for children, thus contributing to a richer, more diverse society than would otherwise result (Wald, 1976, pp. 639-641). Neither of these rationales assumes that parental autonomy produces uniformly good results in every individual case; some children un-doubtedly would be better off if they had been raised in a different family, or with greater state supervision. The rationales posit, however, that most children, individually and collectively, are better off because of the autonomy parents have in raising their own children. This commitment to parental autonomy means that Sandra and Walter, while living together, would be allowed to raise their twins without reading them books, feeding them meat, or allowing them to join a Scout troop or listen to the radio. They would be allowed to spend money on vacations and fancy cars without setting aside money for the higher education of their children. They would be allowed to raise their children in two different religious faiths at the same time, or to teach the superiority of the white race, that women's place is in the home, or that fluoridated water is the work of the devil. They would be allowed to let their children stay up all night, to enter their daughter at age 4 into a beauty contest wearing makeup and seductive clothing, or to take over control of an airplane at age seven.

At divorce, in theory at least, all aspects of parental decision-making come under greater state scrutiny. As noted above, unconventional parenting philoso-phies or practices may count against a parent who is competing against the more conventional parent for primary custodial responsibility. Even when parents are

agreed about residential arrangements for the child at divorce, parental autonomy is abridged by the requirement that a parental agreement be judicially
reviewed, to determine if is in the child's best interests (*Miller v. Miller,* 1993;
Schwab v. Schwab, 1993). The stated reason for judicial review is that while
parents can bargain way their own rights, they cannot bargain away those of
their children, which the court has an obligation to protect (*Miller v. Miller,*
1993). Implied in this rationale is a suspicion that parents are not themselves
while going through a divorce, that they have their own interests to protect, and
that they may be willing to compromise the interests of their children in favor
of their own. Another concern is that of domestic violence, which increases the
possibility that parental agreements are neither voluntary, nor in the children's
best interests (Bruch, 1988, pp. 120).

Despite the law requiring court review, most courts do not have the time or
resources to give meaningful review to proposed settlements (Maccoby &
Mnookin, 1992, pp. 41-42). Approximately 90% of divorce cases involving
children are settled by agreement of the parents, and review of these agreements
is, at best, pro forma (Id., pp. 41). This means, on the one hand, that courts may
intrude on the decision-making processes of well-meaning parents who are
likely to know best what will serve the interests of their children. Court-ordered
investigations of such families discourage settlement efforts and may help to
transform an amicable resolution of issues relating to the child into a dispute.
Such investigations may also lead to orders which the court has no practical
means to enforce, over the objection of both parties (Maccoby & Mnookin,
1992, pp. 48-49). At the same time, a system in which all cases are subject to
judicial review to determine whether an agreement is in a child's best interests
means that cases in which special protections to enhance the safety of a parent
or a child are warranted are unlikely to be identified. In short, judicial review
is unnecessarily intrusive in cases in which it might occur, while coercion and
domestic violence are likely to go unchecked in the cases in which they exist.

Protection Versus Privacy

A tension also exists between the state's interest in protecting individuals
from harm and the freedom of families to have their privacy undisturbed. There
is increasing awareness of the prevalence and danger of domestic abuse both to
the physical security of individuals and to domestic tranquility (Klein & Orloff,
1993). Yet the primary importance of the family in private lives, as well as its
significance in U.S. constitutional case law, is reflected in the very limited

degree of official oversight and control over relationships in its internal relationships (*Meyer v. Nebraska,* 1923, at p. 399; *Prince v. Massachusetts,* 1944,
at p. 166; *Griswold v. Connecticut,* 1965, at p. 495). The challenge for the law
is to provide protection for individuals, within an institution valued primarily
for the privacy from law that it provides.

Biological Versus Functional Parenthood

A final tension concerns how the legal status of parenthood is assigned
between legal and functional parents. The law usually assigns the child's
biological parents—one mother and one father—full and exclusive parental
rights (Bartlett, 1984, pp. 883-885). When this assignment is not made because
of the unavailability or unfitness of the parents, the law's ideal is to substitute
a different set of parents—adoptive parents—to whom the full package of rights
and responsibilities can be transferred.

In practice, stepparents, grandparents, spousal or spouse-like partners, and
other adults function as coparents, without completely replacing the legal
parents. The law resists formal recognition of these individuals because it would
weaken the commitment society has to legal parents, on which the ideology of
responsible parenting is based. Thus, traditionally, only when a parent has been
shown to be unfit or to have abandoned the child may a parent's rights be
compromised (Mo. Ann. Stat. 452.375(5)(3)(a), 1997; Wis. Stat. Ann.
767.24(3)(a), 1994; *Petersen v. Rogers,* 1994; *McDonald v. Wrigley,* 1994).

Some courts have understood that ignoring de facto parenting relationships
may deprive the child of his or her most important source of stability and
continuity. Acting on this understanding, these courts have stretched or evaded
existing law, in order to protect the child's relationship to a significant parent
figure (*Carter v. Brodrick,* 1982; *In re Allen,* 1981; *Collins v. Gilbreath,* 1980;
Gribble v. Gribble, 1978). Only a few states have passed statutes authorizing
visitation or custody by a child's de facto parents. For example, Michigan, in
response to the Baby Jessica case (*In re Baby Girl Clausen,* 1993), enacted a
statute providing that children should not be removed from an "established
custodial environment" unless there is clear and convincing evidence that
moving them is in their best interests (Mich. Comp. Laws Ann. 722/27(1)(c),
1995). Louisiana allows custody to be awarded to a person "with whom the
child has been living in a wholesome and stable environment" other than a
parent, if custody in either parent would result in substantial harm to the child
(La. Civ. Code art. 133, 1997). In Hawaii, a "person who has had de facto

custody of the child in a stable and wholesome home" has a "prima facie" right to custody (Haw. Rev. Stat. 571-46(2), 1995).

In most jurisdictions, however, parenthood cannot be shared. It is an all-or-nothing status; a person is either a parent, with all of the legal rights as parent, or a nonparent, with no rights or responsibilities. One exception stands out: grandparents. Grandparents in virtually every state have the ability to obtain visitation rights to their grandchildren, if they can show that visitation is in the child's best interests. In most states these rights exist whether or not the grandparents ever lived with the child, and in some states, they exist even if the parents remain together (Bostock, 1994, pp. 337-338; Harpring, 1994, pp. 1660-1661). A few courts have begun to find such application constitutionally objectionable (*Peterson v. Peterson,* 1997; *Brooks v. Parkerson,* 1995; *Hawk v. Hawk,* 1993) or have limited application of grandparent visitation statutes to divorce custody actions (*In re Troxel,* 1997; *Castagno v. Wholean,* 1996; *McIntyre v. McIntyre,* 1995); the supreme court of one state implied a presumption against court-ordered grandparent visitation where both divorced parents agree that the visitation is not in the children's best interests (*Steward v. Steward,* 1995). The area remains in flux, however, as states fumble to reconcile their commitment to exclusive, legal parenthood on the one hand, with their sympathies for those providing other sources of emotional support of a familial nature on the other.

RESOLVING THE TENSIONS

The tensions described above are best addressed not with separate proposals, each addressing the particular dilemmas the tension poses, but with a package of reforms designed to take account of the tensions together, or in various combinations. A single, relatively straightforward concept goes a long way toward resolving each of them: past caretaking patterns. Past caretaking patterns provide a basis for determinacy that derives from the individualized circumstances of a family, rather than from a standard solution thought to be best for all postdivorce families. The concept helps to resolve the tension between finality and flexibility by insisting on planning for the child's future, by those who have been raising the child, and by requiring that those plans take account of future changes and potential conflicts. Putting priority on the past experience of the family means accepting voluntary arrangements made by parents for the future of their children, just as they have been responsible for past arrangements. Finally, the concept guides the identification of those limited situations in which past caretaking patterns warrant an exception to the usual rule that a child's biological or adoptive parents have full and exclusive parental rights.

This section begins by developing the "approximation standard" as the background rule for allocating responsibility for children between parents at divorce. This standard tracks past caretaking patterns by allocating postdivorce custodial responsibility for children in rough approximation to the relative shares of caretaking time each parent invested in the child prior to their separation. Exceptions are made (a) to accommodate a guaranteed minimum amount of postdivorce access by parents who have acted as responsible parents, even when they have not spent a significant amount of time providing caretaking functions for their children; (b) to take into account the firm and reasonable preferences of older children; and (c) to protect the child's welfare when there has been domestic abuse or when there is a gross disparity between the parents in terms of in the quality of emotional attachments with their children or their parental abilities that does not conform to past caretaking patterns. The remainder of the section spells out further proposals that support and extend the approximation standard, in light of the overall priority on past caretaking patterns. At the heart of these proposals is a requirement for parenting plans, not only to resolve present issues but also to specify how future ones will be handled. Additional rules for both expand and limit what adults, besides a child's biological or adoptive parents, may on occasion be allocated caretaking responsibility, based on their past exercise of caretaking functions.

The Approximation Standard

Any legal standard in this area of law serves primarily as the "shadow" within which parents negotiate their own agreements (Mnookin & Kornhauser, 1979). It is generally thought that a legal standard that corresponds reasonably well to what parents in most cases would already expect to have happen encourages settlement (Scott, 1992). For decades in the United States custody cases were resolved by a maternal presumption that yielded predictable results that were generally considered sound by most people (Mason, 1994; Grossberg, 1985; Goldstein, 1994). The factual assumption that mothers are inherently better parents than fathers is now an obsolete notion, but the importance of who cares for a child in determining the quality and strength of parent-child relationships is not. In focusing on actual caretaking relationships, the approximation standard provides a predictable guide to postdivorce custodial arrangements that corresponds to the expectations and experience of the particular family, rather than to some state-imposed ideal of what divorced families should look like, or to generalizations about what is good for children generally based on the experience of families in the aggregate.

Subject to the exceptions detailed below, the approximation standard requires courts to make residential arrangements for children, when parents do not otherwise agree, based on the proportion of caretaking responsibilities each parent was exercising before the parents separated (Scott, 1992, pp. 630-643). Approximating past caretaking functions means that if one parent performed the lion's share of caretaking functions before the parents separated, that parent ordinarily should be allocated the majority of custodial responsibility after the separation. If the arrangements were more evenly divided, responsibility at divorce would be divided in some rough correspondence to these alternative patterns.

The responsibilities that should matter most in determining how custodial responsibility is shared between parents at divorce should be the day-to-day caretaking functions most closely associated with living with and caring for a child. Washington takes this approach, requiring that "greatest weight" be given to the past responsibility assumed for parenting functions "relating to the daily needs of the child" (Wash. Rev. Code Ann. 26.09.187(3)(a)(I), 1996). Day-to-day functions include waking, feeding, dressing, bathing, disciplining and educating the child and attending to the child's other physical, medical, educational, and maturational needs. They include taking a child to a soccer game, as well as feeding them meals; recreational play, as well as staying home with the child when he or she is sick; help with homework as well as getting dressed. All are tasks that can be performed by fathers as well as mothers, even though in this culture, women perform them at a disproportionate rate; insofar as the approximation standard provides an incentive for fathers to play larger caretaking roles, it should have the effect of reducing this disproportionality over time.

The approximation approach should eliminate much of the conflict between Sandra and Walter. Sandra would receive a majority share of custodial responsibility for the twins at divorce since she served as the primary caretaker while married to Walter. There may be disputes between the parents, of course, about who did what during the marriage; research shows substantial discrepancies in the spousal reports of the percentage of household work each has performed. (Galinsky & Bond, 1996). Still, questions of historical fact are issues courts are accustomed to resolving, in contract to speculation about the future predictions which the best-interests test requires but which courts are notoriously ill-equipped to make (Mnookin, 1975, pp. 251-252; Wexler, 1985, p. 762). Precise quantification is not necessary—only a rough approximation. Whether Sandra performed 60 percent or 90 percent of the caretaking functions, she should receive an allocation of primary caretaking responsibility, and Walter's threats to fight all the way to the supreme court will simply not be credible or effective.

The approximation standard does not aim for exact replication of predivorce parenting roles. If Sandra read the kids their bedtime stories at night while Walter supervised their teeth-brushing, obviously this division of labor cannot continue. Rough proportionality is the aim. Using past parenting practices as a guide, however, means looking to choices made by the parents, not by the state. It gets the state out of deciding what parenting practices are best for a child: courts will have no need to decide whether creativity or discipline is more important for the child, or whether the child is benefitted by going to church. Focusing on past caretaking roles puts out of bounds matters pertaining largely to values, such as Sandra's affair, her lack of a church, or her "permissive" child rearing practices. It also gets the state out of deciding whether sole custody with reasonable visitation, or joint custody, is best for Sandra's and Walter's children. The court takes its cues from what they have done in the past, consistent with the deference ordinarily afforded to parent choices about their children.

An emphasis on past caretaking arrangements is also consistent with deference to parental agreements: if Sandra and Walter can no longer agree about the future, the past allocation of responsibility is the most reliable indicator of the parties' joint judgment about the needs and welfare of the child. Insofar as parental preferences matter in custody cases, the past allocation of responsibility between parents also provides better evidence of their actual long-term preferences than the strategic positions taken by the parties in postseparation litigation (Scott, 1992, pp. 630-633).

Perhaps the main advantage of the caretaking functions factor is that it is likely to correlate well with various qualitative factors relevant to a child's interests that are otherwise quite difficult to measure, such as the strength of each parent's emotional ties with the child, parental competence, and the willingness of each party to put the child's welfare first. This concentration on the past reduces the expenses and uncertainty produced by expert witnesses hired to testify on such matters. The resources of experts can be better spent helping Sandra and Walter make plans and deal constructively with each other and their children at divorce than on exposing the strengths and weaknesses of each parent and the child in the litigation process.

There are some necessary qualifications on the emphasis to be given to past caretaking functions. While the "secondary" parent should have as much access to the child as his past share of caretaking functions warrant, the law should ensure that a responsible parent has sufficient access at divorce to maintain a meaningful relationship with the child even if that parent has not been substantially engaged in caretaking functions. In other words, any parent who has been exercising a reasonable share of responsibilities as a parent, perhaps as the family breadwinner, ordinarily should be presumed entitled to a prescribed amount of access to a child at divorce, as a minimum. The precise amount of the presumptive guaranteed amount of access should be established on a state-by-state basis, through specific guidelines, which may well vary by the child's age. Utah now has such guidelines, providing 6 hours of visitation per month for children under five months of age, preferably divided into three visitation periods in the custodial home. The period increases to 9 hours for children 5 to 10 months old, an 8-hour visit and a 3-hour visit for children between 10 and 18 months, gradually increased to one weekday evening and alternating weekends for children over the age of 5. Holiday time is also provided for the nonresidential parent, starting when the child is five months with two hours on designated days in alternating years, preferably at the child's residence, and extending to longer holiday and vacation periods and telephone time as the child grows older. (Utah Code Ann. 30-3-34, 1995). Texas also provides specific visitation guidelines for children over the age of three (Tex. Fam. Code Ann. 153.251(d), 153.254, 1996). A guaranteed minimum recognizes that both parents are usually important to a child, regardless of whether both have been active in daily caretaking, and can be achieved without overly intruding on the continuity of any primary caretaking relationship.

In addition, it should ordinarily be presumed that parents who have acted responsibly toward their children in the past, even if not equally engaged in caretaking functions, should share decision-making authority, traditionally called "legal" custody. A number of states have presumptions in favor of joint legal custody (Idaho Code 32-717B(1), 1996; Iowa Stat. Ann. 598.41(2)(b), (5), 1996). Under such an approach, even if residential responsibility is unevenly divided Walter should be allowed to participate equally with Sandra in making health care, education, and other major decisions for his children. This presumption should be considered rebutted only when domestic violence is present or when there has been excessive conflict between the parents which impairs their ability to share in decision-making, when practical factors limit their ability to communicate, or when their actual experience demonstrates that they cannot reach decisions cooperatively.

The second qualification on the approximation standard concerns not the other parent, but the child. The court should accommodate the preferences of an older child who has firm and reasonable preferences. A specific age, probably in the range between 11 and 15, should be designated for this purpose. The reasons for giving weight to the preferences of an older child are largely pragmatic. Older, mature children have the capacity to evaluate their own interests, which makes it less necessary for the law to rely on past patterns of care of the child to determine the child's best interests. In addition, forcing older children to adjust to arrangements to which they are keenly opposed is often unrealistic and counterproductive. In one study of cases in a state that did not give special weight to an older child's preference, 90% of the judges surveyed felt that the preference of a child aged fourteen or older was either dispositive, absent unusual circumstances, or extremely important (Scott et al., 1988, p. 1050).

There is a reasonable range within which a state may choose an age at which a child's preferences should be given strong consideration. In Georgia and West Virginia, the child's preference is controlling if the child is 14 or older, unless the parent preferred by the child is determined to be unfit (Ga. Code Ann. 19-9-3(a)(4), 1996; W. Va. Code 44-10-4, 1982). In New Mexico, the only factor the court is required to consider with respect to the custody of children who are 14 years old or older is the "desires of the minor" (N.M. Stat. Ann. 40-4-9(B), 1994). Mississippi has a presumption similar to that applied in Georgia and West Virginia, applicable to children 12 or older (Miss. Code Ann. 93-11-65, 1994). Other states require greater consideration of the preferences of children or require that greater weight to be given to children of a specified age such as 14 (Ind. Code Ann. 31-3-11.5-21(3), 1996) or 12 (Tenn. Code Ann. 36-6-106(7), 1995; Tex. Fam. Code Ann. 153.134(a)(6), 1996).

A third limit on the approximation standard should apply when a custodial arrangement that approximates past caretaking patterns would harm a child because the quality of emotional attachments or the respective abilities of each parent are grossly incongruent with those patterns. In such unusual cases, exceptions to the otherwise appropriate allocation should be made. The threshold disparity in parental attachments or abilities necessary to trigger this exception should be high so as not to undermine the basic rule. Walter should not be able to threaten Sandra's ability to retain primary caretaking status based on the assessment of an expert that, on balance, the children feel somewhat closer to him than to Sandra, or that Walter has a greater natural aptitude for parenting. The evidence should be clear and strong, and it should support a conclusion that Walter's far superior capacities as a parent would make an allocation of primary caretaking responsibility to Sandra detrimental to the children.

Another limitation on the priority to be given past caretaking patterns is that the arrangements should be practical. The proximity of the parents' residences, their availability to care for the child and the conflict level between them all may limit the viability of arrangements meant to reflect past parenting roles, especially when those roles have been equal. In some cases, practical limitations will mean that the postdivorce caretaking arrangements simply cannot reflect predivorce caretaking, even in a rough general sense. For example, if two parents will live in different states after divorce, it is unlikely that custodial responsibility for their children can be divided equally, even if their past caretaking roles had been equal. In such cases, the best-interests test—for all of its shortcomings—would be as a second-best but necessary fallback.

The best-interests test would also come back into play in other cases as well in which past caretaking patterns are not determinative. For example, past caretaking patterns will not resolve the case between two parents if they equally shared caretaking responsibilities in the past but both agree at divorce that the children would be better off living primarily with one parent. In other cases, historical patterns may be so complex or unstable as to be unhelpful as a guide. An infant may too young for there to have been established a pattern of past caretaking. In such cases, the less satisfactory, best-interests-of-the-child test becomes, again, a necessary, second-best alternative.

The most frequent objection to the approximation standard is that it locks into place a division of caretaking responsibilities that was based on circumstances that will change with the divorce. For example, when Sandra increases her work to full-time hours, she may no longer be more available to the twins than Walter. Since one of the principal justifications for the standard is continuity for the child, the question arises whether a legal standard based on prior circumstances can provide best for continuity when those circumstances change.

While this argument has some initial appeal, the fact that circumstances inevitably change at divorce is not a factor unaccounted for in the approximation standard; it is one of the underlying assumptions. The approximation standard assures the continuity of the child's primary parent-child relationships notwithstanding inevitable changes that will occur at divorce. The example of the full-time working parent who previously did not work outside the home, or worked only part-time, is particularly instructive. As a threshold matter, it should be noted that the number of mothers who enter the work force on account of divorce is not as great as may often be assumed: close to three-fourths (70%) of married mothers work, as compared to 75% of divorced mothers (U.S. Department of Commerce, 1996). For those whose work patterns do change substantially, it cannot be assumed that such changes make a parent unavailable to be a primary caretaking parent. Many primary caretaking parents, in fact, work outside the home, full-time. We *can* assume that Sandra, who previously was more available to her children, will have less time to spend with her children when she increases her paid labor force participation. But presumably Walter, whose participation in caretaking was always less because of his paid workforce participation, will *also* be working full-time after the divorce. The question, then, is how the shrinking amount of overall parental availability to the children should be allocated. What is often at stake is evening and weekend time, now that the children will be in school or with third-party providers during the day.

The approximation standard in this set of circumstances recognizes that continuity for the children is already threatened by the fact that Sandra will have less time with the children, both because she and Walter are living in different households and because she is spending more time in paid employment. Giving Sandra a *lesser share* of caretaking responsibility than she exercised before the divorce—all to give Walter a *greater share* of time (and possibly even a greater *amount*) than he was previously exercising—is not a good solution because it undermines the continuity of the primary parent-child relationship. Continuity of both parent-child relationships, however, can be preserved by maintaining roughly the same *shares* of caretaking responsibilities the parents were exercising during the marriage (subject, as noted above, to the guaranteed presumptive amount to Walter, since he was financially supporting the family by working outside the home). In sum, notwithstanding the change in Sandra's employment status, it still makes sense to give her the majority of weekend and evening responsibility. Only if Walter's work circumstances change as well as Sandra's, enabling Walter to care for the child during significant periods when Sandra is working, would it make sense to think about a significant reordering of the shares of residential time that each parent has with the twins. Even then, it is difficult to imagine a scenario in which Walter's greater availability would make it more reasonable for him, rather than Sandra, to be the primary caretaker during the periods of time in which she was available to the children.

The evidence that shared arrangements that have been ordered by courts are less stable than others, and are more likely to change over time, supports an approach to custody that relies primarily on past caretaking patterns. A study of California couples, for example, showed a considerable drift away from joint custody arrangements that had been ordered by the court, with 38% of "joint physical custody" cases amounting to de facto residence with the mother at a point 3 years after the order was issued (Mnookin & Maccoby, 1992, p. 166). It can be assumed that one reason these arrangements are never established, or do not endure, is that they are often not "continuous" with caretaking patterns established during an intact marriage. The goal of the approximation standard is to respect the continuity of predivorce caretaking patterns, even though other circumstances cannot stay the same.

Parenting Plans

A parenting plan provides the mechanism for determining how caretaking arrangements will be continued in the postdivorce family. It goes beyond the customary order which gives "custody" to one parent and "reasonable visitation" to the other; it specifies the child's residential arrangements in some detail, including the days of each parent's responsibility or a method for choosing those days, as well as provisions for day care, the child's education, health care, and other matters significant to the parents and to the child. It should be a dynamic instrument, anticipating changes that may occur and how arrangements will be altered in response to those changes. It also provides for unanticipated change and conflict, by specifying how disputes between the parties over matters anticipated and not anticipated should be resolved. Given the importance of focusing on future plans for the children at the time of divorce, the law should require that they be submitted, either jointly or, if the parents cannot agree on a plan, individually, as alternative proposals for the court's consideration.

To date, only about nine states require parenting plans and most of these do so only as a condition of a joint custody order (Ariz. Rev. State. Ann. 25-332(D), (G), 1995; Ill. Ann. Stat. ch. 750, para. 5/602.1(b), 1996; Mass. Ann. Laws. ch. 208, 31, 1994); Mo. Ann. Stat. 452.375(subd. 8), 1997; N.M. Stat. Ann. 40-4-9.1(F), 1994; Ohio Rev. Code Ann. 3109.04(G), 1994; Okla Stat. Ann. tit. 43, 109(C), 1990). Only Montana and Washington require a parenting plan in every case (Mont. Code Ann. 40-4-221(2), 1995; Wash. Rev. Code Ann. 26-09.191(1), 1996).

With a parenting plan requirement, Sandra and Walter would each have to submit a plan, which would force them to undergo the useful exercise of articulating concrete plans in terms of their children's interests. The law should require that they be supplied with information about mediation and other forms of dispute resolution. In about 15 states, parenting classes may be required, in order to counsel parents and inform parents of the effects of a family breakdown on children (e.g., Conn. Gen. Stat. Ann. 46b-69b(b), 1995; Del. Code Ann. tit. 13, 727(b)(2), 1993; Fla. Stat. Ann. 61.21(2), 1997). Court programs may also instruct the parents about the benefits of mediation and other alternative dispute resolution mechanisms. Mediation, however, should not be required. Mediation presupposes voluntary agreement and its benefits, which have been established in voluntary settings (Bohmer & Ray, 1994; Meierding, 1992; Mathis & Yingling, 1992; Kelly, 1989), have simply not been established when the parties have not entered it voluntarily.

Judicial Review of Joint Parenting Plans

If Sandra and Walter *do* come up with a joint parenting plan, the court should accept it. Despite some unfairness in the bargaining processes in which some couples engage, courts are unlikely to play a useful role in uncovering unfair or unwise agreements as part of a routine review requirement.

Elimination of mandatory review in all cases leaves courts more available to give meaningful review to agreements produced in circumstances in which there is special reason for concern about coercion of one of the parties or detriment to the child. Cases involving a history of domestic abuse are one such set of cases; some mechanism for a threshold review of cases for evidence of domestic abuse should exist in every jurisdiction, which may include routine crosschecking with other court records or regular screening by court officials when a divorce case is filed.

The narrowing of judicial review to a select group of cases involving issues of special concern would require a significant shift in existing law. Most statutes that require court acceptance of a parental agreement apply only to agreements for joint custody (e.g., Nev. Rev. Stat. Ann. 458:17(II)(a), 1992; Me. Rev. Stat. Ann. tit. 19, 752(6), 1995). Michigan has the strongest agreement-favoring rule, imposing a presumption not only when joint custody is agreed to, but whenever there is parental agreement. The presumption can be overcome only by "clear and convincing evidence" that the terms are contrary to the child's best interests (Mich. Comp. Laws Ann. 722.27a(2), 1995). This approach represents the right direction for legal reform.

Provisions for Resolution of Future
Dispute and Plan Modifications

An important requirement of the parenting plans in some states is that procedures be specified by which proposed changes and future disputes may be handled (e.g., Ariz. Rev. Stat. Ann. 25-332(G)(3), (4), 1995; Ill. Ann. Stat. ch. 750, para. 5/602.1(b), 1996; Neb. Rev. Stat. 43-2913, 1995). If required in all cases, these procedures would help to achieve flexibility in the context of a more or less final planning document. For example, Sandra and Walter could designate arbitration, or a particular family dispute resolution center, to handle future disputes over the children; if several years later they can't agree about where their children would go to high school, the specified process could be invoked without the need for further court action. The one limitation on the finality of these procedures is that when they are imposed by court order, without agreement of the parents, existing rules relating to the obligation of courts to decide questions involving the welfare of children may require that the outcomes of these procedures be subject to *de novo* review (*Dick v. Dick,* 1995; *Kirshenbaum v. Kirshenbaum,* 1997).

Regardless of the dispute resolution procedures designated in a parenting plan, some matters that arise go beyond issues of implementation of the plan, and may require modification of the underlying plan itself. For example, while the decision where Sandra's and Walter's children should go to school may be submitted to arbitration when they cannot agree over how to exercise their joint decision-making authority, it may be appropriate for the court to modify the joint decision-making authority if it is demonstrated after repeated disputes that must be sent to arbitration that the joint decision-making provisions are not working.

With regard to requested plan modifications, the law should distinguish between changes that recognize and reinforce existing caretaking arrangements—i.e., those that help to maintain continuity and those that threaten the child's continuity. A modification should be allowed relatively freely when the parents have agreed to it (e.g., Minn. Stat. Ann. 518.18(d)(i), 1996; Wis. Stat. Ann. 767.329, 1993), when it reflects the actual parenting arrangements that have evolved since adoption of the plan (e.g., Minn. Stat. Ann. 518.18(d)(ii), 1996; Wash. Rev. Code Ann. 26.09.260(2)(b) 1996), when it involves only minor adjustments in existing arrangements (e.g., Del. Code Ann. tit. 13, 729(2)(b), 1993), or when it accommodates an older child's reasonable and firm preferences. Allowing modifications more readily in these circumstances should relieve the pressure on the otherwise strict standards that are required to maintain stability in parenting plans. On the other hand, modifications that would upset continuing arrangements should be rarely granted, under legal standards requiring a showing of substantial need or harm to the child.

A recurring, difficult modification issue concerns the proposed relocation of a parent. A parent seeking to move may have the stronger relationship to the child and a significant personal stake in the move, such as an important career opportunity or remarriage to a spouse who lives elsewhere. The other parent, however, may have a relationship with the child that will be significantly compromised by the move. Assume, for example, that Sandra decides to move from Maryland back to Lincoln, Nebraska, where she grew up, to be closer to her family. Walter wants her to stay in Maryland or, if she wants to move, to leave the children behind with him.

There is not a good solution to relocation conflicts when both parents have been active in the child's upbringing. Many courts apply a balancing test designed to weigh the benefits and costs of the relocation to the child (*Ireland v. Ireland*, 1997; *Tropea v. Tropea*, 1996; *D'Onofrio v. D'Onofrio*, 1976). Such an approach is flexible, but like all flexible tests, leaves much up to the individual discretion of the judge, thereby increasing uncertainty, unpredictability, and the opportunity for bias.

Some courts have been strict in requiring a relocating parent to bear the burden of demonstrating that a relocation with the child is in the child's best interests (e.g., *Hertzak v. Hertzak*, 1993; *McAlister v. Patterson*, 1982; see also Ill. Ann. Stat., ch. 750, para. 5/609, 1993). These courts may condition continued custody on the custodial parent remaining in the home jurisdiction, without determining whether the change of custody would be justified under the rules applicable to custody modifications (e.g., *Sullivan v. Sullivan*, 1993; *Maeda v. Maeda*, 1990; *Lozinak v. Lozinak*, 1990). Such an approach, instead of accepting the fact of the relocation and deciding what arrangement is best for the child in light of it, treats the relocation as itself an open issue. In so doing, it gives priority to the noncustodial parent's interest in staying in a particular location, over the custodial parent's interest in relocating.

An approach more consistent with past caretaking patterns gives priority to the relationship of the parent who has been exercising primary caretaking responsibility. It would allow a parent who has been exercising the greater share of custodial responsibility to relocate with the child, for a legitimate reason and to a location reasonable in light of that reason, with appropriate adjustments to the parenting plan to maintain the child's relationship with the other parent. Such a law would be consistent with the current trend, which permits relocation by a parent who has been exercising primary custodial responsibility for a child unless the relocation is for the purpose of frustrating the other parent's access to the child or can be shown to be harmful to the child (e.g., *In re Marriage of Burgess,* 1996; *Trent v. Trent,* 1995; *Aaby v. Strange,* 1996). No statute currently specifies what reasons will be considered legitimate reasons for a relocation; doing so would be extremely helpful in eliminating guesswork on this score or bias against parents, especially mothers who are more likely than fathers to be viewed as acting "selfishly" when they make certain kinds of decisions, such as those that improve their own career opportunities. Legitimate reasons should include employment or educational opportunities for a parent or a parent's spouse, moving to be close to family or other support networks, significant health reasons, and protection of a child or parent from domestic abuse. Nondesignated reasons could also be established by a relocating parent, but the legitimacy of any additional reasons would have to be individually established. Under such an approach, since Sandra's reason for relocating is on the approved list, she should be able to move with the children so long as she has maintained primary caretaking responsibility for them, without the special burden of having to establish that the relocation would actually be beneficial to their welfare.

This approach to relocation may appear to give the relocating, primary caretaking parent excessive discretion, without sufficient consideration to the importance of the child's relationship with the other parent. The problem is that the alternative—to condition the continuing caretaking role of the primary parent on remaining in the location of the marital domicile—goes overboard in the other direction, sacrificing the interests of the parent who has played the primary caretaking role in favor of the parent who has played the lesser role. Insofar as one parent's interests will necessarily be compromised in favor of the other's in any relocation dispute, the approach reasonably favors the parent with the greater parenting role, so long as the relocation is reasonable in the respects described above. To the extent possible, the new arrangements should make adjustments to allow for visitation to reduce the impact on the relocation on the nonrelocating parent.

When a relocation does not fall within the criteria outline above, there is little alternative—other than a coin flip—but for the court to reconsider the basic residential framework under the fallback, best-interests-of-the-child test.

Thus, if Sandra and Walter had been sharing caretaking for the children on a more or less equal basis, Sandra will not be able simply to relocate with the children because she has a good reason. In such a case, past caretaking is not dispositive of the question, and Sandra should bear the burden of showing that, given her relocation, it is in the best interests of the children to come with her.

Protection From Domestic Abuse

Domestic abuse does not end, and may even worsen, when family members separate (Mahoney, 1991, pp. 71). Moreover, access to a child is often used by an abuser as a way of continuing to control the other party (Fischer et al., 1993). The safety of both the victimized parent and the child is threatened by domestic abuse, since even when abuse is limited to a child's parent and is not aimed directly at the child, it can damage the child's sense of security and establish poor models for adult behavior (Davidson, 1995, pp. 357-358; Straus, 1995, pp. 237-238; *In re Marriage of Brainard,* 1994).

Although in recent years, the law has exhibited greater appreciation of the direct and indirect risks of domestic abuse to children, the rules enacted to protect the victims of domestic violence are frequently disregarded, or under-enforced (Family Violence Project, 1995, pp. 216-217, 221-222; Czapanskiy, 1993, pp. 255-257; Klein & Orloff, 1993, pp. 958; Cahn, 1991, pp. 1072; Association of Family and Conciliation Courts Research Unit, 1988, pp. 82 and selected tables). A past history of domestic violence is one of the few circumstances in which courts should be required to conduct a meaningful review of a parental agreement. All other rules governing disputes over children should also be subject to provisions designed to guarantee the protection of children and parents who are victims of domestic abuse. Courts should not be permitted to ignore domestic abuse, or assume that it will never happen again now that the parties are separating.

Where domestic abuse is shown, the law must impose upon courts the affirmative obligation to consider a range of options to protect the victim, including reduction in the amount of residential contact and supervision of the contact that occurs, mandatory treatment programs, and no-drinking, no-drug limitations during periods of access. In addition, temporary protective orders should be easier to get. Mediators should be required to screen for domestic abuse and either refuse to mediate or to take steps to ensure meaningful consent to the mediation, a voluntary agreement, and safety of the victim. There should be a good faith defense to contempt proceedings brought against parents who interfere with access by the other parent in the good faith belief that interference is necessary to protect the safety of the child even if it turns out, once the matter is adjudicated, that the feared danger cannot be proved. Also, although independent legal representation for a child usually does not play a reliably constructive role in custody proceedings (Representing Children, 1995, pp. 2-3), a guardian ad litem or attorney for the child should be appointed in cases of domestic abuse since this is one likely area in which the parents cannot be counted upon to protect their child's interests.

The law has made significant recent progress in ensuring protection of a child and parent from domestic abuse. At least 16 states impose presumptions against assigning either sole custody, joint custody, or both, to parents who have committed domestic abuse (e.g., Del. Code Ann. tit. 13, 705A(a), (b), 1994; La. Rev. State. Ann. 9:364(A), 1996). At least two thirds of states require consideration of evidence of domestic violence in determining how custodial responsibility should be allocated at divorce (Family Violence Project of The National Council of Juvenile and Family Court Judges, 1995, pp. 199). In addition, many states make exceptions from other rules, such as mandatory mediation, when domestic abuse has occurred (e.g., Colo. Rev. Stat. Ann. 13-22-311(1), 1995; La. Rev. Stat. Ann. 9:363, 1996; Minn. Stat. Ann. 518.619(1), 1996; Mont. Code Ann. 40-4-301(2), 1995). As the reality of domestic abuse becomes better recognized, such measures should become even more widespread.

Functional Parents

Current categories of adults who may be allocated responsibility for children are both too broad and too narrow. The law should narrowly define a category of stepparents, relatives, and other adults who have functioned as a child's parent, who should be allocated some responsibility for children in appropriate circumstances when parents separate. This category should include only those individuals who have previously lived with the child for a significant period and regularly performed the majority, or near-equal, share of the caretaking functions, with the consent of a legal parent. This is a category defined by function, not legal relationship. It excludes paid babysitters, roommates, and loving grandparents who have not lived with the child (Bostock, 1994, pp. 370-372; Harpring, 1994, pp. 1688-1689). It includes some individuals, including coparents and involved stepparents, even if that inclusion means the child will have more than one mother, or father (Bartlett, 1984, pp. 944-951).

When the category of functional parents is narrowly enough circumscribed to cover only those who have actually served as parent for a meaningful length of time, the law can afford to treat them very seriously, as parents. A preference for biological parents should still be maintained, especially with respect to who is allocated primary custodial responsibility. Continuing contact of some sort with an adult whose role in the child's life has been functionally equivalent to the role expected of a legal parent, however, may often be an extremely important factor in the continuity and stability of a child's life. The law should not rely on courts to protect these interests by stretching existing laws that define parenthood as an exclusive status. The problem requires explicit rules carefully defining the relevant status to be protected and the extent of the protections.

CONCLUSION

This chapter ends with a word on the limits of law. The law is given both too much blame for what goes wrong at divorce, and too much credit for how it might make things better. The empirical research does not support the stereotypical view of lawyers stirring up conflict, prolonging disputes, or helping their clients take advantage of the other side, in disregard of the interests of the children. Austin Sarat and William Felstiner, in their study of lawyer behavior in divorce cases, found that lawyers attempted to refocus the attention of clients—who were otherwise hung up on the emotional issues and short-term strategic considerations—on the long- term goals of the client and the need of the postdivorce family for stability and fairness (Sarat & Felstiner, 1986, pp. 125-132).

Experience also does not support the hope that the law can supply a framework that can insure that divorces go well. The law cannot prevent embittered or adversarial adults from waging battle over children. It cannot guarantee the future behaviors of adults or responses by children. Most of all, the law cannot guarantee that children will obtain the love and nurture that they most need.

Too often reform efforts focus on the narrow minority of high conflict cases whose results are likely to be poor, no matter what the law is. Judged by the outcomes in those cases, no law will seem sound. Reforms in the law should not ignore the results it might produce—indirectly—in the 85% to 90% of cases where parties can be assisted, and affirmed, in acting reasonably. An approach that builds on choices these parents have made in the past and that expects them to plan reasonably and with some flexibility for the future not only achieves greater stability and continuity in some of the more difficult cases courts face, but it reinforces the importance of these values in the larger majority of cases as well.

REFERENCES

Association of Family and Conciliation Courts Research Unit (1998, March). *Sexual abuse allegations project: Final report.*

Bartlett, K. T. (1988). Re-expressing parenthood. *Yale Law Journal, 98,* 293-340.

Bartlett, K. T. (1984). Rethinking parenthood as an exclusive status: The need for legal alternatives when the premise of the nuclear family has failed. *Virginia Law Review, 70,* 879-963.

Becker, M. (1992). Maternal feelings, myth, taboo, and child custody. *Southern California Review of Law and Women's Studies, 1,* 133-224.

Bohmer, C., & Ray, M. L. (1994). Effects of different dispute resolution methods on women and children after divorce. *Family Law Quarterly, 28,* 223-245.

Bostock, C. (1994). Does the expansion of grandparent visitation rights promote the best interests of the child?: A survey of grandparent visitation laws in the fifty states. *Columbia Journal of Law and Social Problems, 27,* 319-373.

Brinig, M. F., & Alexeev, M. V. (1993). Trading at divorce: Preferences, legal rules and transaction costs. *Ohoi State Journal of Dispute Resolution, 8,* 279-297.

Bruch, C. A. (1988). And how are the children? The effects of ideology and mediation on child custody law and children's well-being in the United States. *International Journal of Law and the Family, 2,* 106-126.

Cahn, N. R. (1991). Civil images of battered women: The impact of domestic violence on child custody decisions. *Vanderbilt Law Review, 44,* 1041-1097.

Chambers, D. L. (1985). Rethinking the substantive rules for custody disputes in divorce. *Michigan Law Review, 83,* 477-569.

Crippen, G. (1990). Stumbling beyond best interests of the child: Reexamining child custody standard-setting in the wake of Minnesota's four year experiment with the primary caretaker preference. *Minnesota Law Review, 75,* 427-503.

Czapanskiy, K. (1993). Domestic violence, the family, and the lawyering process: Lessons from studies on gender bias in the court. *Family Law Quarterly, 27,* 247-277.

Davidson, H. A. (1995). Child abuse and domestic violence: Legal connections and controversies. *Family Law Quarterly, 29,* 357-373.

Elster, J. (1987). Solomonic judgments: Against the best interest of the child. *University of Chicago Law Review, 54,* 1-45.

Family Violence Project of the National Council of Juvenile and Family Court Judges (1995). Family violence in child custody states: An analysis of state codes and legal practice. *Family Law Quarterly, 29,* 197-227.

Fineman, M. (1988). Dominant discourse, professional language, and legal change in custody decisionmaking. *Harvard Law Review, 101,* 727-774.

Fischer, K., Vidmar, N., & Ellis, R. (1993). The culture of battering and the role of mediation in domestic violence cases. *Southern Methodist University Law Review, 46,* 2117-2174.

Galinsky, E., & Bond, J. T. (1996). Work and family: The experience of mothers and fathers in the labor force. In C. Costello & B. K. Krimgold (Eds.), *American woman, 1996-1997, Where we stand: Women and work.*

Glendon, M. A. (1986). Fixed rules and discretion in contemporary family law and succession law. *Tulane Law Review, 60,* 1165-1197.

Goldstein, J., & Fenster, C. A. (1994). Anglo-American criteria for resolving child custody disputes from the eighteenth century to the present. *Journal of Family History, 19,* 35.

Grillo, T. (1991). The mediation alternative: Process dangers for women. *Yale Law Journal, 100,* 1545-1610.

Grossberg, M. (1985). *Governing the hearth: Law and family in nineteenth-century America.* Chapel Hill: University of North Carolina Press.

Harpring, S. N. (1994). Wide-open grandparent visitation statutes: Is the door closing? *University of Cincinnati Law Review, 62,* 1659-1694.

Henry, R. K. (1994). "Primary caretaker": Is it a ruse? *Family Advocate, 17,* 53-56.

Hollinger, J. F., (1995). Adoption and aspiration: The Uniform Adoption Act, the DeBoer-Schmidt case, and the American quest for the ideal family. *Duke Journal of Gender of Law and Policy, 2,* 15-40.

Kelly, J. B. (1989). Mediated and adversarial divorce: Respondents' perceptions of their process and outcomes. *Mediation Quarterly, 24,* 71-88.

Klein, C. F., & Orloff, L. E. (1993). Providing legal protection for battered women: An analysis of state statutes and case law. *Hofstra Law Review, 21,* 801-1189.

Maccoby, E. E., & Mnookin, R. H. (1992). *Dividing the child: Social and legal dilemmas of custody.* Cambridge, MA: Harvard University Press.

Mahoney, M. R. (1991). Legal images of battered women: Redefining the issue of separation. *Michigan Law Review, 90,* 1-94.

Mason, M. A. (1994). *From father's property to children's rights: The history of child custody in the United States.* New York: Columbia University Press.

Mathis, R. D., & Yingling, L. C. (1992). Analysis of pre- and post-test gender differences in family satisfaction of divorce in mediation couples. *Journal of Divorce and Remarriage, 17,* 75-85.

Meierding, N. R. (1993). Does mediation work? A survey of long-term satisfaction and durability rates for private mediated agreements. *Mediation Quarterly, 11,* 157-170.

Melli, M. S., Erlanger, H. S., & Chambliss, E. (1988). The process of negotiation: An exploratory investigation in the context of no-fault divorce. *Rutgers Law Review, 40,* 1133-1172.

Mnookin, R. H. (1975). Child-custody adjudication: Judicial functions in the face of indeterminacy. *Law and Contemporary Problems, 39,* 226-293.

Mnookin, R. H., & Kornhauser, L. (1979). Bargaining in the shadow of the law: The case of divorce. *Yale Law Journal, 88,* 950-997.

Neely, R. (1984). Child custody and the dynamics of greed. *Yale Law and Policy Review, 3,* 168-186.

Representing children: Standards for attorneys and Guardians ad litem in custody or visitation proceedings (with Commentary) (1995). *Journal of the American Academy of Matrimonial Lawyers, 13,* 1-179.

Sack, L. (1992). Women and children first: A feminist analysis of the primary caretaker standard in child custody cases. *Yale Journal of Law and Feminism, 4,* 291-328.

Sarat, A., & Flestiner, W. B. (1986). Law and strategy in the divorce lawyer's office. *Law and Society Review, 20,* 93-134.

Schneider, C. E. (1991). Discretion, rules and law: Child custody and the UMDA's best interest standard. *Michigan Law Review, 89,* 2215-2298.

Scott, E. S. (1992). Pluralism, parental preferences, and child custody. *California Law Review, 80,* 615-672.

Scott, E. S., Reppucci, N. D., & Aber, M. (1988). Children's preference in adjudicated custody decisions. *Georgia Law Review, 22,* 1035-1078.

Straus, R. B. (1995). Supervised visitation and family violence. *Family Law Quarterly, 22,* 229-252.

US Department of Commerce (1996). *Statistical abstract of the United States, 1996.* Washington, DC: Government Printing Office.

Wald, M. (1976). State intervention on behalf of "neglected" children: Standards for removal of children from their homes, monitoring the status of children in foster care, and termination of parental rights. *Stanford Law Review, 28,* 623-706.

Wexler, J. G. (1985). Rethinking the modification of child custody decrees. *Yale Law Journal, 94,* 757-820.

CASES

Aaby v. Strange, 924 S.E.2d 623 (Tenn. 1996).

In re Allen, 626 P.2d 16 (Wash. App. 1981).

Bienenfeld v. Bennett-White, 605 A.2d 172 (Md. Ct. Spec. App. 1992).

Bottoms v. Bottoms, 457 S.E.2d 102 (Va. 1995).

In re Marriage of Brainard, 523 N.W.2d 611 (Iowa Ct. App. 1994).

Brooks v. Parkerson, 454 S.E.2d 769 (Ga. 1995).

In re Marriage of Bukacek, 907 P.2d 931 (Mont. 1995).

Burchard v. Garay, 724 P.2d 486 (Cal. 1986).

In re Marriage of Burgess, 913 P.2d 473 (Cal. 1996).

Burnham v. Burnham, 304 N.W.2d 58 (Neb. 1981).

In re Baby Girl Clausen, 502 N.W.2d 649 (Mich. 1993).

Carter v. Brodrick, 644 P.2d 850 (Alaska 1982).

Collins v. Gilbreath, 403 N.E.2d 91 (Ind. Ct. App. 1980).

Dempsey v. Dempsey, 306 S.E.2d 230 (W. Va. 1983).

Devine v. Devine, 398 So.2d 686 (Ala. 1981).

Dick v. Dick, 534 N.W.2d 185 (Mich. Ct. App. 1995).

In re Marriage of Diehl, 582 N.E.2d 281 (Ill. App. Ct. 1991).

D'Onofrio v. D'Onofrio, 365 A.2d 27 (N.J. Super.Ch. Div. 1976).
In re Fennell, 485 N.W.2d 863 (Iowa Ct. App. 1992).
Foreng v. Foreng, 509 N.W.2d 38 (N.D. 1993).
Fox v. Fox, 904 P.2d 66 (Okla. 1995).
Garska v. McCoy, 278 S.E.2d 357 (W. Va. 1981).
Gribble v. Gribble, 583 P.2d 64 (Utah 1978).
Griswold v. Connecticut, 381 U.S. 479 (1965).
Hawk v. Hawk, 855 S.W.2d 573 (Tenn. 1993).
Hertzak v. Hertzak, 616 So.2d 727 (La. Ct. App. 1993).
Ireland v. Ireland, 696 A.2d 1016 (Conn. 1997).
Kenneth L.W. v. Tamyra S.W., 408 S.E.2d 625 (W. Va. 1991).
Kirshenbaum v. Kirshenbaum, 929 P.2d 1204 (Wash. Ct. App. 1997).
Lacaze v. Lacaze, 621 So.2d 298 (Ala. Civ. App. 1993).
Linda R. v. Richard E., 561 N.Y.S.2d 29 (N.Y. App. Div. 1990).
Lozinak v. Lozinak, 569 A.2d 353 (Pa. Super. Ct. 1990).
McAlister v. Patterson, 299 S.E.2d 322 (S.C. 1982).
McDonald v. Wrigley, 870 P.2d 777 (Okla 1994).
McIntyre v. McIntyre, 461 S.E.2d 745 (N.C. 1995).
Maeda v. Maeda, 794 P.2d 268 (Haw. Ct. App. 1990).
Meyer v. Nebraska, 262 U.S. 390 (1923).
Miller v. Miller, 620 A.2d 1161 (Pa. 1993).
Palmore v.Sidoti, 466 U.S. 429 (1984).
Patricia Ann S. v. James Daniel S., 435 S.E.2d 6 (W. Va. 1993).
Petersen v. Rogers, 445 S.E.2d 901 (N.C. 1994).
Peterson v. Peterson, 474 N.W.2d 862 (Neb. 1991).
Peterson v. Peterson, 559 N.W.2d 826 (N.D. 1997).
Prince v. Massachusetts, 321 U.S. 158 (1944).
Prost v. Greene, 652 A.2d 621 (D.C. 1995).
Pusey v. Pusey, 728 P.2d 117 (Utah 1986).
S.E.G. v. R.A.G., 735 S.W.2d 164 (Mo. Ct. App. 1987).
Schwab v. Schwab, 505 N.W.2d 752 (S.D. 1993).
Seymour v. Seymour, 433 A.2d 1005 (Conn. 1980).
Steward v. Steward, 890 P.2d 777 (Nev. 1995).
Sullivan v. Sullivan, 594 N.Y.S.2d 276 (N.Y. App. Div. 1993).
Trent v. Trent, 890 P.2d 1309 (Nev. 1995).
Tropea v. Tropea, 665 N.E.2d 145 (N.Y. 1996).
In re Troxel, 940 P.2d 698 (Wash. App. 1997).
Tucker v. Tucker, 910 P.2d 1209 (Utah 1996).
Van Driel v. Van Driel, 525 N.W.2d 37 (S.D. 1994).

STATUTES AND MODEL ACTS

Alaska Stat. 25.24.150(c) (1995).
Ariz. Rev. Stat. Ann. 25-331.01(3), 25-332(D), (E), (G), (L) (Supp. 1995).

Cal. Fam. Code 3080 (West 1994).

Colo. Rev. Stat. 13-22-311(1) (West Supp. 1995); 14.10-131(1) & (2) (1987).

Conn. Gen. Stat. Ann. 46b-56a(b), 46b-69b(b) (West 1995).

Del. Code Ann. tit. 13, 727(b)(2), 729(2)(b), (c)(1993); 705A(a) (Supp. 1994).

D.C. Code Ann. 16-911(a)(5) (Supp. 1996).

Fla. Stat. Ann. 61.13(2)(b)(2), 61.21(2), 61.121 (Supp. 1997).

Ga. Code Ann. 19-9-3(a)(4) (Supp. 1996); 19-9-6(3) (1991).

Haw. Rev. Stat. 571-46(2) (Supp. 1995).

Idaho Code 32-717B(1), (2), (4) (Michie 1996).

Ill. Ann. Stat., ch. 750, para. 5/602.1(b), para. 5/609, para. 5/610(a) (Smith-Hurd Supp. 1996).

Ind. Code Ann. 31-1-11.5-21(3) (Burns Supp. 1996).

Iowa Code Ann. 598.41(2), (5) (Supp. 1996).

Kan. Stat. Ann. 60-1610(a)(4)(A) (Supp. 1993).

Ky. Rev. Stat. Ann. 403.340(1) (Baldwin Supp. 1995).

La. Civ. Code, articles 132, 133, 335(B) (West Supp. 1997).

La. Rev. Stat. Ann. 9:363; 9:364(A) (West Supp. 1996).

Mass. Ann. Laws ch. 208, 31 (Law. Co-op 1994).

Me. Rev. Stat. Ann., tit. 19 752(6) (West Supp. 1994).

Mich. Comp. Laws Ann. 722.26a(1), 722.27(1)(c), 722.27a(2) (West Supp. 1995).

Minn. Stat. 518.18(1), (2), 518.619(1) (West Supp. 1996).

Miss. Code Ann. 93-5-24(4), 93-11-65 (1994).

Mo. Ann. Stat. 452.375(5)(3)(a), (8) (West 1997).

Mont. Code Ann. 40-4-223(2), 40-4-224(1), 40-4-301(2) (1995).

N.M. Stat. Ann. 40-4-9.1(A), (B), (F) (Michie 1994).

Nev. Rev. Stat. Ann. 125.490(1) (Michie 1993).

Ohio Rev. Code 3109.04(E)(1), (G) (Baldwin 1995).

Okla. Stat. Ann. tit. 43, 109(C) (West 1990).

Tenn. Code Ann. 36-6-106(7) (Supp. 1995).

Tex. Fam. Code Ann. 153.134(a)(6), 153.251(d), 153.254 (West 1996).

Uniform Marriage and Divorce Act, 409 (1970).

Utah Code Ann. 30-3-34 (1995).

Vt. Stat. Ann. tit. 15, 664(1) (1989).

Wash. Rev. Code Ann. 26.09.187(3)(a)(i), 26.09.191(1), 26.09.260(2)(b) (West Supp. 1996).

Wis. Stat. Ann. 767.24(3); 767.325(1); 767.329 (West 1994).

W. Va. Code 44-10-4 (1982).

PART III

Nonresidential Parenting

In most postdivorce families, custodial parents assume the predominant role in the daily care of children, while nonresidential parents assume a visiting relationship. But each adult is a parent and, in most circumstances, children should be able to enjoy meaningful, satisfying relationships with each parent after divorce. For most of this century, of course, mothers have typically become custodial parents after divorce and fathers have become nonresidential parents. In recent years the role of fathers in postdivorce life has been vigorously debated as evidence accumulates that many men fail to visit offspring or maintain fidelity to their child support obligations. Popularized images of the "deadbeat dad" and absent father have contributed to legislative initiatives to strengthen child support enforcement and encourage more committed fathering. A society that is concerned with the disengagement of men from their children should seek constructive roles for fathers in the postdivorce family. Two contributors to this section seek to clarify the reasons that some fathers remain involved in their children's lives and others increasingly distance themselves from the needs of offspring.

In the initial chapter, Michael Lamb considers noncustodial fathers and their impact on their children in the context of the incentives and constraints that characterize nonresidential parenting. His focus is on the visiting relationship that the large majority of fathers assume after divorce, and his concern is with the time distribution arrangements and physical circumstances of visitation that make it difficult for fathers to maintain meaningful parenting relationships with their offspring. But how much do children really benefit from regular contact with their noncustodial fathers? In reflecting on research indicating only a small association between visitation frequency and child well-being, Lamb indicates that a father's gradual disappearance from a child's life has multifaceted consequences, and that the benefits of visitation are contingent on factors such as the quality of the father-child relationship, the extent of ongoing conflict between the child's parents, and the economic assistance that accompanies visitation. In the end, he argues that despite the potential benefits to children of policies that enhance fathers' parenting involvement, the allocation of parenting responsibility in the postdivorce family probably reflects features of the "marital compact" that defined caregiving roles prior to marital dissolution.

In the next chapter, Dan Meyer considers fathers' compliance with child support orders after divorce and after nonmarital childbearing when paternity has been established. In each case, he indicates that various factors can influence a father's fidelity to child support orders, including the father's ability to pay, the "burden" of the support order (i.e., the ratio of the order amount to total income), the strength of enforcement mechanisms, the strength of family ties between the father and his offspring (such as the length of marriage and the number of children), and the perceived economic need of the custodial parent and children (including the mother's remarriage). Using data from the Wisconsin Court Records Database collected by the Institute for Research on Poverty at the University of Wisconsin, Meyer concludes that noncompliance with child support orders remains a serious problem, and that some men are capable of paying but refuse to do so. However, his findings also indicate that a meaningful proportion of fathers are incapable of making their child support payments, suggesting that there may be eventual limits to the efficacy of current enforcement mechanisms and that new policy directions may be needed for strengthening the economic conditions of children in postdivorce life, such as increasing the earning power of low-income fathers.

Chapter 5

Noncustodial Fathers and Their Impact on the Children of Divorce

Michael E. Lamb

Joan and David Berg were married in 1984 as they graduated from college. Both took entry-level management jobs in large corporations. They were paid sufficiently well and they were able to buy a small suburban home in 1986. When Benjamin was born in late 1987, David took a week's leave to help at home and Joan was able to get a partially paid maternity leave for 3 months. Realizing that the family needed two incomes to meet its expenses, Joan returned to work when Ben was 3 months old. A woman recommended by the couple's neighbors agreed to care for Ben, along with two toddlers and her own three children. To minimize the cost of childcare, which Joan and David had not adequately anticipated when Joan got pregnant, David arranged to start work early and forego his lunch break so he was able to pick Ben up each day at 3 p.m. Joan fed, dressed, and dropped Ben off each day at 9 a.m., working until 6 p.m. This arrangement appeared to work well for all concerned, and April, Ben's younger sister, experienced the same pattern of care when she was born in 1989.

Joan and David began to notice strains in their marriage shortly after April's birth, and they separated in the spring of 1991. Both parents sued for divorce and full custody of the two children, each arguing that he or she was the primary caretaker. David's lawyer was highly regarded in the county, but he was uncertain whether he could prevail, arguing that the judge was likely to award custody of such young children to their mother. He eventually persuaded David to accept an arrangement in terms of which the children stayed with Joan but spent every other weekend with David. The judge quickly accepted this compromise as the basis for

AUTHOR'S NOTE: I am grateful to Paul Amato, Kathleen Sternberg, and Ross Thompson for helpful comments on earlier drafts of this chapter.

a formal order issued in October 1993, and used the state guidelines to establish David's child support responsibilities.

It was difficult for David and Joan to maintain two households on the same incomes they had needed to support one, and Joan soon decided to move closer to her parents, who offered to provide cost-free childcare during the time she worked at her new job. David initially continued to visit Ben and April every other weekend, although they grumbled about the 2-hour commute in each direction and Ben complained about missing his Saturday soccer games. In 1995, David accepted a transfer within the company that moved him to the state capital, a 5-hour drive away. The increased pay made it easier to meet his child support obligations, but he began skipping his weekend visits, particularly after the children began talking excitedly about Bill, who moved into Joan's apartment with his puppy in November 1995.

Unfortunately, variations on this theme play out in families and courtrooms throughout America with amazing frequency. Although the rates of divorce have leveled recently, it remains the case that about half of the children in America will experience the separation of their parents before they reach adulthood. Although children are no longer stigmatized by their parents' divorce as they were in earlier decades, divorce is not a victimless experience, and the adverse effects on children have attracted the greatest attention, as noted later in this chapter. Recognition of these adverse effects, along with increased awareness of the vast number of children affected by divorce, have fueled efforts to both understand and minimize the adverse effects, and a discussion of these issues is at the heart of this chapter.

In 1998, as in 1958, divorce is typically followed by a period of time in which children live with their mothers, visiting their fathers on specified occasions. Many, perhaps most, fathers visit their children less and less frequently as time goes by, and father absence is frequently represented as the root cause of the children's difficulties and subsequent adjustment. This conclusion has been controversial, and the identification of resultant fatherlessness as the worst consequence of divorce has spawned a series of questions. Is the magnitude of the effects a linear correlate of the extent of fatherlessness, such that children who see their fathers extensively after divorce suffer fewer adverse consequences than children who see their fathers every other weekend, or those who seldom, if ever, see their fathers? How can nonresident fathers be encouraged to continue seeing their children? Why do so many fathers agree to postdivorce arrangements that afford them few opportunities to be with their children? Many mothers argue that they should be awarded primary custody of their children because they were the primary careproviders prior to divorce; fathers counter that this was only because the couple agreed to divide responsibilities in this way and that it is unfair to punish them by depriving them of access to their children both before and after divorce. Are issues of fairness really pertinent? Should courts not focus only on protecting the best interests of dependent children? And since divorce wreaks such profound effects on all involved parties, is it really meaningful to focus on predivorce arrangements when postdivorce arrangements are certain to be different, whichever parent takes (or is granted) primary responsibility?

We cannot answer all these questions in this brief chapter, particularly as the relevant evidence, for the most part, is not yet available. My more modest goal is to explore the role that noncustodial fathers play and might play in the lives of their children. It is important to recognize, however, that noncustodial fathers do not operate in a vacuum; their roles, responsibilities, and behavior are influenced by social expectations and practices that cannot be ignored.

THE REDISCOVERY OF FATHERHOOD

The contemporary concern with noncustodial fathers (often better known as "deadbeat dads" or "absent fathers") has not always been evident. In fact, more than two decades ago, I wrote a paper entitled, "Fathers: Forgotten contributors to child development" (Lamb, 1975). The title, like the paper itself, reflected my frustration with the way that developmental psychologists had ignored the possible roles that fathers might play in children's development. By the 1970s, fathers were seldom evident in the theories and practices of clinical psychologists as well, although of course fathers continued to hold central roles in psychoanalytic theory. According to most psychoanalysts, however, it mattered little who the father was and what he actually did. Rather, it was important that somebody be identified as a father who could enter into the child's fantasy life and be imagined doing things with, to, and for the child. Ironically, this fantastic and mythical father figure was the one who mattered most, particularly in the Oedipal phases of development (Mächtlinger, 1981).

In the ensuing 25 years, social scientists in general and psychologists in particular have come to see fatherhood quite differently (Lamb, 1981, 1997). These changing perspectives have converged most recently to create a strong belief among social scientists and in the popular media that fatherhood and father-child relationships are extremely important to and for children. Books like David Blankenhorn's (1995) *Fatherless America,* David Popenoe's (1996) *Life Without Father,* and Adrienne Burgess' (1997) *Fatherhood Reclaimed,* as well as popular articles like that by Barbara Dafoe Whitehead (1993), have proclaimed and recounted the exceptional importance of fathers. Among those with a special interest in social policy, however, the focus has fallen not on fatherhood, but on fatherlessness, and the underlying concern has been with the number of children handicapped because they do not have fathers involved in their lives (see Knitzer & Bernard, 1997, for a survey of policy initiatives at the state level). The following excerpt from Blankenhorn's (1995, p. 26) book represents well an increasingly common refrain, with an extraordinary emphasis placed on the devastating effects of fatherlessness:

> In short, the key for men is to be fathers. The key for children is to have fathers. The key for society is to create fathers. For society, the primary results of fatherhood are right-doing males and better outcomes for children. Conversely, the primary consequences of fatherlessness are rising male violence and declining child well-being. In the United States at the close of the twentieth century, paternal disinvestment has become the major source of our most important social problems, especially those rooted in violence.

In his book, Blankenhorn acknowledges that fatherlessness has many different origins, and it is important to remember that many of the children growing up in fatherless families were born into these situations, not placed there by the separation or divorce of their parents (Smith, Morgan, & Koropeckyj-Cox, 1996). These different types of fatherless families are associated with different demographic characteristics, at least some divergent developmental processes, and different outcomes (Zill, 1996). Specifically, single-parent families created by divorce as opposed to nonmarital childbirth at minimum differ with respect to racial background (those created by divorce are disproportionately white) and socio-economic circumstances (unmarried mothers tend to be worse off). From the perspective of the individuals themselves, furthermore, experiencing the disruption of a relationship is quite different psychologically than never having had such a relationship. I am concerned in this chapter with children living in fatherless families created by the disruption of relationships between the parents and the relevance of this discussion to children in other fatherless contexts is unknown. My inattention to the plight of children born to single mothers reflects my particular concern here, not with the effects of fatherlessness per se, but with understanding how divorce affects children, and how changed policies and practices regarding custody and visitation might prove beneficial to children.

To this end, I devote the next section of the chapter to a brief review of the evidence regarding the effects of divorce and fatherlessness on children's development. I then turn attention to the implications of these findings for those making decisions about the amount and type of contact children are permitted to have with their noncustodial parents. My explicit thesis is that the modal child experiencing his or her parent's divorce would benefit from arrangements which facilitated greater paternal participation. Unfortunately, many contemporary time distribution plans, wittingly or unwittingly, restrict the quality of father-child relationships, and may drive fathers away from rather than draw them closer to their children. In the final section, I note that the postdivorce division of time between the two parents often reflects implicit predivorce marital contracts, or the courts' assumptions about such arrangements. The slow pace of change in the implicit contracts between mothers and fathers provides an important backdrop against which custody awards and reforms of the judicial and legal decision-making processes should be viewed.

THE EFFECTS OF FATHER ABSENCE FOLLOWING DIVORCE

Although interpretation of the findings has been controversial for three decades, there is substantial consensus that children are better off psychologically and developmentally in two-parent rather than single-parent families (see reviews by Amato, 1993; Amato & Keith, 1991; Amato, Loomis, & Booth, 1995; Cooksey, 1997; Downey, 1994; Goodman, Emery, & Haugaard, 1998; Hetherington & Stanley-Hagan, 1997; Hines, 1997; McLanahan & Sandefur, 1994; McLanahan & Teitler, in press; Seltzer, 1994; Thomson, Hanson, & McLanahan, 1994). The now-voluminous literature reveals a number of developmental domains in which children growing up in fatherless families are disadvantaged relative to peers growing up in two-parent families. Specifically, the research literature is replete with studies focused on psychosocial adjustment, behavior and achievement at school, educational attainment, employment trajectories, income generation, involvement in antisocial and even criminal behavior, and the ability to establish and maintain intimate relationships, but because the literature has been reviewed so frequently and so extensively, my goal in this chapter is not to provide another comprehensive review. Much remains to be learned about the ways in which limitations on father-child contact affect child adjustment, however, and I therefore examine hypothesized and causal mechanisms quite closely. There is widespread consensus that the magnitude of the simple or bivariate associations between father absence or contact and child outcomes is much weaker than many commentators would have us believe, and my aim is to probe these associations further in an effort both to explain why the effects of post divorce father-child contact may sometimes appear small and to articulate the implications for legal and judicial practice.

Along with social scientists such as Biller (1981, 1993), Blankenhorn offers a simple and straightforward interpretation of the association between father-lessness and its effects. Simply stated, Blankenhorn believes that absolute and relative father absence affect children not because their households are poorer, or their mothers are stressed, but because they lack a father figure—a model, a disciplinarian, and a male figure—in their lives. Like me, many social scientists question this interpretation because it fails to acknowledge the many salient and often traumatic events experienced by children when their parents divorce. Typically, for example, divorce disrupts one of the child's most important and enduring relationships, that with his or her father. Second, the family's financial status is adversely affected by the loss of a major source of income, usually the principal breadwinner. Third, because mothers need to work more extensively outside the home when their partners leave, adults are less likely to be present and the supervision and guidance of children becomes less intensive and reliable in single-parent families. Fourth, conflict between the parents commonly precedes, emerges or increases during the divorce process, and often continues beyond it. Fifth, single parenthood is associated with a variety of social and financial stresses with which individuals must cope, largely on their own. Researchers have shown that all of these factors (the disruption of parent-child relationships, marital conflict, stress, economic hardship, and undersupervision) have adverse effects on children's adjustment, and it is thus not surprising to find that divorce, representing the co-occurrence of these factors, has adverse consequences for children. Less clear are the specific processes by which these effects are mediated, yet an understanding of how divorce and custody arrangements affect child development is absolutely crucial if we as a society are to minimize or reverse the adverse effects of divorce on children. Stepparenthood and remarriage further complicate efforts to understand the effects of diverse postdivorce custody arrangements on child well-being (Hanson, McLanahan, & Thomson, 1996; Hetherington & Henderson, 1997; Isaacs & Leon, 1988).

As Amato (1993; Amato & Gilbreth, in press) has shown with particular clarity, the associations between father absence and postdivorce father-child contact and their contrasting effects are much weaker than one might expect. Indeed,

Amato and Gilbreth's (in press) recent meta-analysis revealed no significant association between the frequency of father-child contact and child outcomes, and similar conclusions have been reached by several other reviewers of the literature (Amato, 1993; Furstenberg & Cherlin, 1991; Furstenberg, Morgan, & Allison, 1987; McLanahan & Sandefur, 1994; Seltzer, 1994). In part, this may well reflect variation in the exposure to other pathogenic circumstances (e.g., changing family economic status, stress, marital conflict) as well as data sets with distributional properties that can obscure statistical associations, but it likely reflects in addition the diverse types of father-child relationships represented in the samples studied. Specifically, abusive, incompetent, or disinterested fathers are likely to have much different effects than devoted, committed, and sensitive fathers, and high-quality contacts between fathers and children are surely more beneficial than encounters that lack breadth and intensity. Consistent with this, Amato and Gilbreth (in press) reported that children's well-being was significantly enhanced when their relationships with nonresidential fathers were positive and when the nonresidential fathers engaged in "active parenting." Likewise, Simons (1996) reported that contact with nonresidential fathers who engaged in active parenting was beneficial and data from the National Center for Education Statistics (*Father Times,* 1997) demonstrated that both resident and nonresident fathers enhanced their children's adjustment when they were involved in the children's schooling. The clear implication is that postdivorce arrangements should specifically seek to maximize positive and meaningful paternal involvement rather than simple visitation or contact between all fathers and children. Such postdivorce arrangements would focus on the needs of the children concerned, and would make no effort to "reward" or punish" the parents differentially depending on their relative parental involvement prior to divorce. These implications are pursued more fully in the next section.

IMPLICATIONS FOR DIVORCING PARENTS AND DECISION MAKERS

Divorce and the extent of postdivorce father-child contact do not affect all children similarly. This variability is important, inasmuch as it underscores the complexity of the processes mediating the associations between contact and adjustment and the fact that children vary with respect to the pathogenic circumstances they encounter as well as the buffering or protective factors that reduce their vulnerabilities.

As suggested in the previous section, as well as by Robert Emery in Chapter 1, five factors are particularly important when considering and seeking to predict the effects of divorce on children: (1) the level of involvement and quality of relationships between residential or custodial parents and their children; (2) the level of involvement and quality of the relationships between nonresidential parents and their children; (3) the amount of conflict between the two parents; (4) the amount of conflict between the children and their parents; and (5) the socioeconomic circumstances in which the children reside. Social scientists may argue about the relative importance of these factors, but such debates are not particularly fruitful because these factors are all highly interrelated, and this precludes research that could untangle and quantitatively evaluate the magnitude of independent effects. Although we can play statistical games, selectively partialling out the effects of individual factors or groups of factors, we need to remember that these statistical exercises cannot truly estimate relative importance when measurement is poor and the factors themselves are inextricably linked in the real world.

On the issue of measurement, note controversy about the validity of varying measures of adjustment, and continuing debates about the divergent perspectives of differing informants (Dremen & Ronen-Eliav, 1997; Sternberg, Lamb, & Dawud-Noursi, 1998). Overt behavior problems can be measured reliably, but how well do they index the "psychological pain" experienced by children affected by divorce (Emery, 1994)? Possible measures of socioeconomic circumstances abound, but their intercorrelations are far from perfect, and few take into account such crucial factors as the discrepancy between predivorce and postdivorce circumstances, the qualitative consequences (e.g., residential moves within or to other school districts and neighborhoods), the availability and quality of noneconomic and economic support from relatives and friends, or even the timing of economic deprivation, which now appears quite important (e.g., Duncan & Brooks-Gunn, 1997). Conflict is almost ubiquitous in modern divorces; how much and what types of conflict are tolerable and how much is pathogenic (Cummings & Davies, 1994; Cummings & O'Reilly, 1997)? Most experts agree that conflict localized around the time of litigation and divorce is of less concern than conflict that was and remains an intrinsic and unresolved part of the parents' relationship and continues after their divorce (Cummings & Davies, 1994). Reports of and perspectives on paternal responsibility, conflict, and violence differ; which reports should be used by researchers attempting to measure conflict and how should researchers judge severity and chronicity and even the extent of contact or the reliability of child support payments (Braver, Wolchik, Sandler, Fogas, & Zvetina, 1991; Sternberg & Lamb, 1999; Sternberg et al., 1998)? Stress is usually measured by assessing exposure to stress-inducing events, but these measures typically ignore potentially important differences in individual resources and coping styles. Can stress be measured in ways that capture its phenomenological significance?

Setting aside measurement problems such as these, consider the interrelations among important constructs. Child adjustment is correlated with the quality of the relationships that children have with both their custodial and noncustodial parents (e.g., Amato & Gilbreth, in press; Simon, 1996; Thompson & Laible, 1999). Child adjustment is also correlated quite consistently with the amount of child support received (Amato & Gilbreth, in press; Furstenberg & Cherlin, 1991; McLanahan & Sandefur, 1994; Seltzer, 1994) and in at least some circumstances, it is associated with the amount of contact children have with their noncustodial parents (Amato & Gilbreth, in press). The amount of child support is greater when there is joint custody, fathers are more involved in decision making, and when fathers see their children more often (e.g., Braver, Wolchik, Sandler, Sheets, Fogas, & Bay, 1993; Seltzer, 1991, 1996; Zill & Nord, 1996), yet although the extent of visitation affects the opportunities for parental conflict, joint custody is not associated with increased levels of conflict (Pearson & Thoennes, 1990). Exposure to violence between the parents can be harmful, but significant numbers of children have warm and supportive relationships with parents who have violent relationships with one another, so we must be careful when reports of parental conflict are allowed to influence decisions about parent-child contact (Holden, Geffner, & Jouriles, 1998; Sternberg & Lamb, 1999). In sum, whether the associations are large or small in magnitude, the existing data suggest that the factors influencing child well-being work together in ways that make it impossible to design simple and universal decision rules that ignore individual circumstances. Although it is possible that increased child support may potentiate visitation and thereby enhance child adjustment (Zill & Nord, 1996), for example, it is also plausible that adequate contact and the resultant perceptions of paternal relevance and inclusion promote economic child support which in turn enhances child well-being, and even well adjusted happy children make noncustodial parents want to be with and support them financially. Clearly, we have a constellation of correlated factors and in the absence of intensive and reliable longitudinal data, it is difficult either to discern casual relationships definitively and unambiguously or to establish the relative importance of different factors.

In addition, the statistical associations are surely not linear, and the factors may operate together in complex ways. Voluntary child support may have more reliable associations with visitation frequency and child well-being than court-ordered support (Argys, Peters, Brooks-Gunn, & Smith, 1997; Zill & Nord, 1996), for example, and when there is substantial conflict between the parents, contact with noncustodial parents may not have the same positive effect on children that it is does when levels of conflict are lower (Johnston, Kline, & Tschann, 1989). Unfortunately, our adversarial legal system has a way of promoting conflict around the time of divorce and as a result most divorcing families experience at least some conflict. According to Maccoby and Mnookin (1992), somewhere around a quarter of divorcing families experience high levels of conflict around the time of divorce, and perhaps 10% of them may have conflict that is sufficiently severe and sufficiently intractable that it is probably not beneficial for the children concerned to have contact with their noncustodial parents (Johnston, 1994, 1995). These statistics obviously represent selective samples and we do not have access to more representative data concerning the incidence of high conflict in the broader population of divorcing couples, although Johnston has made especially careful efforts to differentiate among types of conflictful families, noting that conflict is intrinsically harmful to children in a minority of conflictful families. Unfortunately, mere allegations of conflict or even marital violence can be powerful tools in our adversarial system, frequently resulting in reduced levels of court-approved contacts between fathers and children (Sternberg, 1997). Until the relevant data are gathered, it appears that somewhere around 10% of the divorcing families in America experience parental conflict so severe that contact between children and their noncustodial parents is not desirable.

The quality of the relationships between noncustodial parents and their children is also crucial. There are some families in which noncustodial fathers and children have sufficiently poor relationships that "maintenance" of interaction or involvement may not be of any benefit to the children, but we do not know how many relationships are like this. Unrepresentative data sets, such as those collected by Greif (1997) in the course of research designed to study fathers and mothers who lose (and frequently avoid) contact with their children after divorce, suggest that perhaps 10% to 15% of parents do not have either the commitment or individual capacities to establish and maintain supportive and enriching relationships with their children following divorce. Taken together, Johnston's and Greif's estimates suggest that 15% to 25% of the children who experience their parents' divorce would not benefit—and might perhaps be harmed—by contact with their noncustodial parents. Stated differently, of course, this suggests that at least three quarters of the children experiencing their parents' divorce *could* benefit from (and at least not be hurt by) having and maintaining relationships with their noncustodial parents, although the benefits could be obscured if researchers did not distinguish between these types of families when studying the effects of postdivorce contact.

Unfortunately, most contemporary custody and visitation decrees do not foster the maintenance of relationships between children and their noncustodial parents. Table 5.1 presents illustrative data from Maccoby and Mnookin's (1992; Maccoby, 1995) Stanford Child Custody Project which focused on divorce and custody awards handed down in two California counties, San Mateo and Santa Clara. The table describes the amount of time children were allowed to spend with their fathers (typically, the noncustodial parents) per two-week period. A quarter of the children were permitted essentially no contact with their noncustodial fathers; we can only hope that the majority of these children were in fact those who were unlikely to benefit from continual contact, not simply those whose interests were poorly protected by the judicial system. More disconcertingly, the table also shows that a substantial number of children were allowed by the courts to have very limited contact with their noncustodial parents; only a third of the total were allowed to spend three or more nights per two-week period with their fathers, and some of these were allowed to spend two or fewer nights with their noncustodial mothers, further increasing the number of children apparently deemed unlikely to benefit from relationships with their noncustodial parents. Should we be alarmed that 25% to 35% of the children in this large sample were allowed to spend little time with their noncustodial parents (and that 40% to 50% were allowed to have no overnights with these parents) when the best estimates based on Johnston's and Greif's data suggest that pervasive conflict or parental inadequacy should have justified minimal contact in less than half this number of cases?

The available data further suggest that the situation that exists around the time of separation or divorce is about "as good as it gets." Typically, even when the amount of contact between children and noncustodial parents is as small initially as Table 5.1 indicates, it actually declines over time, with increasing numbers of children having less and less contact with their noncustodial parents as time goes by (Furstenberg & Cherlin, 1991; Furstenberg, Nord, Peterson, & Zill, 1983). To the extent that contact is beneficial, of course, such data suggest that many children are placed at risk by the gradual (and sometimes less gradual) withdrawal of their noncustodial fathers.

TABLE 5.1 Court-Ordered Time With Father (Stanford Child Custody Project)[1]

Category	Percentage of children
No contact	24
No overnights	15
1 overnight	9
2 overnights	19
3-7 overnights	21
8-11 overnights	3
12-14 overnights[2]	10

NOTES: 1. These data were provided by Peters (1997; Table 2).
2. According to Maccoby and Mnookin (1992, Table 4.1), 2.8% have no regular contact with their mothers and an additional 2.6% have no overnights with their mothers.

What might account for the behavior of these men? Many fathers, most fathers' rights activists, and some scholars point to the fact that even when children do see their fathers regularly, these men are unable to play parental roles. Although it has not yet been demonstrated empirically, critics argue that many fathers drift away from their children after divorce because they are deprived of the opportunity to be parents rather than visitors. Most noncustodial parents are awarded *visitation* and they function as visitors, taking their children to the zoo, to movies, to dinner, and to other special activities in much the same way that grandparents or uncles and aunts behave. Children may well enjoy these excursions, and may not regret the respite from arguments about completing homework, cleaning up their rooms, behaving politely, having their hair cut (or *not* having their hair cut!), going to bed on time, getting ready for school, and respecting their siblings' property and their parents' limited resources, but the exclusion of fathers from these everyday tribulations is crucial, ultimately transforming the fathers' roles and making these men increasingly irrelevant to their children's lives, socialization, and development. Many men describe this as a sufficiently painful experience that they feel excluded from and pushed out of their children's lives (Clark & McKenry, 1997).

Among the experts who drafted a recent consensus statement on the effects of divorce and custody arrangements on children's welfare and adjustment, there was agreement that parents not only need to spend adequate amounts of time with their children, but also need to be involved in a diverse array of activities with their children:

To maintain high-quality relationships with their children, parents need to have sufficiently extensive and regular interactions with them, but the amount of time involved is usually less important than the quality of the interaction that it fosters. Time distribution arrangements that ensure the involvement of both parents in important aspects of their children's everyday lives and routines . . . are likely to keep nonresidential parents playing psychologically important and central roles in the lives of their children. (Lamb, Sternberg, & Thompson, 1997, p. 400)

If noncustodial parents are to maintain and strengthen relationships with their children, in other words, they need to participate in a range of everyday activities that allow them to function as parents rather than simply as regular, genial visitors. Unfortunately, those constructing custody and visitation awards do not always appear to understand what sort of interaction is needed to consolidate and maintain parent-child relationships, and as a result, their decisions seldom ensure either sufficient amounts of time or adequate distributions of that time (overnight and across both school and nonschool days) to promote healthy parent-child relationships. The statistics popularized by Furstenberg and Cherlin (1991) may show fathers drifting away largely because they no longer have the opportunities to function as fathers in relation to their children.

This pattern of visitation actually overstates the involvement of nonresidential fathers in raising their children. Even . . . where children are seeing their fathers regularly, the dads assume a minimal role in the day-to-day care and supervision of their children . . . most outside fathers behaved more like close relatives than parents . . . [R]outine parent-child activities were [un]common. (Furstenberg & Cherlin, 1991, p. 36)

Summary

The issues discussed in this section help explain the unexpectedly small and somewhat unreliable associations between various measures of child development and the amount of contact between children and their noncustodial fathers. Evidently, contact between a minority of children and their noncustodial parents may be harmful, so the quality of the relationships need to be taken into account when making decisions about the amount of interaction to encourage. Furthermore, it appears that most children do not simply need more contact, but rather contact of an extent and type sufficient to potentiate rich and multifaceted parent-child relationships. When nonresidential fathers are fully and richly integrated into their children's lives, they appear more likely to contribute economically to their children's support, and this too is associated with benefits for children.

The concrete implications for custody evaluators and decision makers are clear. First, they should determine whether the relationships between noncustodial parents and their children are worthy of support and protection; sadly, some adults are incapable even of mediocre or adequate parenting. Second, they should determine whether the conflict between the parents is sufficiently intense, overt, and likely to continue indefinitely. In some such cases, even minimal visitation may be undesirable. Third, when contact is not contraindicated, evaluators should ensure that noncustodial parents are able to participate in a broad range of everyday activities with their children, particularly those demanding chores and contexts that "visiting" parents often avoid. Fourth, custody evaluators should aim for voluntary agreements and ensure that the actual custody orders both specify transitions and blocks of time in detail, and anticipate changes in the joint parenting plan as children's developmental needs change (Zill & Nord, 1996). Fifth, when voluntary arrangements cannot be reached, evaluators must avoid misinterpreting failures to compromise as symptoms of severe underlying conflict too intense to permit coparenting. As long as evaluators continue to make this mistake, they will continue to encourage mothers who feel they have the upper hand to avoid meaningful compromises, relying instead on allegations of conflict to help them "win" custody. Overall, custody awards should promote children's best interests; they should not reward or punish parents for real or alleged histories of involvement.

THE MARITAL COMPACT

As Mnookin and Kornhauser (1979) noted several years ago, most decisions about the custody of divorcing parents are made, not by judges, but by parents "bargaining in the shadow of the law." These parents, like their attorneys, counselors, relatives, and the judges who may be forced to decide a small minority of the cases, search for compromises about the children's future care while reviewing their former arrangements and broader societal expectations about the divergent roles and responsibilities of mothers and fathers. In many cases, such examinations may be helpful, elucidating the genuine commitments and propensities of the divorcing parents. For many others, however, the exercise can be misleading, inasmuch as it (a) shifts focus from the children's best interests to "justice" for the parents, (b) incorrectly implies that predivorce patterns of behavior are good predictors of postdivorce patterns or possibilities, or (c) ignores that the predivorce division of responsibilities between the parents represented different types rather than different degrees of commitment to the children's welfare. Nevertheless, parents, judges, and counselors continue to focus extensively on the histories of those contesting the custody of their children.

In this society, many parents enter and conduct their marital relationships with some implicit understanding about the ways in which the two adults will contribute to their marriages. Over the last 30 years, however, we have moved from a society in which fathers were the primary breadwinners and mothers the primary parents to a society in which mothers are both breadwinners and parents. Fathers have not assumed responsibility for parenting and childcare commensurate with the changes in maternal responsibility for breadwinning. As long as these differences in the relative predivorce responsibility of mothers and fathers persist, we are likely to continue seeing postdivorce time-distribution arrangements that do not support or facilitate meaningful father-child relationships because they pay too much attention to the histories of parental participation in day-to-day child care and too little attention to the future needs and best interests of children.

In much of the preceding discussion, I have argued that broad, positive, and multifaceted relationships between noncustodial fathers and their children are both attainable and desirable except in the minority of cases in which conflict between the parents is too high or the parents' capacities and motivation are too limited. It is important to recognize, however, that minimal father-child contact following divorce can often represent merely the continuation of parental roles that were adopted by the parents when explicit or implicit decisions about their duties and responsibilities were made years earlier. In most cases, predivorce divisions of labor and responsibility included breadwinning responsibilities for fathers and little expectation that they would spend much time interacting with or caring for their children. As a result, many fathers in two-parent families have tenuous and somewhat superficial relationships with their children, although many others play important roles in their children's everyday lives, even when they are clearly less involved than their partners.

The data compiled and summarized by Pleck (1997) document both the extent of paternal participation in average two-parent families, as well as the secular changes that have taken place over the last two decades. Continuing controversies about the types of activities that involve parent-child *interaction* as opposed to *accessibility* (watching TV together? attending a movie or baseball game? working in the yard together?) make it difficult to quantify the average levels of paternal involvement, but when we represent the amounts of time spent by fathers as a proportion of the average amounts of maternal involvement, the resulting statistics reveal increases over time in the average levels of both interaction/engagement and accessibility. Specifically, the average American father in a two-parent family now spends about 40% as much time as the average mother engaged in interaction with his children and about two-thirds as much time as the average mother accessible to those children (Pleck, 1997).

Statistics on parental *responsibility*—executive decision making regarding children, their welfare, and their care—paint a somewhat different picture, with fathers on average much less likely than mothers to assume such responsibility. Indeed, Pleck indicates that more than three quarters of the fathers in two-parent families *never* spent time as the primary parent present, the one with ultimate responsibility. Secular changes in paternal responsibility have taken place, however, and a small but significant number of fathers (at least 10%) regularly assume primary responsibility for the care of their young children, often while mothers are at work (Hofferth, Brayfield, Deich, & Holcomb, 1991; Presser, 1988, 1992). Such arrangements are nonnormative, however, and should not prevent recognition of the large number of fathers in two- parent families who assume very limited parental responsibilities.

Just as it is relatively easy to conclude that abusive and incompetent fathers would likely harm rather than benefit their children and therefore should not be granted unsupervised access, so is it easy to conclude that fathers who have assumed regular responsibility and have positive relationships with their children should be allowed to maintain and develop these relationships after divorce. The tougher decisions concern those fathers who have spent little time with their children although they have been committed breadwinners, working additional hours so that their partners can afford to work less. The limited evidence available to us suggests that those who have developed positive relationships and want to remain involved in their children's lives should be encouraged to do so, even when the postdivorce plans demand different types of parental commitment (including more extensive hands-on parenting) than the predivorce history discloses (Amato & Gilbreth, in press). Indeed, positive paternal involvement appears beneficial whether or not parents divorce, and social reformers should thus focus their attention on the division of responsibilities in two-parent families as well (Amato & Gilbreth, in press; Lamb, 1997; Pleck, 1997).

CONCLUSION

Overall, there is substantial reason to believe that most (though not all) children would benefit following divorce from the opportunity to build and maintain relationships with both their noncustodial and custodial parents. Unfortunately, most custody decrees today permit limited and restricted opportunities for children to spend time with their noncustodial parents; these parents are thus peripheralized and their relationships weakened. As a result, time-distribution plans wittingly or unwittingly lead many noncustodial fathers to drift away from and out of the lives of their children. These trends might well be ameliorated by changing the typical postdivorce time distribution plans, ensuring that they facilitate involvement by both parents. The proportion of families and children likely to benefit from more thoughtful time distribution plans will also increase as secular changes in maternal and paternal roles continue. As long as the division of parental responsibilities within two-parent families is grossly unequal, we are unlikely to witness major changes over time in the role of noncustodial parents after divorce. Further changes in the roles and responsibilities of fathers and mothers in two-parent families appear to be a prerequisite for widespread changes in the nature of postdivorce relationships. As practices within two-parent families continue to change, we should expect to see postdivorce parenting plans changing. Critics who aim to reform judicial decision-making processes should thus focus their attention as well on potential changes in predivorce marital distributions of responsibility and their likely implications for postdivorce or postseparation custody arrangements.

REFERENCES

Amato, P. R. (1993). Children's adjustment to divorce: Theories, hypotheses, and empirical support. *Journal of Marriage and the Family, 55,* 23-38.

Amato, P. R., & Gilbreth, J. G. (in press). Nonresident fathers and children's well-being: A meta-analysis. *Journal of Marriage and the Family.*

Amato, P. R., & Keith, B. (1991). Parental divorce and the well-being of children: A meta-analysis. *Psychological Bulletin, 110,* 26-46.

Amato, P. R., Loomis, L. S., & Booth, A. (1995). Parental divorce, marital conflict, and offspring well-being during early adulthood. *Social Forces, 73,* 896-916.

Argys, L. M., Peters, H. E., Brooks-Gunn, J., & Smith, J. R. (1997). *Contributions of absent fathers to child well-being: The impact of child support dollars and father-*

child contact. Unpublished manuscript, Department of Economics, University of Colorado, Denver.

Biller, H. B. (1981). Father absence, divorce, and personality development. In M. E. Lamb (Ed.), *The role of the father in child development* (Rev. ed., pp. 489-551). New York: Wiley.

Biller, H. B. (1993). *Fathers and families: Paternal factors in child development.* Westport, CT: Auburn House.

Blankenhorn, D. (1995). *Fatherless America.* New York: Basic Books.

Braver, S. H., Wolchik, S. A., Sandler, I. N., Fogas, B. S., & Zvetina, D. (1991). Frequency of visitation by divorced fathers: Differences in reports by fathers and mothers. *American Journal of Orthopsychiatry, 61,* 448-454.

Braver, S. H., Wolchik, J. A., Sandler, I. N., Sheets, V. L., Fogas, B. S., & Bay, R. C. (1993). A longitudinal study of noncustodial parents: Parents without children. *Journal of Family Psychology, 7,* 9-23.

Burgess, A. (1997). *Fatherhood reclaimed: The making of the modern father.* London: Vermilion Press.

Clark, K., & McKenry, P. C. (1997). *Unheard voices: Divorced fathers without custody.* Unpublished manuscript, Department of Family Relations and Human Development, Ohio State University, Columbus, OH.

Cooksey, E. C. (1997). Consequences of young mothers' marital histories for children's cognitive development. *Journal of Marriage and the Family, 59,* 245-261.

Cummings, E. M., & Davies, P. (1994). *Children and marital conflict: The impact of family dispute and resolution.* New York: Guilford.

Cummings, E. M., & O'Reilly, A. W. (1997). Fathers in family context: Effects of marital quality on child adjustment. In M. E. Lamb (Ed.), *The role of the father in child development* (3rd ed., pp. 49-65, 318-325). New York: Wiley.

Downey, D. B. (1994). The school performance of children from single-mother and single-father families: Economic or interpersonal deprivation. *Journal of Family Issues, 15,* 129-147.

Duncan, G. J. & Brooks-Gunn, J. (Eds.). (1997). *Consequences of growing up poor.* New York: Russell Sage Foundation.

Dremen, S., & Ronen-Eliav, H. (1997). The relation of divorced mothers' perceptions of family cohesion and adaptability to behavior problems in children. *Journal of Marriage and the Family, 59,* 324-331.

Emery, R. E. (1994). *Renegotiating family relationships: Divorce, child custody, and mediation.* New York: Guilford.

Fathers' involvement in their children's schools (1997, Winter). *Father Times, 6*(2), 1, 4-6.

Furstenberg, F. F., Jr., & Cherlin, A. J. (1991). *Divided families: What happens to children when parents part.* Cambridge, MA: Harvard University Press.

Furstenberg, F. F., Jr., Morgan, S. P., & Allison, P. D. (1987). Paternal participation and children well-being after marital dissolution. *American Sociological Review, 52,* 695-701.

Furstenberg, F. F., Jr., Nord, C. W., Peterson, J. L., & Zill, N. (1983). The life course of children of divorce. *American Psychological Review, 48,* 656-668.

Goodman, G. S., Emery, R. E., & Haugaard, J. J. (1998). Developmental psychology and law: The cases of divorce, child maltreatment, foster care, and adoption. In W. Damon, I. Sigel, & A. Renninger (Eds.), *Handbook of child psychology* (5th ed., Vol. 4). *Child psychology in practice* (pp. 775-874). New York: Wiley.

Greif, G. L. (1997). *Out of touch: When parents and children lose contact after divorce.* New York: Oxford University Press.

Hanson, T. L., McLanahan, S. S., & Thomson, E. (1996). Double jeopardy: Parental conflict and step-family outcomes for children. *Journal of Marriage and the Family, 58,* 141-154.

Hetherington, E. M., & Henderson, S. H. (1997). Fathers in stepfamilies. In M. E. Lamb (Ed.), *The role of the father in child development* (3rd ed., pp. 212-226, 369-373). New York: Wiley.

Hetherington, E. M., & Stanley-Hagan, M. M. (1997). The effects of divorce on fathers and their children. In M. E. Lamb (Ed.), *The role of the father in child development* (3rd. ed., pp. 191-211). New York: Wiley.

Hines, A. M. (1997). Divorce-related transitions, adolescent development, and the role of the parent-child relationship: A review of the literature. *Journal of Marriage and the Family, 59,* 375-388.

Hofferth, S. L., Brayfield, A., Deich, S., & Holcomb, P. (1991). *National child survey, 1990.* Washington, DC: Urban Institute.

Holden, G. W., Jouriles, E. W., & Geffner, R. (Eds.) (1998). *Children exposed to family violence.* Washington, DC: American Psychological Association.

Isaacs, M. B., & Leon, G. H. (1988). Remarriage and its alternatives following divorce: Mother and child adjustment. *Journal of Marital and Family Therapy, 14,* 163-173.

Johnston, J. R. (1994). High-conflict divorce. *The Future of Children, 4,* 165-182.

Johnston, J. R., Kline, M., & Tschann, J. (1989). Ongoing postdivorce conflict in families contesting custody: Effects on children of joint custody and frequent access. *American Journal of Orthopsychiatry, 59,* 576-592.

Knitzer, J., & Bernard, S. (1997). *Map and track: State initiatives to encourage responsible fatherhood.* New York: National Center for Children in Poverty, Columbia University School of Public Health.

Lamb, M. E. (1975). Fathers: Forgotten contributors to child development. *Human Development, 18,* 245-266.

Lamb, M. E. (Ed.). (1981). *The role of the father in child development* (Rev. ed.). New York: Wiley.

Lamb, M. E. (Ed.). (1997). *The role of the father in child development* (3rd ed.). New York: Wiley.

Lamb, M. E., Sternberg, K. J., & Thompson, R. A. (1997). The effects of divorce and custody arrangements on children's behavior, development, and adjustment. *Family and Conciliation Courts Review, 35,* 393-404.

Maccoby, E. E. (1995). Divorce and custody: The fights, needs, and obligations of mothers, fathers, and children. In G. B. Melton (Ed.), *The individual, the family, and social good: Personal fulfillment in times of change* (pp. 135-172). Lincoln, NE: University of Nebraska Press.

Maccoby, E. E., & Mnookin, R. H. (1992). *Dividing the child: Social and legal dilemmas of custody.* Cambridge, MA: Harvard University Press.

Mächtlinger, V. J. (1981). The father in psychoanalytic theory. In M. E. Lamb (Ed.), *The role of the father in child development* (Rev. ed., pp. 113-154). New York: Wiley.

McLanahan, S. S., & Sandefur, G. (1994). *Growing up with a single parent: What hurts, what helps.* Cambridge, MA: Harvard University Press.

McLanahan, S. S., & Teitler, J. (1999). The consequences of father absence. In M. E. Lamb (Ed.), *Parenting and child development in "nontraditional" families* (pp. 83-102). Mahwah, NJ: Erlbaum.

Mnookin, R. H., & Kornhauser, L. (1979). Bargaining in the shadow of the law: The case of divorce. *Yale Law Journal, 88,* 950-997.

Pearson, J., & Thoennes, N. (1990). Custody after divorce: Demographic and attitudinal patterns. *American Journal of Orthopsychiatry, 60,* 233-249,

Peters, H. E. (1997). *Child custody and monetary transfers in divorce negotiations: Reduced form and simulation results.* Unpublished manuscript, Department of Economics, Cornell University.

Pleck, J. H. (1997). Paternal involvement: Levels, sources, and consequences. In M. E. Lamb (Ed.), *The role of the father in child development* (3rd ed., pp. 66-103). New York: Wiley.

Popenoe, D. (1996). *Life without father.* New York: Free Press.

Presser, H. B. (1988). Shift work and child care among young dual-earner American parents. *Journal of Marriage and the Family, 50,* 133-148.

Presser, H. B. (1992). Child care and parental well-being: A needed focus on gender and trade-offs. In A. Booth (Ed.), *Child care in the 1990s: Trends and consequences* (pp. 180-189). Hillsdale, NJ: Erlbaum.

Seltzer, J. (1991). Relationships between fathers and children who live apart: The father's role after separation. *Journal of Marriage and the Family, 53,* 79-101.

Seltzer, J. A. (1994). Consequences of marital dissolution for children. *American Review of Sociology, 20,* 235-266.

Seltzer, J. A. (October 1996). *Father by law: Effects of joint legal custody on nonresident fathers' involvement with children.* Paper presented to the NICHD conference on Father Involvement, Bethesda, MD.

Simons, R. L. (1996). *Understanding differences between divorced and intact families.* Thousand Oaks, CA: Sage.

Smith, H. L., Morgan, S. P., & Koropeckyj-Cox, T. (1996). A decomposition of trends in the nonmarital fertility ratios of Blacks and Whites in the United States. *Demography, 33,* 141-151.

Sternberg, K. J., & Lamb, M. E. (1999). Violent families. In M. E. Lamb (Ed.), *Parenting and child development in "nontraditional" families* (pp. 305-325). Mahwah, NJ: Erlbaum.

Sternberg, K. J., Lamb, M. E., & Dawud-Noursi, S. (1998). Understanding domestic violence and its effects: Making sense of divergent reports and perspectives. In G.

W. Holden, R. Geffner, & E. W. Jouriles (Eds.), *Children exposed to family violence* (pp. 121-156). Washington, DC: American Psychological Association.

Thompson, E., Hanson, T. L., & McLanahan, S. (1994). Family structure and child well-being: Economic resources versus parental behaviors. *Social Forces, 73,* 221-242.

Thompson, R. A. (1994). The role of the father after divorce. *The Future of Children, 4,* 210-235.

Thompson, R. A., & Laible, D. J. (in press). Noncustodial parents. In M. E. Lamb (Ed.), *Parenting and child development in "nontraditional" families* (pp. 103-123). Mahwah, NJ: Erlbaum.

Whitehead, B. D. (1993). Dan Quayle was right. *Atlantic Monthly, 271,* 47-50.

Zill, N. (1996). Unmarried parenthood as a risk factor for children. *Testimony before Committee on Ways and Means, House of Representatives, March 12, 1996* (Serial 104-52, pp. 50-65). Washington DC: Government Printing Office.

Zill, N., & Nord, C. W. (November 1996). *Causes and consequences of involvement by noncustodial parents in their children's lives: Evidence from a national longitudinal study.* Paper presented to the National Center on Fathers and Families Roundtable, New York City.

Chapter 6

Compliance With Child Support Orders in Paternity and Divorce Cases

Daniel R. Meyer

A frequently cited problem with the child support system has been (and continues to be) the low rate of compliance with child support obligations. National data confirm that compliance is a problem: of mothers with child support orders, only half receive the full amount owed, and a quarter receive nothing at all (U.S. Bureau of the Census, 1995). A prevailing view has been that the cause of low compliance is nonresident parents choosing to pay less than they could afford to pay (the "deadbeat dads" of the press).

Since the mid-1970s, the child support system has come under increased scrutiny. The scrutiny arose in part because the increase in nonmarital births and divorces meant that child support now affects more children, in part because of concerns that public welfare was having to support children who could have

AUTHOR'S NOTE: I thank my colleague and collaborator Judi Bartfeld, who contributed greatly to this paper and this line of research. This research was supported in part by a contractual agreement between the Wisconsin Bureau of Child Support in the Department of Workforce Development and the Institute for Research on Poverty. This contractual arrangement also supported the collection of the data used in this paper. Any views expressed in this paper are those of the author and not necessarily those of the Department or the Institute.

been supported by their fathers, and in part because of ongoing concerns about the economic vulnerability of mother-only families. Over this period, lawmakers have undertaken a number of initiatives aimed at improving the functioning of the child support system, including efforts to enhance compliance with support obligations. In seeking to increase compliance with support orders, legislation has generally focused on enforcement strategies (such as withholding support obligations from the incomes of nonresident parents, placing liens on property, garnishing tax refunds, and revoking licenses in response to nonpayment, etc.) rather than on enhancing the earnings capacity of nonresident parents. But if the compliance problem is more related to unrealistic expectations of the amount of child support that nonresident parents can pay than to their unwillingness to pay, then these policy efforts to increase compliance are likely to provide little increase in collections at a relatively high cost.

Previous work using a unique data set in Wisconsin has focused on the impact of four kinds of variables on a nonresident father's compliance with child support orders.[1] The variables include (1) those reflecting his ability to pay support, (2) the stringency of the enforcement system, (3) the strength of the family ties between the father and his ex-spouse and children, and (4) the economic needs of the mother and children. These examinations have been conducted separately for marital (divorce) and nonmarital (paternity) cases. This chapter summarizes the findings from this line of research and extends it by reviewing the more recent compliance literature, incorporating more recent Wisconsin data and by making explicit comparisons between divorce and paternity cases.

FRAMEWORK: FACTORS
ASSOCIATED WITH COMPLIANCE

In this chapter I focus on factors associated with whether nonresident fathers are complying with their child support orders (that is, the amount paid divided by the amount due). I do not focus here on the dollar amount paid, for several reasons. First, the amount paid can be usefully divided into two processes, the amount that *should* be paid (the order amount), and the amount that *is* paid, given the order. The two processes occur at different times, and policies governing the two steps differ, suggesting that separate analyses are appropriate. Second, empirical research examining the amount paid typically finds that the key determinant is the amount owed (Beller & Graham, 1993), suggesting that questions about the factors associated with compliance are more interesting than questions about the amount paid. Finally, if researchers and policymakers are interested in how the enforcement system is working, they need to focus on the enforcement step, not the order-setting step. As we will see below, the two steps are interrelated; in particular, if the order is set too high, compliance may be lower.

The first step, the setting of an appropriate child support order, has been controversial. When the child support system was first examined, one of the problems that was found was that child support orders were often inconsistent: similar cases were treated differently (Meyer, Bartfeld, Garfinkel, & Brown, 1996). In part this occurred because orders were set on a case-by-case basis in a judicial system. The policy solution was to require each state to establish a presumptive numerical guideline, that is, a formula that is to be used to determine the amount of the child support order unless the formula-required amount is specifically found to be inappropriate. The formulae selected by the states were nearly all based on the concept of "income sharing," that is, the amount of the order was based on the amount parents share with their children when they live together. In all states the order was to increase as the nonresident parent's income increased and increase as the number of children increased (Williams, 1994). Once a child support order amount is set, it seldom changes, in part because a change typically required legal action.[2] Thus it is quite possible that an order that was initially set according to the guidelines could become too high or too low as circumstances change; moreover, the guidelines may or may not have been used to set the initial order.

When child support orders are set, a decision is also often made about the extent to which the nonresident parent can visit the child. But a firm policy wall has been erected between the two parts of the child support system: if the resident parent obstructs visitation, the nonresident parent is not allowed to hold back child support payments; similarly, if the nonresident parent does not pay, this is presumably not an acceptable reason for the resident parent to hold back access to the children. But in reality a great deal of policy attention is paid to noncompliance with child support payment agreements, and noncompliance can have potentially serious consequences, while noncompliance with visitation agreements seldom has consequences.

When a formal child support order is established, payments now typically go through a central governmental agency, rather than directly to resident parent. In all cases decided after January 1, 1994, the amount of the child support order is supposed to be automatically withheld from the income of the nonresident parent. But whether withholding actually occurs in every case is unknown, and moreover, when the nonresident parent changes jobs, a new withholding order would be needed, and this is not always forthcoming. The public collection of child support enables a monitoring of payments and allows the child support agency to take specific actions if a parent becomes delinquent in making the required payments; for example, a lien could be placed on the nonresident parent's property, or any income tax refund due the nonresident parent could be taken, etc.

Given this policy framework, what factors might be associated with whether a nonresident parent complies with a child support order? One theoretical article on factors associated with child support payments suggests that nonresident fathers have different levels of commitment to financially supporting their children (Weiss & Willis, 1985), and this leads to different levels of support. Moreover, nonresident fathers have little control over how child support is spent, and thus even fathers who want to support their children may pay less if they believe that child support would be spent on the resident parent, not the children. This theoretical approach has guided some of the empirical research on this question. In this section, I review the empirical research, then comment on its limitations, then outline which of these limitations will be addressed in this research. For the empirical research review, I use a conceptual framework that classifies the factors associated with compliance into four broad categories: (1) the ability of the nonresident father to pay support, (2) the stringency of the enforcement system, (3) the strength of family ties between the father and the mother and children, and (4) the economic need of the mother and children. I primarily review literature in which compliance with child support orders is defined as the amount of child support paid divided by the amount due; I also examine literature focusing on the dollar amount of child support that is paid.

Ability to Pay

If child support orders perfectly reflect the nonresident father's ability to pay, then ability to pay may not necessarily affect whether orders are paid. But this is not the finding of the empirical research: a father's ability to pay has been found to be quite important to both orders and compliance. Typically, researchers have operationalized "ability to pay" as the income of the father, and have found that higher income is associated with higher compliance (Garfinkel & Klawitter, 1990; O'Neill, 1985; Sonenstein & Calhoun, 1990). For example, Garfinkel and Klawitter (1990), using data from court records in Wisconsin, found that higher incomes at the time of the order were associated with higher compliance over a subsequent several-year period, and O'Neill (1985), using the Current Population Survey, found that mothers' reports of fathers' incomes were a predictor of higher compliance.

Researchers have also used other variables that are related to the ability to pay, including the father's employment status, educational attainment, marital status, and the percent of income owed in support. Several studies indicate that compliance is higher among employed fathers (Nichols-Casebolt & Danziger, 1989; Peters, Argys, Maccoby, & Mnookin, 1993). Because multivariate analyses are typically used in this research, these findings suggest that employment leads to higher compliance even among fathers with similar levels of income. This may be because employment reflects an ability to pay beyond what is reflected in the income level, because income has typically been measured poorly in prior research, or because the child support system works better at collecting support when the source of the nonresident parent's income is employment than when it is self-employment or asset income (in which case the source of income is more related to an analysis of the enforcement system than to ability to pay). Compliance is also higher among those with higher educations (Peters et al., 1993). This may be because education is a better measure of social class than income is, and social class may affect the ability to pay, or the desire to pay.

Enforcement System

A substantial body of research suggests that the use of specific enforcement techniques, primarily the routine (immediate) withholding of child support from income (rather than waiting for the parent to miss a payment before withholding occurs), is associated with increased compliance. Garfinkel and Klawitter (1990) estimated that routine income withholding increases the compliance rate by 11% to 30% in Wisconsin. Meyer and Bartfeld (1992a) found that the effect of routine withholding decreases over time, and speculate that this may be due to an inability of withholding orders to track employment changes. In a recent national study, Garfinkel and Robins (1994) identified several state-level policy variables, including routine withholding, advertisement of child support services, collection of support through a public agency, and higher public expenditures on child support enforcement, that have a positive impact on compliance. Using a similar approach, Beller and Graham (1993) found that routine withholding, criminal penalties, tax intercepts, and the ability to place liens against property all increased the amount paid.

Standard experimental designs have generally not been used in this empirical research. Instead, sometimes quasiexperimental techniques have been used (e.g., Garfinkel and Klawitter, 1990), and sometimes researchers have focused more on describing whether enforcement techniques are associated with compliance rather than attempting to ascertain causality.

Strength of Family Ties

This category includes a cluster of factors related to the relationships among the nonresident parent, the resident parent, and the children. Measuring the impact of family ties on compliance is more difficult than measuring the impact of factors such as ability to pay and enforcement, in that the concept is more abstract. Moreover, researchers have found it difficult to determine whether family ties cause compliance, paying child support causes more contact or family ties, or both are caused by other unmeasured factors. Recent analyses of these issues have found somewhat conflicting results, with Veum (1993) finding no effect of changes in the amount of visitation on changes in the amount of child support paid, and others finding that the amount of contact nonresident fathers have with their children is associated with the amount of child support paid (Teachman, 1991) as well as compliance with a child support order (Peters et al., 1993), and Seltzer and her colleagues (Seltzer, Schaeffer, & Charng, 1989; Seltzer, 1991b) finding a significant correlation between child support payments and visitation by nonresident fathers, even after controlling for demographic variables. Other factors reflecting family ties that have been found to influence child support payments or compliance with child support orders include proximity (Peters, et al., 1993; Teachman, 1991), time since divorce (Garfinkel & Robins, 1994, see also Peters et al., 1993), having a contested divorce (Peters et al., 1993), and having a good postdivorce relationship (Wright & Price, 1986).

Other potential variables related to family ties have not consistently been linked to greater compliance. Fathers with joint legal custody do not have higher compliance or higher payments, net of other factors (Peters et al., 1993; Seltzer, 1991a; Sonenstein & Calhoun, 1990). Peters et al. (1993) and Turner and Sorensen (1997) found that remarried fathers have the same compliance rates as fathers remaining divorced, but Sonenstein and Calhoun (1990) found that remarried fathers actually had higher compliance rates.

Little previous work explicitly compares compliance of paternity and divorced fathers. To the extent that paternity (nonmarital) fathers, who typically have not lived with their children, have lower compliance than divorced fathers, this may reflect the importance of family ties.

Economic Needs of Mother and Children

The relationship between economic needs of the mother and children and the rate of compliance has not been consistently supported by empirical research. Higher mother's income has been found to be linked to both lower compliance and probability of payment (Peterson & Nord, 1990; Sonenstein & Calhoun, 1990), although other researchers have found no effect (Seltzer et al., 1989; Teachman, 1991). The effect of the mother remarrying also has inconsistent effects (Beller & Graham, 1993; Peters et al., 1993; Seltzer et al., 1989; Sonenstein & Calhoun, 1990). Some ethnographic research suggests that some nonresident fathers whose children are poor support them informally, rather than through the formal child support system, particularly if they are receiving cash welfare (Edin, 1995; Johnson & Doolittle, 1998). This may occur because most child support collected on behalf of welfare recipients goes to offset welfare costs rather than to the resident parent. Little empirical research has examined this question.[3]

Other Factors

The prior research has typically had limited information on parent's attitudes about child support. Lin (1997) has recently analyzed compliance data in which there was also information on the extent to which the nonresident father thought the child support order was fair. She finds that fathers who think their order is fair tend to have higher compliance rates, but this result only holds for cases in which there is no routine withholding. For cases in which there is routine withholding (and thus the father has little discretion over whether he pays), there is no relationship between perceived fairness and compliance. Her results suggest that as the child support system allows less flexibility, parental attitudes will become less important.

Limitations of Prior Research

In two previous papers, Judi Bartfeld and I have examined compliance with child support orders in Wisconsin, one paper focusing on paternity cases

(Bartfeld & Meyer, 1994), and the other on divorce cases (Meyer & Bartfeld, 1996). We did this because the prior research on compliance contained several gaps. First, research on the impact of the enforcement system had generally paid minimal attention to the relative importance of nonpolicy variables. The exclusive focus on enforcement made it difficult to assess the importance of enforcement relative to other contributing factors that had been documented in the broader compliance literature. Thus an important objective of our work has been to examine the role of enforcement within a framework that also places emphasis on case-level factors including ability to pay, economic need of the resident-parent family, and strength of family ties.

Another limitation in the prior compliance research was that nonresident parent's ability to pay support had often been measured inadequately. Income measures have often been from a time not corresponding to when compliance is measured (Garfinkel & Klawitter, 1990; Nichols-Casebolt & Danziger, 1990; Teachman, 1991), or based on the reports of the resident parent (O'Neill, 1985). In our previous work, and in the analyses reported on here, a more accurate and timely income measure, income as reported on state tax returns, is used.

Third, in examining the importance of ability to pay, researchers had typically not accounted for the "burden" of the support order, that is, the amount of support owed relative to the nonresident parent's income. In this paper and our previous work, we explicitly consider the burden of the support order because it sheds light on the importance of ability to pay in affecting compliance. From a policy standpoint it also provides important information, in that state child support guidelines are based on varying percentages of the nonresident parent's income. Thus far, the policy debate over child support guidelines has generally focused on the impact of guidelines on support orders, with the implicit assumption that increasing orders will lead to increased payments.

In this chapter, I extend our prior work by using more recent cases and by examining both paternity and divorce cases, conducting an explicit comparison of factors affecting compliance among the two case types. Some of the limitations of the prior work are also not addressed in this work. For example, I have no information on attitudes toward the child support order for most of my cases, nor do I have much information on family ties. Second, I have no information on race or education (although because I control for income, any indirect effects through income will be incorporated). Finally, in the prior work it has been hard to disentangle the extent to which a factor actually *causes* compliance or whether it is merely *associated with* compliance. In this chapter, I do not attempt to disentangle the question of causality, and thus this analysis is better understood as describing factors associated with compliance, rather than factors that cause compliance.

DATA, METHODS, AND VARIABLES

Data

Research on compliance using this framework requires information on child support orders and payments, the nonresident father's income, the resident mother's income, and a variety of characteristics of the parents, children, and the enforcement system. No national dataset has these variables.

The primary data used in this analysis are from the Wisconsin Court Records Database (WCRD), collected and maintained by the Institute for Research on Poverty. This database consists of information from the court records of divorce and paternity cases involving at least one child under age 18 from 21 Wisconsin counties. Twelve cohorts of cases have been collected in each county. Cases were selected according to a sequential sampling scheme, with a specified number of cases collected within each county-cohort. (For detailed discussion of the data and sampling procedures, see Brown & Roan, 1997.) Information in the court records includes information on both parents, the children, and characteristics of child support orders. Because all who owe child support in Wisconsin are supposed to pay through the Clerk of the Court, the court records also include longitudinal data on child support payments. I therefore can construct the total amount of child support paid and the total amount due in any year in which data were collected.

I merge these data with income information from the Wisconsin Department of Revenue (DOR) by matching social security numbers. Personal taxable income information, as well as marital status, is available annually from 1980 through 1994 for parents in the WCRD who filed Wisconsin income tax returns. In any given year, tax data are missing for a subset of the parents; those who have moved out of state, those who are avoiding paying income taxes, and those with incomes too low to file a return. Because Wisconsin offers refundable tax credits, many low-income people who are not obligated to file tax returns do so, which may reduce the extent of missing data among low-income parents. I also merge these data with records of payments in the Aid to Families with Dependent Children (AFDC) program.

In this analysis, I select a subset of the cases that entered the courts between July 1980 and June 1992. The sample includes divorce and paternity cases in which a child support order was in effect for the entire calendar year following the year of the first order. I exclude cases in which the amount of support ordered or paid could not be determined from the data. I include only cases in which the father is the designated payer and the mother has sole physical custody because these are the most common kinds of cases, and because the determinants of compliance may differ in other kinds of cases. (Note that I do not make any exclusions based on *legal* custody, so that the sample includes cases in which both parents share legal custody, as well as those in which the mother has sole legal custody.) The sample for the descriptive data that follows contains 6,027 cases (1,905 paternity and 4,122 divorce) with order dates ranging from 1980 to 1992 and therefore the year in which compliance is measured ranging from 1981 to 1993. For the multivariate model, I select only the 3,609 cases (952 paternity and 2,657 divorce cases) in which the father's income is known. All dollar amounts are adjusted to 1988 dollars, using the Consumer Price Index.

Methods and Variables

Methods

As mentioned, I focus on compliance with child support orders, not the dollar amount of child support paid. I define compliance with child support orders as the ratio of the amount paid to the amount owed in the calendar year following the year in which child support is first ordered. I begin by presenting simple descriptive information on compliance, the percentage of cases with zero, partial, and full payments. I then examine the compliance ratio (the amount paid divided by the amount due, coded as 1 when payments exceed obligations) in a multivariate context. For this analysis I use maximum likelihood estimation to estimate a two-sided tobit model (Maddala, 1983). This model takes into consideration the fact that the dependent variable is limited to a range of 0 to 1 and may have many observations at these limit points. The model is of the form:

(1) $Y^* = \beta_1 X_1 + \beta_2 X_2 + \beta_3 X_3 + \beta_4 X_4 + \beta_5 C + e$

and $Y =$ 0 if $Y^* \leq 0$
            Y if $0 < Y^* < 1$
            1 if $Y^* \geq 1$

where Y = the ratio of child support paid to owed;

     Y^* = an unobserved variable underlying Y;

     X_1 = variables representing the father's ability to pay support;

     X_2 = variables representing the strength of the enforcement system;

     X_3 = variables that reflect the strength of family ties;

     X_4 = variables that reflect the economic need of the mother and children;

     C = a vector of control variables.

In the final analysis, I take a closer look at fathers who are not complying with child support orders, examining their income and the burden of their support order.

Variables Reflecting Ability to Pay

I use three measures of ability to pay—total income, income source, and the percentage of current income owed in child support. I refer to the latter as the "burden" of the order. Both income and burden are entered as a series of dummy variables to allow for nonlinear relationships. Income and burden are measured over the same time period as compliance is measured, the first calendar year following the order. The source of income is measured as of the date of the divorce or paternity action and is taken from the court records. Note that these variables measure actual rather than potential ability to pay; I am unable to estimate the latter because the data do not contain enough information on items related to human capital.

Variables Reflecting Child Support Enforcement Efforts

I primarily use two variables to capture the stringency of the child support enforcement system: the year in which compliance is measured, and the use of routine income withholding. The year ranges from 1981 to 1993, a period in which the emphasis on child support enforcement increased dramatically, both at the state and federal levels. Thus, the year variable at least in part reflects the stringency of the enforcement system. (The year variable could also reflect factors such as changing caseloads and changes in the economy that, if not adequately controlled, would confound the interpretation of the coefficient on the year variables. I attempt to control for some of these factors in the analysis.)

The second enforcement variable is the use of routine income withholding. Routine withholding was first introduced in Wisconsin in 1984 on a pilot basis and has been mandatory statewide since September 1987. A recent analysis of Wisconsin cases indicates that routine withholding was used even before such use was mandated, but it is still not used universally. Use is most common when the parents have been married for a relatively short time and when the father's primary source of income is an employer, although there remains considerable variation across counties after controlling for these and other factors (Meyer & Bartfeld, 1992b).

I define use of routine withholding at the case level, and control for factors that have been shown to be correlated with its use. I also allow the impact of withholding to vary according to the father's primary income source at the time the order was established, estimating separate effects for employed fathers, self-employed fathers, and fathers with no income or income from other miscellaneous sources such as Unemployment Compensation or other transfer programs.

A third variable related to the enforcement system is an indicator variable denoting whether the order was expressed as a percentage of the nonresident father's income or expressed as a dollar amount. Percentage-expressed orders may be more difficult to enforce than fixed-dollar orders, although research suggests that they result in higher collections (Bartfeld & Garfinkel, 1996).

Variables Reflecting the Strength of Family Ties

I include several variables that may reflect the strength of family ties: case type (divorce versus paternity), the length of marriage, the number of children, the age of the oldest child, the remarriage of the father and mother, and legal custody. Due to data limitations, I am not able to include a measure of the extent of postdivorce contact between fathers and children.

Variables Reflecting the Economic Needs of the Mother and Children

I measure the economic status of the mother and children with a series of variables reflecting different categories of the mother's pre-child support income. A variable denoting whether the mother remarried, which may affect the strength of family ties, may also be related to economic needs in that fathers may perceive less financial need when the mother has a new spouse. I also include a variable that indicates whether the mother's family received AFDC benefits during the year in which compliance is measured. As mentioned, because a large portion of child support payments on behalf of AFDC recipients are used to offset AFDC costs rather than to increase the mothers' income, fathers may perceive that their payments are not assisting with their children's needs.

Control Variables

I include indicator variables for counties because child support orders are established, monitored, and enforced at the county level, and compliance rates may therefore vary substantially among counties even after controlling for case-level characteristics. I include several other case-level variables because previous research has indicated that they may affect compliance, and because there may be caseload changes over the period that could confound the interpretation of the year variables. I have not included economic indicators such as county unemployment rate because I assume that any effect of economic performance on compliance would operate through an effect on income. The appendix provides the means of all independent variables.

Generalizability of the Results

Because the data are from Wisconsin, results may not be generalizable to the nation. I expect generalizability to be more of a problem in the last analysis, which looks at the characteristics of noncompliers, than in the primary analysis which focuses on the determinants of compliance. I have no theoretical reason to expect that ability to pay, the need of the mother's family, and family ties would have different effects in Wisconsin than elsewhere. On the other hand, the effects of enforcement may vary considerably among states, as the type of strategies used and the way such strategies are implemented.

RESULTS

Descriptive Information

Figure 6.1 shows the time trend in compliance in the first year of the child support order among paternity cases. Over this entire period, 33% of nonresi-

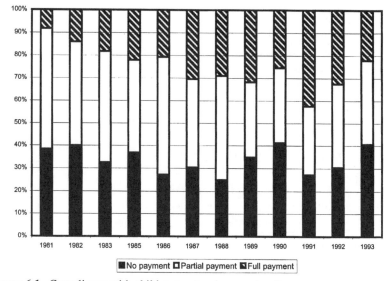

Figure 6.1. Compliance with child support orders—paternity cases

dent fathers paid nothing, 40% made partial payments, and 27% paid the full amount. From 1981 through 1991 there was general improvement in compliance rates, with the share of fathers paying the full amount increasing from less than 10% to more than 40%. However, the last 2 years of data show a downturn, with only 22% of cases being full payers in 1993.

Figure 2 shows the time trend among divorce cases. Overall, compliance is much higher among divorce cases than among paternity cases, with only 16% of divorce cases paying nothing, 37% making partial payments, and 47% making a full payment. These data also show improvements over time, with about 60% of the cases paying in full in 1992, up from less than one-quarter in 1980. However, even among divorce cases, the 1993 rates are worse than the 1992 rates.

Multivariate Analysis of Compliance Rates

Because the variables that may affect compliance are correlated with each other, the true effects cannot be discerned without a multivariate approach. For the multivariate analysis, I use only cases in which the income of the father is known ($n = 3,609$). Because of the importance of income as a determinant of

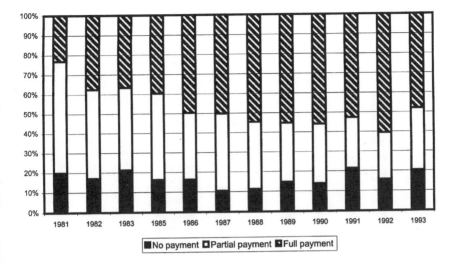

Figure 6.2. Compliance with child support orders—divorce cases

compliance, and the nonrandom nature of missing income information (i.e., fathers who did not file a tax return in Wisconsin in the relevant year), including missing income cases would yield biased coefficients.

Table 6.1 shows the results of the tobit model. The first columns show the results for paternity and divorce cases separately. Variables reflecting the ability to pay show a strong relationship to compliance. Controlling for other factors, both paternity and divorce fathers with incomes below $20,000 have lower compliance, especially fathers with incomes below $10,000. Above $20,000, there is no discernable relationship between compliance and income. The burden of the order also appears important. For paternity cases, orders above 20% of income are associated with lower compliance; for divorce cases it is only orders above 30% of income. Paternity fathers who are employed have higher rates of compliance than those not employed.

The coefficients on the variables reflecting the enforcement system generally show that more stringent enforcement leads to higher compliance. While compliance has not generally been increasing over time among paternity cases (controlling for other factors), compliance among divorce cases is higher in every year after 1981, although the coefficients do not increase in magnitude from year to year. Thus, the model does not suggest that, net of the impact of

(text continues on p. 146)

TABLE 6.1 Multivariate Analysis of Compliance With Child Support Order

	Paternity		Divorce		All	
	Coefficient	Standard Error	Coefficient	Standard Error	Coefficient	Standard Error
Variables Reflecting Ability to Pay						
Father's Income, Compared to Income $30-$50,000						
Income $0-$10,000	-0.48***	0.10	-0.45***	0.05	-0.46***	0.05
Income $10-$20,000	-0.28***	0.10	-0.17***	0.04	-0.18***	0.04
Income $20-$30,000	-0.13	0.11	-0.05	0.04	-0.06	0.04
Income $50,000 +	0.09	0.28	0.01	0.05	0.02	0.05
Case Type-Income Interactions						
Paternity, Income $0-$10,000					-0.03	0.07
Paternity, Income $10-$20,000					-0.07	0.06
Father's Burden, Compared to Burden of 15%-20%						
Burden 0-10%	0.03	0.06	0.02	0.05	0.02	0.05
Burden 10-15%	0.07	0.06	0.02	0.04	0.02	0.04
Burden 20-25%	-0.19**	0.09	-0.02	0.04	-0.02	0.04
Burden 25-30%	-0.28***	0.10	-0.03	0.04	-0.03	0.04
Burden 30-35%	-0.31***	0.12	-0.11*	0.06	-0.11*	0.06
Burden 35-50%	-0.39***	0.11	-0.12**	0.05	-0.10**	0.05
Burden 50-75%	-0.58***	0.11	-0.13*	0.07	-0.12*	0.07
Burden 75% +	-0.67***	0.11	-0.20***	0.07	-0.19***	0.07
Case Type-Father's Burden Interactions						
Paternity, Burden 0-10%					-0.04	0.07
Paternity, Burden 10-15%					0.02	0.07
Paternity, Burden 20-25%					-0.17*	0.10
Paternity, Burden 25-30%					-0.22**	0.11

	Model 1 Coef	Model 1 SE	Model 2 Coef	Model 2 SE	Model 3 Coef	Model 3 SE
Paternity, Burden 30-35%	0.27**	0.13			-0.26**	0.13
Paternity, Burden 35-50%	0.27	0.20			-0.31**	0.12
Paternity, Burden 50-75%	0.24	0.17			-0.48***	0.13
Paternity, Burden 75% +	-1.01***	0.35			-0.51***	0.13
Father's Income Source, Compared to no source						
Source Employment			0.03	0.12	-0.11	0.09
Source Self-Employment			0.15	0.13	0.21**	0.10
Source Unemployment Compensation			-0.05	0.14	0.04	0.10
Source Miscellaneous			-0.10	0.17	-0.22	0.14
Variables Reflecting Enforcement System						
Year Compliance Measured, Compared to 1981						
1982	-0.16	0.15	0.24***	0.06	0.16***	0.06
1983	0.02	0.14	0.21***	0.06	0.18***	0.06
1985	0.02	0.16	0.19***	0.07	0.17***	0.06
1986	0.09	0.15	0.24***	0.07	0.23***	0.06
1987	0.12	0.15	0.21***	0.07	0.21***	0.06
1988	0.22	0.15	0.32***	0.08	0.33***	0.07
1989	0.26	0.16	0.23***	0.09	0.27***	0.07
1990	0.10	0.16	0.30***	0.08	0.29***	0.07
1991	0.29*	0.16	0.30***	0.08	0.34***	0.07
1992	0.11	0.16	0.32***	0.08	0.31***	0.07
1993	0.06	0.17	0.24**	0.09	0.26***	0.08
Use of Routine Withholding, by Income Source, Compared to No Routine Withholding						
Routine Withholding, Employment	0.07	0.06	0.18***	0.03	0.15***	0.03
Routine Withholding, Self-Employment	-0.54**	0.27	0.12	0.12	0.00	0.11
Routine Withholding, Other	0.05	0.07	0.14***	0.06	0.10**	0.04

143

TABLE 6.1 Continued

	Paternity		Divorce		All	
	Coefficient	Standard Error	Coefficient	Standard Error	Coefficient	Standard Error
Order Type, Compared to Fixed-Dollar Order						
Percentage-Expressed Order	-0.07	0.10	-0.11**	0.05	-0.12***	0.04
Variables Reflecting Ties Between Nonresident Father and Resident-Parent Family						
Case Type-Marriage Length-Number of Children, Compared to Divorce, One Child, Marriage Length Less Than One Year						
Paternity					-0.05	0.14
Divorce, Two Children			0.07**	0.03	0.06**	0.02
Divorce, Three + Children			0.06	0.04	0.06	0.04
Divorce, Married 1-3 Years			-0.04	0.13	-0.05	0.13
Divorce, Married 4-6 Years			0.05	0.13	0.01	0.13
Divorce, Married 7-10 Years			0.03	0.13	-0.02	0.13
Divorce, Married 11 + Years			0.02	0.13	-0.04	0.13
Age of Oldest Child, Compared to Oldest Age 11-17						
Oldest Age 0-2	-0.18	0.19	0.13**	0.06	0.08	0.05
Oldest Age 3-5	-0.15	0.20	-0.01	0.05	-0.01	0.05
Oldest Age 6-10	-0.18	0.23	0.04	0.04	0.04	0.04
Remarriage, Compared to Father Remarried						
Father Not Remarried	0.00	0.05	0.00	0.04	-0.01	0.03
Remarriage, Compared to Mother Remarried						
Mother Not Remarried	-0.10	0.10	0.00	0.06	-0.02	0.05

Legal Custody, Compared to Sole Mother Custody

Joint Custody	-0.01	0.17	-0.01	0.03	-0.02	0.03
Variables Reflecting Economic Need of Mother and Children						
Mother's Income, Compared to $20,000 + for Paternity; Compared to $20-$30,000 for Divorce and Both						
Mother's Income 0-$5,000	-0.21	0.15	-0.04	0.06	-0.06	0.05
Mother's Income $5-$10,000	-0.17	0.15	0.07	0.05	0.05	0.05
Mother's Income $10-$15,000	0.09	0.16	0.03	0.05	0.04	0.05
Mother's Income $15-$20,000	0.11	0.17	0.05	0.05	0.06	0.05
Mother's Income, $30,000 +			-0.04	0.08	-0.04	0.07
Mother's AFDC Receipt, Compared to No History of AFDC						
Mother Received AFDC	0.03	0.05	-0.04	0.03	-0.03	0.03
Intercept	1.05***	0.34	0.56***	0.21	0.62***	0.18
Sigma	0.49***	0.02	0.53***	0.01	0.53***	0.01
Log likelihood	-703.9		-2033.4		-2790.6	
N	952		2657		3609	

NOTES: Model also includes dummy variables denoting counties and variables denoting missing father's income source, missing marriage length, missing oldest child's age, missing father's or mother's remarriage, missing legal custody, missing mother's income, and missing AFDC status.

*** Coefficient significantly different from 0, p < .01

** Coefficient significantly different from 0, p < .05

* Coefficient significantly different from 0, p < .10

routine withholding, a general attention to enforcement has led to steadily increasing compliance. The coefficients on the withholding variables also differ somewhat between paternity and divorce cases. Among paternity cases, income withholding does not have a discernable positive effect; among divorce cases, the coefficients indicate that routine withholding in cases in which the father is either employed or has miscellaneous income sources are associated with higher compliance, compared to cases without routine withholding.[4] The coefficients on the variables indicating the county of the court case are significant as a group (results not shown on table), suggesting that enforcement systems (or some other feature of counties) may be important.

There is little evidence in this model for the importance of family ties in influencing compliance. Among divorce cases, fathers of two children have somewhat higher compliance rates than fathers of one child; the coefficient for three children is similar in magnitude to the coefficient for two children but is not statistically significant. Among divorce cases, parents of very young children have higher compliance than those whose children are older. None of the other variables reflecting family ties—marriage length, father's or mother's remarriage, or legal custody—have statistically significant coefficients.

Finally, there is no evidence that fathers have higher compliance rates when the mother has greater economic need. Note that there are potential endogeneity problems with the economic need variables in that these variables may be indirectly caused by child support payments. For example, if low child support compliance increases the probability of AFDC receipt, there would be a negative coefficient on AFDC receipt. Despite this downward bias, there is no evidence of lower compliance among ex-husbands of AFDC recipients. Mothers' income may also be endogenous; there is some evidence that mothers decrease their labor supply in response to child support receipt (Graham & Beller, 1989), so that higher mothers' income could be a result rather than a cause of lower compliance. However, the labor supply responses found by Graham and Beller (1989) were quite small, and the income categories used in the model range from $5000 to $10,000; it seems unlikely that small labor supply adjustments would cause substantial shifts across these categories.

Are the factors that affect compliance among paternity and divorce cases similar? The approach I use to answer this question is to begin with a model with no interaction terms and then add selected interactions, conducting a chi-squared log-likelihood test for whether the addition of the interaction terms significantly improves the fit of the model at the .01 level. The final columns of the table show the results of my final model. Variables reflecting the father's ability to pay are important to compliance, with low income fathers and fathers with higher burdens having lower compliance. While income does not have a different effect for paternity and divorce cases, burden does, with compliance declining more steeply as the burden increases for paternity cases. While the time trends between paternity and divorce cases do appear different, adding interaction terms between case type and year does not significantly improve the fit of the model. The first variable listed under family ties shows that once the other variables are included, paternity cases have no different compliance rates than divorce cases.

Predicted Compliance in Prototypical Cases

Compliance rates for several prototypical cases can be predicted using the combined model. I present cases that differ in income level, percentage of income owed, use of routine withholding, year, and county, and set all variables not specifically mentioned at their mean. This approach is useful in illustrating the relative impact of the various factors.

As the earlier discussion suggests, the predicted compliance rate varies substantially with the father's ability to pay. Income increases compliance among both paternity and divorce cases; when income increases from less than $10,000 to a range of $30,000 to $50,000, predicted compliance rates increase from 56% to 83% among paternity cases and from 61% to 85% among divorce cases. The burden of the child support order has a very strong effect for paternity cases: the predicted compliance rate declines from around 70% if the child support order is less than 20% of income to 48% if the order is 30% to 35% of income. In contrast, the predicted compliance rate does not decline much for divorce cases, declining from 78% to 71% for analogous burden rates. For divorce cases, the model predicts that increasing orders from below 15% of income to 30% to 35% of income could lead to higher payments because the limited decline in compliance rates would be more than offset by the increase in the amount owed. (Of course, many factors enter a decision on the appropriate amount of a child support order, not merely a pragmatic question of how much is likely to be paid.)

Routine withholding does increase the predicted compliance rate when the main source of income is employment or unemployment compensation, but the effect is not large. Predicted compliance increases over time, from 61% in 1981 to 79% in 1992. Finally, predicted compliance rates differ dramatically across counties, with the two extremes showing predicted rates of 55% and 84%.

Who Are Noncompliers?

The previous analyses generally confirm the importance of ability to pay and enforcement among both paternity and divorce cases. In this section, I take a closer look at noncompliers (both nonpayers and partial payers), presenting distributional information on income and percentage of income owed in support. For these analyses, I return to the first sample used, which includes cases with unknown incomes as well as those in which incomes are known.

Figure 6.3 shows the income distribution of nonpayers and partial payers in the sample. Unfortunately, income information is missing for a substantial share of cases, especially the nonpayers, precluding definitive conclusions. Among nonpayers with known income, the income of fathers in paternity cases is substantially below that of fathers in divorce cases. Of nonpaying fathers with known income, 74% of paternity fathers have incomes below $10,000, compared to 24% of divorced fathers. Similarly, while only 2% of these paternity fathers have incomes above $20,000, more than half of divorced fathers do, with nearly one-fourth having incomes over $30,000. Among fathers who pay part of the amount due and have known income, paternity fathers again have lower incomes: 54% of paternity fathers have incomes below $10,000, compared to 27% of divorced fathers. Similarly, of the partially-paying fathers with known income, 12% of the paternity fathers have incomes above $20,000, compared to 42% of the divorced fathers.

While the amount of missing information limits conclusions, it appears that a portion of divorce cases that are not paying their full order have moderate incomes. Among paternity cases, those not paying their full order have substantially lower incomes.[5]

When income is unknown, the relationship of the order to income is also unknown. Among noncomplying cases in which the "burden" is known, there is substantial variation. For both nonpayers and partial payers, orders range from below 10% of current income to above 75%. Note that the sample includes cases that entered the courts as early as 1980, when support guidelines were not in effect. Among cases who paid nothing and in which income is known, 31% of paternity cases had orders less than 10% of their incomes, while 37% had orders over 35% of their income; the corresponding figures for divorce cases were 31% and 18%.

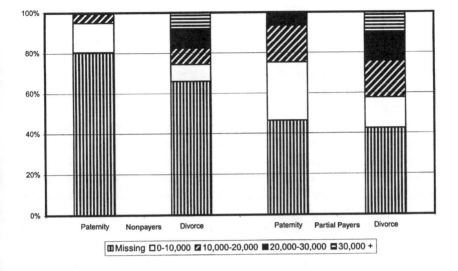

Figure 6.3. Income of Noncompliers

CONCLUSIONS AND POLICY IMPLICATIONS

These data show that noncompliance with child support orders *is* a serious problem: one third of paternity fathers and one sixth of divorced fathers with orders pay nothing in the first year of their order, and another 40% of paternity fathers and 37% of divorced fathers pay only part. While there has been some improvement in these rates since 1980, the most recent years analyzed here show troubling trends. The extent to which the apparent downturn in 1993 has continued is unknown, but if it has, the reasons are not yet well understood. One possible explanation is that the kinds of cases being brought into the child support system are cases in which collection is more difficult, leading to lower collection rates. For example, in the past an unemployed father may not have been asked to pay child support; recent policy changes may require more and more of this type of father. Future research that tries to examine whether the recent compliance rates are lower among similar cases could assist us in addressing these questions.[6]

These results indicate that compliance is strongly associated with the non-resident parent's ability to pay, particularly income and the burden of the order. Enforcement activities may be having a beneficial impact on compliance with child support orders: routine withholding is associated with significantly higher compliance rates among divorced payers and among those for whom employment is their primary income source. I find little evidence that strength of family ties is associated with the compliance rate; note, however, that the family ties variables are crude and do not capture the extent of fathers' interactions with their ex-wives or children. I find no evidence that economic need among the mother and children leads to greater compliance.

Paternity cases and divorce cases have generally similar determinants of compliance, with the important exception of the burden of child support orders. Nonmarital fathers whose orders are between 20% and 30% of their income pay a lower proportion of their orders; in contrast, divorce cases with orders in this range tend to have similar compliance rates to those with orders between 15% and 20% of their incomes. Moreover, among paternity cases, compliance rates decrease much more rapidly as the burden increases.

Unfortunately, the amount of missing income limits the conclusions that can be drawn about the characteristics of noncomplying fathers. The evidence we have suggests a large difference between paternity and divorced fathers, with paternity fathers having much lower incomes. Although divorced fathers are not a high-income group, they are generally not so poor that they can not afford at least some support. Indeed, I believe it is difficult to argue that nonpaying divorced fathers who earn over $20,000 can not afford at least some contribution in child support. On the other hand, the generally low to modest incomes evidenced here do not lend support to the stereotypical portrayal of noncompliers as wealthy men who simply refuse to support their children.

These results have several potential implications for public policy. As discussed earlier, policies aimed at promoting compliance have overwhelmingly emphasized enforcement. The higher compliance in cases with routine withholding orders suggests that this strategy has indeed been effective for fathers with income from wages as well as various earned income sources. However, the bulk of the gains possible from routine withholding, at least as currently carried out, may have already been realized in Wisconsin, since the majority of current noncomplying fathers already have withholding orders. Achieving further gains from withholding may require shifting focus from simply issuing initial withholding orders to making sure withholding continues when the nonresident parent changes employers. One step in this direction was recently enacted in the 1996 Personal Responsibility and Work Opportunities Reconciliation Act, which requires employers to provide information on new hires to state agencies, that then transfer this information to a national registry. This national registry can be used to keep track of when nonresident parents change employers so that withholding orders can stay current.

The relatively higher incomes among noncomplying divorced fathers, compared to noncomplying paternity fathers suggests that the optimal policy response for the two groups may differ. In particular, programs designed to increase the earnings capacity of fathers may be more important for fathers in nonmarital cases, and careful attention to enforcement may be more important for fathers in divorce cases. As noted above, though, a sizable minority of noncomplying divorced fathers do have very low incomes, and for this group an emphasis on earnings capacity may be appropriate. One recent attempt to increase the earnings capacity of fathers is the Parents' Fair Share Demonstration, a multistate pilot program that includes job training, job search groups, enhanced child support enforcement and parenting groups. While the overall literature on the effects of job training programs shows mixed results (e.g., Blank, 1994), initial evaluations of this program show that increasing the earnings capacity of nonresident fathers may be an effective strategy for increasing compliance (Doolittle and Lynn, 1997).

Another policy implication follows from the findings on the relation between the burden of the order and the compliance rate. I find that orders between 1% and 30% of the father's income have similar compliance rates among divorce cases, suggesting that support guidelines up to the top of this range may not have a negative effect on compliance rates. Whereas guidelines that require more than 30% of the father's income may be considered by policymakers, the results suggest that such orders may involve a tradeoff in the form of lower compliance. Furthermore, some of the nonpaying fathers have orders that are very high percentages of their income, percentages beyond those required by most child support guidelines. The extent to which orders are set above the guideline-required amount, and the extent to which orders change when incomes change, are critical issues for future research.

More broadly, not enough is known about the relationship between changes in circumstances and changes in orders. Useful research questions are both descriptive (e.g., In what types of cases do orders change when circumstances change?) and normative (e.g., Should orders change as children age? Should orders decrease if the nonresident parent has new children to support? If the resident parent marries and has more income? Should orders increase automatically when incomes change, or should a separate review occur?).

The focus of this analysis has been compliance during the calendar year after the first support order. Some research shows that average compliance rates decline as the time since divorce increases (e.g., Peters et al., 1993), as does the amount of contact between fathers and their children (e.g., Seltzer, 1991b). One hypothesis is that some fathers are willing to pay child support shortly after their divorce, but as the time since the divorce lengthens, their willingness subsides, and the stringency of the enforcement system becomes more important to the amount of child support that is paid. We now have information on patterns of compliance among Wisconsin cases in the first 5 years postpaternity or postdivorce (Meyer & Bartfeld, 1998). This work shows that compliance in the first year is an important predictor of later compliance, full-payers in year 1 pay an average of 80% of their obligation in years 2 through 5 and nonpayers in year 1 pay an average of 10% to 30% in years 2 through 5. This finding suggests the possibility of experimenting with early interventions. Perhaps nonresident parents who fall behind in their obligations during the first year could be required to attend something like the Parents' Fair Share group sessions. Some sessions would focus on the importance of father involvement (both financial contributions and other support) for their children's well-being, other sessions might provide the rationale behind the formula for setting child support orders (given the research that shows that fathers who thought their orders were fair were more likely to pay), and still other sessions could assist those who need help in initiating a review of the amount of their order. Finally, future research could assist policymakers by extending analyses of factors associated with compliance into a dynamic framework, examining compliance over the life of a case.

Appendix

MEANS OF VARIABLES USED IN MULTIVARIATE ANALYSIS

	Paternity	*Divorce*	*All*
Father's Income $0-$10,000	0.42	0.16	0.23
Father's Income $10-$20,000	0.38	0.29	0.31
Father's Income $20-$30,000	0.15	0.32	0.27
Father's Income $30-$50,000	0.04	0.14	0.12
Father's Income $50,000 +	0.01	0.09	0.07
Burden 0-10%	0.31	0.11	0.16
Burden 10-15%	0.29	0.20	0.22
Burden 15-20%	0.17	0.24	0.23
Burden 20-25%	0.06	0.15	0.12
Burden 25-30%	0.04	0.12	0.10
Burden 30-35%	0.03	0.05	0.04
Burden 35-50%	0.03	0.06	0.06
Burden 50-75%	0.03	0.04	0.04
Burden 75% +	0.04	0.03	0.03
Father's Source Employment	0.66	0.73	0.71
Father's Source Self-Employment	0.02	0.06	0.05
Father's Source Unemployment	0.02	0.02	0.02
Father's Source Miscellaneous	0.01	0.01	0.01
Father's Source Missing	0.26	0.18	0.20
Father's Source None	0.03	0.01	0.01
1981	0.01	0.06	0.04
1982	0.09	0.12	0.11
1983	0.15	0.13	0.14
1985	0.05	0.09	0.08
1986	0.13	0.13	0.13
1987	0.15	0.16	0.16
1988	0.09	0.07	0.07
1989	0.05	0.04	0.04
1990	0.06	0.06	0.06
1991	0.07	0.06	0.06
1992	0.07	0.05	0.06
1993	0.08	0.03	0.05
No Routine Withholding	0.32	0.46	0.42
Routine Withholding, Employment	0.53	0.46	0.48
Routine Withholding, Self-Employment	0.01	0.01	0.01

(continued)

	Paternity	Divorce	All
Routine Withholding, Other	0.14	0.07	0.09
Fixed-Dollar Order	0.96	0.89	0.91
Percentage-Expressed Order	0.04	0.11	0.09
Paternity			0.26
Divorce, One Child		0.45	0.33
Divorce, Two Children		0.43	0.32
Divorce, Three + Children		0.12	0.09
Divorce, Married < 1 Year		0.01	0.01
Divorce, Married 1-3 Years		0.15	0.11
Divorce, Married 4-6 Years		0.21	0.16
Divorce, Married 7-10 Years		0.25	0.18
Divorce Married 11 + Years		0.37	0.27
Divorce Marriage Length Missing		0.01	0.01
Oldest Child Age 0-2	0.89	0.19	0.38
Oldest Child Age 3-5	0.07	0.23	0.19
Oldest Child Age 6-10	0.02	0.29	0.22
Oldest Child Age 11+	0.01	0.28	0.20
Oldest Child Age Missing	0.02	0.01	0.01
Father Not Remarried	0.84	0.88	0.87
Father Remarried	0.14	0.11	0.12
Father Marital Status Missing	0.02	0.01	0.01
Mother Not Remarried	0.33	0.59	0.52
Mother Remarried	0.04	0.04	0.04
Mother Marital Status Missing	0.63	0.37	0.44
Sole Mother Custody	0.93	0.63	0.71
Joint Legal Custody	0.01	0.34	0.25
Legal Custody Missing	0.06	0.03	0.04
Mother's Income $0-5,000	0.15	0.10	0.11
Mother's Income $5-10,000	0.11	0.12	0.12
Mother's Income $10-15,000	0.06	0.15	0.13
Mother's Income $15-20,000	0.03	0.13	0.10
Mother's Income $20-30,000		0.10	0.08
Mother's Income $20,000 +	0.02		
Mother's Income $30,000 +		0.03	0.02
Mother's Income Missing	0.63	0.37	0.44
Mother Received AFDC	0.65	0.25	0.36
Mother Did Not Receive AFDC	0.25	0.72	0.59
AFDC Status Missing	0.10	0.03	0.05

NOTE: Panel columns may not add to 1 because of rounding.

NOTES

1. The empirical work has focused on compliance in the most common situation, when children live with mothers and fathers are ordered to pay support. Little empirical work has been conducted on the determinants of compliance with child support orders among nonresident mothers.

2. The Family Support Act of 1988 required state child support offices to review every 3 years the orders of cases receiving welfare and to offer reviews to child support office cases not receiving welfare. Pilot studies revealed that many orders needed updating, but that few nonwelfare cases were modified (Kost et al., 1996).

3. Since 1984, the first $50 per month collected was "passed through" to the family with the remainder used to offset welfare costs. The 1996 Personal Responsibility and Work Opportunity Reconciliation Act allows states to set whatever level of "pass through" they want. While nearly every state has thus far chosen to either continue the $50 per month or eliminate it, Wisconsin is experimenting with passing the entire amount on to the resident-parent family. This experiment will be evaluated, so there will eventually be empirical research associated with the effects of the "pass-through."

4. Among divorce cases, the coefficient on percentage-expressed orders is significant and negative. However, some research has shown that the types of cases given percentage-expressed orders have some characteristics that are also associated with lower compliance. This suggests that further research is needed before drawing conclusions about the relationship between percentage-expressed orders and compliance. (For a more comprehensive treatment of this issue see Bartfeld and Garfinkel, 1996.)

5. To what extent might the missing income information bias these results? We have some information in the court records about income in the year the case came to court. Such information is available for about one fourth of paternity fathers and about half of divorced fathers for whom income is not available in the tax records. Cases with income information in the court records but not the tax records tend to show slightly lower incomes than do cases with information in both the court record and the tax record.

6. Note that in the multivariate results the coefficient on 1993 is not significantly different from 1992, which would suggest that it is the types of cases in the system rather than enforcement techniques becoming less effective.

REFERENCES

Bartfeld, J., & Garfinkel, I. (1996). The impact of percentage-expressed child support orders on payments. *Journal of Human Resources, 31,* 794-815.

Bartfeld, J., & Meyer, D. R. (1994). Are there really dead-beat dads? The relationship between enforcement, ability to pay, and compliance in nonmarital child support cases. *Social Service Review, 68,* 219-35.

Beller, A. H., & Graham, J. W. (1993). *Small change: The economics of child support.* New Haven, CT: Yale University Press.

Blank, R. M. (1994). The employment strategy: Public policies to increase work and earnings. In S. H. Danziger, G. D. Sandefur, & D. H. Weinberg (Eds.), *Confronting poverty: Prescriptions for change.* Cambridge, MA: Harvard University Press.

Brown, P., & Roan, C. L. (1997, March). *Sampling report, Wisconsin child support demonstration project, public use data.* Institute for Research on Poverty, University of Wisconsin-Madison.

Doolittle, F., & Lynn, S. (1997). *What happens with increased child support enforcement of the obligations of low income noncustodial parents?* New York: Manpower Demonstration Research Corporation.

Edin, K. (1995). Single mothers and absent fathers: The possibilities and limits of child support policy. *Children and Youth Services Review, 17,* 203-30.

Garfinkel, I., & Klawitter, M. M. (1990). The effect of routine income withholding of child support collections. *Journal of Policy Analysis and Management, 9,* 155-177.

Garfinkel, I., & Robins, P. K. (1994). The relationship between child support enforcement tools and child support outcomes. In I. Garfinkel, S. S. McLanahan, & P. K. Robins (Eds.), *Child support and child well-being* (pp. 133-171). Washington, DC: Urban Institute Press.

Graham, J. W. & Beller, A. H. (1989). The effect of child support payments on the labor supply of female family heads: an econometric analysis. *Journal of Human Resources, 24,* 664-688.

Johnson, E. S., & Doolittle, F. (1998). Low-income parents and the Parents' Fair Share program: An early qualitative look at improving the ability and desire of low-income noncustodial parents to pay child support. In I. Garfinkel, S. S. McLanahan, D. R. Meyer; J. A. Seltzer (Eds.), *Fathers under fire.* New York: Russell Sage Foundation.

Kost, K. A., Meyer, D. R., Corbett, T., & Brown, P. R. (1996). Revising old child support orders: The Wisconsin experience. *Family Relations, 45,* 19-26.

Maddala, G. S. (1983). *Limited-dependent and qualitative variables in econometrics.* Cambridge, MA: Harvard University Press.

Meyer, D. R. & Bartfeld, J. (1996). Compliance with child support orders in divorce cases. *Journal of Marriage and the Family, 58,* 201-212.

Meyer, D. R. & Bartfeld, J. (1992a, June). *The effects of the immediate withholding of child support on collections over time.* Institute for Research on Poverty, University of Wisconsin-Madison: Final report to the Wisconsin Department of Health and Social Services.

Meyer, D. R. & Bartfeld, J. (1992b, June). *How routine is "routine" withholding?* Institute for Research on Poverty, University of Wisconsin-Madison: Final report to the Wisconsin Department of Health and Social Services.

Meyer, D. R. & Bartfeld, J. (1998). Patterns of child support payment in Wisconsin. *Journal of Marriage and the Family, 60,* 309-318.

Meyer, D. R., Bartfeld, J., Garfinkel, I., & Brown, P. (1996). Child support reform: Lessons from Wisconsin. *Family Relations, 46,* 11-18.

Nichols-Casebolt, A. & Danziger, S. K. (1989). The effect of childbearing age on child support awards and economic well-being among divorcing mothers. *Journal of Divorce, 12*(4), 34-38.

O'Neill, J. (1985). Determinants of child support. Final report prepared for the Demographic and Behavioral Sciences Branch, National Institute on Child Health and Human Development, under grant no. IR01HD 16840-01. Washington, DC: The Urban Institute.

Peters, H. E., Argys, L. M., Maccoby, E. E., & Mnookin, R. H. (1993). Enforcing divorce settlements: Evidence from child support compliance and award modifications. *Demography, 30,* 719-735.

Peterson, J. L. & Nord, C. W. (1990). The regular receipt of child support: a multistep process. *Journal of Marriage and the Family, 52,* 539-551.

Seltzer, J. A. (1991a). Legal custody arrangements and children's economic welfare. *American Journal of Sociology, 96,* 895-929.

Seltzer, J. A. (1991b). Relationships between fathers and children who live apart: The father's role after separation. *Journal of Marriage and the Family, 53,* 79-101.

Seltzer, J. A., Schaeffer, N. C., & Charng, H. (1989). Family ties after divorce: The relationship between visiting and paying child support. *Journal of Marriage and the Family, 51,* 1013-1032.

Sonenstein, F. L., & Calhoun, C. A. (1990). Determinants of child support: A pilot survey of absent parents. *Contemporary Policy Issues, 8,* 75-94.

Teachman, J. D. (1991). Who pays? Receipt of child support in the United States. *Journal of Marriage and the Family, 53,* 759-72.

U.S. Bureau of the Census. (1995). Current Population Reports, Series P-60, no. 187. *Child support for custodial mothers and fathers: 1989.* Washington, DC: Government Printing Office.

Veum, J. R. (1993). The relationship between child support and visitation: Evidence from longitudinal data. *Social Science Research, 22,* 229-244.

Weiss, Y., & Willis, R. J. (1985). Children as collective goods and divorce settlements. *Journal of Labor Economics, 3,* 268-92.

Williams, R. G. (1994). An overview of child support guidelines in the United States. In M. C. Haynes (Ed.), *Child support guidelines: The next generation* (pp. 1-17). Washington, DC: U.S. Department of Health and Human Services.

Wright, D. W., & Price, S. J. (1986). Court-ordered child support payments: The effect of the former spouse relationship on compliance. *Journal of Marriage and the Family, 48,* 869-874.

PART IV

Divorce and Society

Divorce is a profound change in the most intimate of relationships, but it is infused with societal values and norms. Divorce policies and processes reflect values concerning caregiving roles and relationships, gender, the moral status of marriage, and children and their needs. As society changes, divorce becomes evaluated differently. In recent years, the impact of divorce on society has received increased attention because of the realization that divorce touches the lives of virtually everyone, either directly or indirectly, by changing our views of marriage and childrearing commitments. Although each divorce represents a unique and private decision, marital disruption has become so common that some believe that it has achieved "critical mass," with cumulative consequences for other forms of social organization that intersect with the family. What does this mean for society, and does it have meaningful implications for public policy? The final two chapters of the book place divorce within this broader societal perspective.

In the first, Paul Amato considers how the high rate of marital disruption in the United States may be transforming larger social institutions. The ubiquity of divorce not only brings larger numbers of people into contact with the legal system, but also has potentially profound implications for broader kinship networks, the nature of intimate relationships (including nonmarital cohabitation), intergenerational relations, and the growth of stepfamilies. Amato notes that the economic consequences of divorce are also far reaching, with poten-

159

tially significant implications for gender inequality and the rate of child poverty, as well as women's labor force participation both before and after marital dissolution. Finally, he focuses on the cultural values that not only encourage the acceptance of divorce, but also may be reciprocally influenced by the high rate of divorce, including the emphasis on individualism that has been a focus of cultural critics. Taken together, Amato's portrayal of the consequences of living in a "postdivorce society" is consistent with a systems perspective in which the causes and consequences of social change are interactive, with many of the cultural changes that have allegedly contributed to rising rates of divorce in the past actually being consequences of these rising rates. Notably, Amato's conclusion that the impact of living in a postdivorce society is different depending on whether one is a child or an adult is significant from the standpoint of policy analysis.

In the final chapter of the volume, Ross Thompson and Jennifer Wyatt focus on the values that are reflected in divorce policy. Family law has a uniquely expressive function because it enunciates public values concerning the family, and incorporated within divorce policies are beliefs concerning parental (and marital) roles and responsibilities, the nature of children and their needs, how to divide the human as well as material capital that have become merged during marriage, and the role of the public sector in managing family relationships when couples part. Contemporary concerns about the impact of divorce on society and its consequences for children highlight the intersection of values and research in shaping public policy, and Thompson and Wyatt compare the arguments of conservative and liberal family scholars concerning the future of divorce policy in the United States. The recent adoption of the Louisiana Covenant Marriage Law is profiled as one illustration of the broader debate underlying the "national family wars" over no-fault divorce and the social values it reflects. The chapter closes with consideration of how research can become "usable knowledge" in future policy reform, and returns to the broader themes of this volume with a short commentary on each of the chapters.

Chapter 7

The Postdivorce Society

How Divorce Is Shaping the Family and Other Forms of Social Organization

Paul R. Amato

Dramatic changes have occurred in the American family during the 20th century. The spread of premarital sexuality, the growing popularity of cohabitation, the increase in nonmarital fertility, and the movement of wives and mothers into the paid labor force have affected the most fundamental details of our lives in extraordinary ways. But of all the changes in family life, perhaps the most far-reaching in its implications has been the increase in the rate of divorce. Indeed, the shift from a modal pattern of lifelong marriage to serial marriage punctuated by divorce represents a fundamental change in how most people meet their needs for intimacy over the life course. This shift has also had major implications for the family settings in which children are nurtured and socialized.

A large literature has emerged on the social and historical factors that gave rise to the current high divorce rate (e.g., Cherlin, 1992; Furstenberg, 1994;

AUTHOR'S NOTE: I thank Stacy Rogers, Ross Thompson, and Lynn White for useful suggestions regarding an earlier version of this chapter.

White, 1991). Scholars also have devoted considerable attention to how divorce affects the psychological well-being of individual adults (Kitson, 1990) and children (Amato & Keith, 1991a). In contrast, scholars have devoted relatively little attention to the consequences of marital instability for society more generally. (For an exception see Bumpass, 1990.) And yet, the high rate of marriage breakdown in the last three decades has required numerous adjustments on the part of other social institutions. For example, divorce brings large numbers of people into contact with the legal system, thus increasing the demand for family law attorneys, court personnel, mediators, and counselors. The ubiquity of divorce has also required policy makers to develop new rules for regulating postdivorce family arrangements, such as rules about custody determination, property division, and child support. Indeed, many of the chapters in this volume (especially those by Emery, Bartlett, Maccoby, and Meyer) deal in one way or another with the challenges that divorce is posing for practitioners and policy makers.

Rather than address how divorce affects the adjustment of individual parents and children, my goal in this chapter is to explore how marital instability is affecting the family as an institution, as well as other aspects of American life. Although the consequences of divorce are broad, I restrict my discussion to a few topics of central interest: family bonds (intimate relationships, intergenerational relations, the growth of stepfamilies), inequality (poverty, gender equity), and structural and cultural factors (women's employment, cultural values). I focus on these topics primarily because they concern large numbers of people, and because a reasonable amount of data is available on which to base conclusions.

My discussion follows a social systems perspective. According to this perspective, (1) changes in one part of a social system bring about changes in other parts of the system, (2) most events in a system are determined by a variety of factors acting together, rather than by a single cause, (3) the elements of a system are involved in reciprocal cause-and-effect relationships, and (4) periods of profound change are eventually followed by a new equilibrium. I make four corresponding assumptions about divorce. First, divorce is a factor that has changed the trajectory of many people's lives, and in so doing, has altered the larger social landscape in fundamental ways. Second, although the increase in divorce has changed society in many ways, it has not been the sole cause of these changes. Third, changes in divorce and changes in other social trends have mutually affected (and amplified) one another. And fourth, the high level of marital instability during the last few decades has contributed to a new equilibrium—a social pattern in which high divorce rates are both normative and self-reinforcing. These four assumptions underlie the following discussion, and I return to them in the conclusion.

THE DEMOGRAPHICS

Although outlined somewhat in earlier chapters, I will reiterate the basic picture. At the middle of the 19th century, when statistics on marital dissolution first became available, only about 5% of all first marriages ended in divorce or permanent separation (Preston & McDonald, 1979). In contrast, more than half of all first marriages initiated in recent years will be voluntarily disrupted (Bumpass, 1990). One might expect second marriages to be more successful, if for no other reason than people should have learned from the mistakes they made the first time around. But second marriages have an even higher rate of dissolution than first marriages. In fact, the number of individuals who voluntarily dissolve more than one marriage has increased substantially during this century; currently, about one out of every six adults endures two or more divorces (Cherlin, 1992). Behaviors once associated with Hollywood celebrities have become increasingly common in suburbia.

About 40% of children will experience parental divorce before reaching adulthood (Bumpass, 1984). This represents more than one million children every year. The high rate of marital dissolution has been accompanied, more recently, by a rise in the rate of nonmarital birth. Currently, 31% of all children are born outside of marriage (U.S. Bureau of Statistics, 1996). However, a large proportion of children born outside of marriage (about one fourth) are born to cohabiting parents (Bumpass & Raley, 1995), and many of these children later experience the dissolution of their parents' relationship. This consideration suggests that the impermanence of childbearing unions, rather than divorce itself, is the key issue. (For this reason, I examine the consequences of nonmarital birth along with divorce in some of the discussions later in this chapter.) Overall, the combination of these trends means that at least half of all children in the U.S. will spend some portion of their childhood living in a single-parent household (Castro & Bumpass, 1989). Because most children live with their mothers following divorce, at least half of all fathers in the U.S. will be nonresident fathers for a spell before their children reach adulthood.

Remarriage following divorce is common, with about two thirds of women and three fourths of men eventually remarrying (Cherlin, 1992). Indeed, nearly half of all marriages in the U.S. today are remarriages for one or both spouses.

Currently, about 12% of all children in the U.S. currently live with a stepparent (U.S. Bureau of the Census, 1992), and about 30% to 40% will live with a stepparent prior to reaching age 19 (Glick, 1989).

FAMILY BONDS

Intimate Relationships

One of the main challenges of adulthood is the establishment of long-term, intimate relationships. Secure and mutually-supportive relationships are important because they contribute to people's sense of well-being and mental health. Research consistently shows that married women and men, compared with those who are single, exhibit fewer symptoms of depression and anxiety, are less likely to engage in risky behavior, have better physical health, and live longer (Mastekaasa, 1994; Ross, 1995; Waite, 1995). Married individuals also report more physical and emotional satisfaction with their sex lives than do single people or people in cohabiting relationships (Laumann, Ganong, Michael, & Michaels, 1994). In addition, marriage confers economic benefits on men and women; compared with single individuals, married people have higher household incomes and benefit from economies of scale (Ross, 1995; Waite, 1995). The link between marriage and well-being may be due partly to the fact that people with high levels of psychological and economic resources are especially likely to be selected into marriage. Nevertheless, research strongly suggests that marriage causes most of these benefits.

The process through which adults form intimate relationships has changed in fundamental ways. In the recent past, most people dated, married, and stayed married until their own death or the death of their spouse. Although some people were sexually active prior to marriage, marriage represented, for most people, the beginning of a regular, close, sexual relationship. And marriage was the arrangement into which the great majority of children were born. Today, however, the links between sexual activity and marriage are weak. The proportion of women and men who initiate sexual activity prior to marrying has increased in recent decades; currently, only a minority of adults has sexual intercourse for the first time within marriage (Laumann, Gagnon, Michael, & Michaels, 1994). Similarly, nonmarital cohabitation has become so common that it is virtually normative; more than one half of all people in their 30s have lived in a cohabiting relationship (Bumpass, 1990).

The increase in marital instability, although not the sole cause, has helped to fuel each of these trends. Offspring from divorced families tend to become sexually active at an earlier age than do offspring from nondivorced families (Booth, Brinkerhoff, & White, 1984; Mott, Fondell, Hu, Kowaleski-Jones, & Menaghan, 1996). This difference may be due to the fact that, following divorce, most offspring see their parents engage in dating, and this often involves overnight visits from new partners. Sexually active single parents model behaviors that offspring may be inclined to emulate (Hetherington, 1972). More generally, parents with liberal attitudes about sexual behaviors are more likely than other parents to have sexually active children (Widmer, 1997). In addition, single parents tend to supervise their adolescent children less closely than married parents (Thomson, McLanahan, & Curtin, 1992). The combination of observing sexual models (which increases motivation), and a low level of parental supervision (which increases opportunities), increases the likelihood that adolescents will become sexually active.

Marital dissolution has also increased the frequency of nonmarital cohabitation. People who have seen their own marriage end in divorce are especially likely to cohabit (Bumpass & Sweet, 1989). Similarly, offspring with divorced parents, as young adults, cohabit at higher rates than do offspring with continuously married parents (Amato & Booth, 1997; Laumann, Ganong, Michael, & Michaels, 1994). Among people who have experienced divorce first hand and realize the fragility of marriage, cohabitation is often the arrangement of choice. After all, cohabitation provides an opportunity to experience intimacy and companionship without having to make a formal commitment that may not be sustainable in the long run. For some cautious individuals, cohabitation provides an opportunity to try out relationships prior to marrying. For other skeptical individuals, cohabitation represents an alternative to marriage. For both of these groups, cohabitation reflects a general wariness about the stability of marriage.

Although about 40% of cohabiting couples split up without marrying, most cohabiting couples eventually marry. Bumpass (1990) estimates that half of the marriages contracted in the 1980s were preceded by cohabitation. So, for many people, cohabitation can be viewed as a step in the courtship process—somewhere between dating steadily and marriage. Couples who cohabit and then marry, however, are more likely than other couples to divorce. This tendency may be due to the fact that people who hold nontraditional attitudes are more likely to cohabit as well as to divorce (Booth & Johnson, 1988; Laumann, Ganong, Michael, & Michaels, 1994). In other words, the association between cohabitation and divorce may be spurious. But it is also probable that the experience of premarital cohabitation increases later marital instability. For example, longitudinal studies show that people adopt less traditional attitudes, including more tolerant attitudes toward divorce, following cohabitation (Axinn & Barber, 1997). Consequently, although individuals with nontraditional attitudes are especially likely to cohabit, the experience of cohabitation may bring about a further liberalization of attitudes. And holding positive attitudes toward divorce is a good predictor of marital dissolution (Amato, 1996). In summary, although most cohabiting couples eventually marry, these couples also experience a greater-than-average risk of divorce. Cohabitation, therefore, is not only a response to the high rate of marital instability, but also a factor that reinforces the high rate of marital instability.

Because divorce is common, we can expect frequent and early cohabitation among young adults in the foreseeable future. But because these cohabiting relationships (and the marriages that develop from them) tend to be unstable, the high rate of cohabitation will be accompanied by a high rate of relationship turnover. Most people will cohabit before marrying, and these relationships may or may not result in marriage. Of those who marry, most will see their marriages end in divorce. Of those who divorce, most will cohabit with a second partner, and these relationships may or may not result in marriage. Among those who remarry, most will see their second marriages end in divorce. Many of these individuals will become involved in additional cohabiting or marital relationships in the future. As a result of these complexities, the great majority of people will experience multiple relationships with live-in partners over the course of a lifetime.

One can interpret this shift as a decline in people's ability or willingness to maintain long-term intimate relationships, or as an increase in people's freedom to try out new relationships, leave unsatisfying unions, and seek out better ones. It is not clear, however, if this greater freedom has improved people's sense of well-being. Ending an unhappy relationship is a relief for most people. But divorce is also stressful for both parties, and singlehood—even if it is a temporary status between relationships—is associated with poorer psychological and physical health. Consequently, a pattern in which people shift from one intimate relationship to the next is unlikely to be one that maximizes the well-being of most people. Overall, regardless of how one views these changes, it is clear that the formation of intimate relationships has become more complex, and the outcomes of these relationships less certain, than in previous decades.

Intergenerational Ties

Research consistently indicates that children in divorced families tend to have more problematic relationships with parents than do children in two-parent families. Hetherington and Clingempeel (1990) found that relations between custodial mothers and their young children are often strained after marital separation. Divorced mothers, compared with married mothers, are less affectionate with their children, punish them more harshly, and monitor their behavior less carefully. Although these differences tended to diminish over time, new tensions in the mother-child relationship often emerge when children reach adolescence or when mothers remarry. In addition, it is well known that many noncustodial fathers have relatively little contact with children, especially as time since marital disruption passes (Furstenberg, Nord, Peterson, & Zill, 1983; Seltzer & Bianchi, 1988). As noted by Alan Booth in Chapter 2, many of the strains in mother-child relationships can be traced to marital conflict that precedes divorce; in contrast, father-child ties become weaker following divorce, presumably because fathers and children usually live apart (Amato & Booth, 1997).

Weak ties between parents and children persist well into adulthood. Offspring with divorced parents, compared with those with continuously married parents, tend to feel less affection for parents, see them less often, and exchange less assistance with them (Amato & Booth, 1997; Amato, Rezac, & Booth, 1995, Aquilino, 1994; Cooney, 1994; Furstenberg, Hoffman, & Shrestha, 1995). And although divorce may actually increase the flow of assistance from adult offspring to mothers (especially mothers who do not remarry), it substantially decreases exchanges of assistance with fathers, regardless of whether fathers remarry. Because so many offspring have minimal contact with fathers following divorce, ties with extended kin on the father's side also tend to be weak.

The growing estrangement of fathers from their children comes at a peculiar moment in history, given that social scientists are increasingly recognizing the importance of fathers in children's development (Lamb, 1997). In addition, attitude surveys reveal that the majority of Americans now believe that fathers should be more involved with their children (Thornton, 1989). Consistent with changes in attitudes, some evidence suggests that married fathers are indeed spending more time with children now than in the past (Pleck, 1997). But due to the rise in divorce and single parenthood (along with the drop in fertility), the amount of time that men reside with children over the life course has declined in recent decades (Eggebeen & Uhlenberg, 1985). Demographic changes, therefore, are undermining the cultural push for men to be more involved with children.

Parent-child relationships are potentially important resources throughout the life course. Parents often provide critical support when offspring are establishing their own households; offspring, in return, often provide critical support when parents are in their later years. Furthermore, close and supportive links between adult children and their parents promote the psychological well-being of both generations (Amato, 1994a; Snarey, 1993). Yet, in spite of the importance of these ties, contact between adult offspring and their parents declined during the 1980s (Bumpass, 1990). Of course, divorce is not the only factor undermining intergenerational relations. The greater wealth (and health) of the elderly is making them less dependent on their children. And increasing geographic dispersion of parents and adult offspring has decreased possibilities for contact and everyday exchanges of assistance. Nevertheless, changes in family structure have almost certainly played a role in weakening the ties across generations.

Divorced fathers may be especially vulnerable in later life. As these men near the end of the life cycle, many will not have the benefit of adult offspring to provide emotional and financial assistance. This problem will be exacerbated as the baby boom generation reaches retirement age. It is already clear that the social security system in the United States can no longer afford to provide the same level of benefits that are currently available, and substantial cutbacks will be necessary in coming decades. If government support programs for the elderly are scaled back, and if adult offspring are not willing or able to step in and provide support to their aging parents, then the well-being of the elderly (especially men) is likely to decline in the future.

The Growth of Stepfamilies

If divorce is weakening the bonds across generations, then what will take their place? One possibility is that the loss of ties with parents (especially fathers) is being balanced by new ties with stepparents (especially stepfathers). In fact, parental remarriage creates a variety of quasi-kin relationships, including those between stepparents and stepchildren, between stepgrandparents and stepgrandchildren, and between stepsiblings. Sibling relationships may become especially complex following parental remarriage. For example, a particular child's family may include full siblings, stepsiblings from the stepfather's previous marriage, stepsiblings from the stepmother's previous marriage, half siblings produced by the marriage of the mother and the stepfather, and half siblings produced by the marriage of the father and stepmother. Remarriage, therefore, expands the size of children's kin networks and the pool of people who can provide potential support in later life (Furstenberg & Spanier, 1984). In this context, Furstenberg (1987) referred to stepfamilies as "the new extended family."

Do these new ties with stepparents and other stepfamily members benefit children? The answer to this question is partly positive. The entry of a stepfather substantially increases household income, which improves children's standard of living (Teachman & Paasch, 1994). Nevertheless, in spite of the financial improvement, the presence of a stepparent in the household does not benefit most children's psychological or behavioral adjustment. Children in stepfamilies are no better off, on average, than children in divorced, single-parent families; indeed, they are worse off in some respects (Amato, 1994b).

The absence of positive effects for stepfamilies is due largely to the fact that relations between stepparents and stepchildren are not always close or even cordial. Although some preadolescent boys respond positively to the introduction of a stepfather, adolescents of both genders are likely to react negatively (Hetherington & Jodl, 1994). Many children view the stepfather as an outsider, reject the stepfather's attempts to exert authority, and are jealous of the emotional bond between the stepfather and the custodial parent. Although many new stepfathers initially attempt to establish close and supportive ties with stepchildren, most stepfathers eventually retreat to a safe distance. Compared with the manner in which married fathers interact with their biological children, stepfathers are less involved, provide less emotional support, and exercise less supervision and discipline (Hetherington & Clingempeel, 1992). Most stepfathers play a limited role in the development and socialization of their stepchildren (Hetherington & Henderson, 1997). Indeed, one study showed that when stepchildren were asked to list who was in their family, nearly one third failed to mention stepparents living in the same household (Furstenberg, 1987). Clearly, stepfathers do not replace absent biological fathers in the lives of most children.

Although residential stepfathers often find it difficult to blend in with previously existing families, residential stepmothers find the process to be even more difficult (Buchanan, Maccoby, & Dornbusch, 1996; Hetherington & Jodl, 1994). The special difficulties of stepmothers may be due to traditional views about motherhood, that is, people may expect more from stepmothers than from stepfathers and may hold stepmothers to a higher standard. The greater difficulty experienced by stepmothers may also be related to the fact that noncustodial mothers tend to keep in contact with offspring more frequently than noncustodial fathers (Furstenberg, Nord, Peterson, & Zill, 1987; Buchanan, Maccoby, & Dornbusch, 1996). The continuing presence of the biological mother in children's lives may complicate and undermine the stepmother's attempts to form close and supportive relationships with her stepchildren. Ties between nonresident stepmothers and stepchildren are especially weak. Most noncustodial stepmothers do not look forward to visits from their stepchildren, and many see stepchildren as interfering with their current marriage (Hetherington & Henderson, 1997).

In some stepfamilies, children disengage from their home life and spend much of their time elsewhere (Hetherington & Jodl, 1994). Older children often leave home to establish residential independence. Aquilino (1991) found that stepchildren were more likely than children from nondivorced two-parent families to leave home prior to age 19, and this difference was especially marked if stepsiblings lived in the household. Similarly, Kiernan (1992) found that stepchildren not only leave home earlier than other children, but also are more likely to leave because of family conflict. Of course, when conflict cannot be resolved, it may be the stepparent who leaves the household. White and Booth (1985) found that remarriages with stepchildren living in the household are more likely to end in divorce than are remarriages without stepchildren.

Although tension is common, stepfamily outcomes are not always as negative as the previous description might suggest. In fact, most stepchildren view their stepfathers positively, although not as positively as children view their biological fathers in two-parent families (Amato, 1987; Hetherington and Jodl, 1994). Indeed, after reaching adulthood, many offspring feel closer to their stepfathers than to their noncustodial fathers (White, 1994). When relations between stepparents and stepchildren are close, children appear to benefit. One study found that children have higher school grades when stepfathers help with homework, attend school events, and are in other ways involved in school activities (Bogenschneider, 1997). Another study found that a close relationship with stepfathers is associated with enhanced psychological well-being among young adults (Amato, 1994a). These findings indicate that stepfathers (and presumably stepmothers) have the potential to be important resources for children, even if this potential is often unmet. Ties to stepfathers in adulthood are usually severed, however, if mothers divorce or die, suggesting that these relationships last only as long as the mother is around to mediate them (White, 1994).

Aside from stepparents, we know very little about the roles other stepkin play in children's lives. Some stepgrandparents form close ties with stepgrandchildren, although this is most common when remarriage occurs when children are young (Cherlin & Furstenberg, 1992). In general, relations between most stepgrandparents and stepgrandchildren are cordial rather than close. Similarly, bonds between stepsiblings are usually not as strong as the bonds between biological siblings. White and Riedman (1992) found that people maintain a substantial degree of contact with stepsiblings in adulthood, seeing them, on average, one to three times per year. However, people maintain lower levels of contact with stepsiblings than with biological siblings. Frequent contact with stepsiblings in adulthood is more common among people who spent more (rather than less) time in a stepfamily, lived with a stepfather rather than a stepmother, and have no biological siblings.

Overall, parental remarriage provides a range of new ties from which children can create relationships, resulting in kin networks that are larger than those found in other family types. Parental remarriage, in this sense, benefits children from single-parent households. Most of the relationships in stepkin networks, however, are not as close as those found in the kin networks of continuously married couples with children. Furthermore, networks based on stepkin are less dense, in the sense that a person can have a relationship with two individuals (mother's new husband and father's new wife) who have little or no relationship with each other. In addition, norms of helping are weaker for stepkin than for biological kin (Rossi & Rossi, 1990). These considerations suggest that kin networks based on stepfamily relationships provide lower levels of support than traditional kin networks. Consistent with this notion, White (1994) found that adult offspring exchange moderate levels of assistance with stepparents, but not as much as they do with never-divorced parents. Most stepfamily relationships, therefore, represent weak rather than strong ties. Although people may provide companionship and a moderate level of support to their stepkin, they may not feel that they can turn to their stepkin in a crisis that requires a substantial degree of assistance. Overall, most children have stronger kin support in stepfamilies than in single-parent households. But because of the high rate of divorce and remarriage, kinship networks of the future (to the extent that they contain a substantial number of stepkin) are likely to be larger but less effective than those in the past.

INEQUALITY

Increased Poverty Among Mothers and Children

It is well known that the economic well-being of custodial mothers and their children tends to deteriorate following marital dissolution. Economic decline is common because women earn less money than men, some ex-husbands pay little or no child support, and public benefits are meager. Teachman and Paasch (1994), using the Survey of Income and Program Participation, reported that the household income of mothers with children drops 23% following divorce. The decline in per capita income is somewhat smaller at 8%. Nevertheless, because of this decline, the percentage of families (mothers and children) who fall below the poverty level increases from 21% prior to divorce to 31% following divorce. Although the numbers vary slightly from study to study, other researchers have reported similar results (e.g., Hoffman & Duncan, 1988). These declines in economic well-being following marital dissolution are comparable for Black and White single mothers.

The increase in divorce and single parenthood has been accompanied by a major decline in the economic security of children in the United States. In the decades following World War II, economic expansion and the creation of federal programs to assist the poor resulted in a substantial decline in the number children living in poverty. Child poverty began to increase again, however, during the 1970s. In 1973, only 14% of children under the age of 18 were poor, but in 1994, the corresponding figure was 21% (U.S. Bureau of the Census, 1996). The current poverty rate varies with race and ethnicity: 17% of White children, 44% of Black children, and 42.5% of Hispanic children are poor (U.S. Bureau of the Census, 1996, p. 473). Irrespective of race, however, the poverty rate now is higher among children than among any other age group. The overrepresentation of children among the ranks of the poor stands in sharp contrast to earlier eras when poverty was concentrated among adults, especially the elderly (McLanahan & Booth, 1990).

To what extent is the growth of child poverty linked to changes in family structure? Eggebeen and Lichter (1991) estimate that increases in the number of single-parent households accounted for about one third of the rise in child poverty between 1960 and 1988. The role of family structure was especially pronounced among African Americans; among this group, the growth of single-parent households accounted for 65% of the increase in child poverty. Similarly, Betson and Michael (1997) estimate that about one third of children are poor today because they live with a single parent. (Other factors that contributed to the rise in child poverty include the decline in men's wages since 1973, the relocation of industries away from the central city, and a drop in the real value of public assistance to needy families.) Economic well-being is lower for children born outside of marriage than for children who experience parental divorce. Nevertheless, both causes of single parenthood have contributed to economic hardship among children.

Remarriage improves the economic well-being of custodial mothers and their children. Teachman and Paasch (1994) report that the entry of a stepfather more than doubles family income. (See Hoffman & Duncan, 1988, for similar estimates.) But rates of remarriage following divorce are declining. And having children substantially decreases single women's overall chances on the marriage market. Consequently, spells of poverty tend to be more persistent for children in single-mother households than for children in other living arrangements (Teachman & Paasch, 1994). Even when mothers remarry, many stepfathers are unwilling to commit the large sums of money necessary to finance higher education for their stepchildren. For example, Goldscheider and Goldscheider (1991) found that stepchildren are less likely than children from nondivorced two-parent families to attend college; similarly, stepchildren who attend college are less likely than children from nondivorced two-parent families to receive financial assistance from their parents.

The rise in marital instability, therefore, has contributed to an increase in the economic vulnerability of women and children in the United States. Poor single mothers experience a considerable degree of psychological stress (McLanahan & Booth, 1990). Most studies, however, have focused on the harmful toll that economic hardship takes on children. Research consistently shows that poverty increases the risk of poor nutrition and health problems (Brooks-Gunn & Duncan, 1997; Klerman, 1991), low school grades, repeating a grade, being suspended from school, dropping out of school (Brooks-Gunn & Duncan, 1997), and emotional and behavioral problems, including depression, low self-esteem, conduct disorders, and conflict with peers (McLoyd & Wilson, 1991).

Although an increase in child misery is of great concern, an even more critical issue is whether economic adversity in childhood results in problems that persist into adulthood. Evidence consistently indicates that this is the case. Studies show that adults who experienced poverty as children, compared with adults who did not, attain less education, hold lower status jobs, have more problems in their marriages, and report lower levels of subjective well-being

(Acock & Kiecolt, 1989; Amato & Booth, 1997; Brooks-Gunn & Duncan, 1997). McLanahan and Sandefur (1994) find that young adults who grew up with a single parent have lower levels of educational attainment, are more likely to be idle (no job and out of school), and are more likely to become single parents than are young adults who grew up with two parents. They also find that a large proportion of the estimated effect of growing up with single parents (up to half of the effect in some analyses) can be attributed to economic adversity in the family-of-origin. Their research clearly illustrates the links between single parenthood, poverty, and poor outcomes in adulthood.

The increase in child poverty has problematic implications, not only for individual children, but also for the society that one day will depend on these children. The first generation to experience high divorce rates (and the increase in family poverty) during the 1970s is reaching adulthood in the 1990s. As the baby-boomer cohort ages, the control of major social institutions will eventually be placed in the hands of younger cohorts with less human capital and fewer physical, psychological, and social resources on which to draw. Generational decline is especially disconcerting in the light of changes that are occurring in the U.S. economy. Employers argue that if the United States is to remain globally competitive, then it needs a better educated, more competent workforce to meet industry's growing need for technological and managerial skill (Holzer, 1996). Many children raised in poverty will be unable to meet this challenge.

In conclusion, we should keep in mind that several social trends, such as the decline in married men's wages during the 1970s and 1980s, helped to erode the economic well-being of children during the last few decades. Nevertheless, the growth of divorce and the rise of single- parent families played key roles in this decline. Of course, it also is true that economic hardship is a cause of marital conflict (Conger et al., 1990), as well as divorce (White, 1991) and nonmarital birth (Bianchi, 1995). But single parenthood makes it more difficult for the poor to escape from poverty, pulls many nonpoor into the ranks of poverty, and increases the likelihood that poverty will be reproduced in the next generation. Poverty and marital instability, therefore, are part of a mutually-reinforcing dynamic, with detrimental consequences for the lives of children.

Gender Equity

As the previous discussion implies, changes in family structure have implications for gender stratification. Since 1980, the gap in earned income has narrowed between men and women (Spain & Bianchi, 1996). This is good news, because it indicates that women have made progress in attaining economic parity with men. But although women are earning more money than ever before, they also are more likely to be single mothers. Indeed, demographers project that about one half of all women born in the 1980s will become single mothers prior to age 35, either through divorce or nonmarital birth (Spain & Bianchi, 1996, p. 40). As noted earlier, because most women retain primary financial responsibility for children, divorce typically results in greater economic hardship for women than men. Therefore, in spite of women's increased earnings, there has been a net decline in women's standard of living relative to men's during the last few decades (Spain & Bianchi, 1996, p. 143). The gender poverty gap would be considerably smaller if divorce and single parenthood were less common.

Some studies also suggest that the impact of marital disruption on children's educational attainment is stronger for daughters than for sons (Amato & Keith, 1991b). If this is true, then the generation of young women currently entering the labor force will face an additional obstacle to closing the earnings gap with men. Furthermore, daughters with divorced parents are more likely to become single mothers, either through divorce (Amato, 1996) or nonmarital birth (McLanahan & Sandefur, 1994), thus increasing their risk of economic hardship in adulthood. The high rate of divorce, therefore, is slowing down the pace at which women are able to narrow the gap in economic well-being between themselves and men.

To illustrate the role of family structure in affecting economic well-being, I carried out an analysis using the 1988 National Survey of Families and Households—a national probability sample of individuals in over 13,000 U.S. households (Sweet, Bumpass, & Call, 1988). For each person in the sample, I calculated an income-to-needs ratio, which is the total family income divided by the appropriate federal poverty threshold. (The poverty threshold is based on the number of related adults and children living together in a household.) With the data weighted to represent the U.S. population, the mean income-to-needs ratio was 3.79 for men and 3.35 for women. This result indicates that, overall, men experience a higher standard of living than women. When I controlled for household structure (married couple, cohabiting couple, single-parent household, other family household, single person living alone, and other nonfamily household), the gap between men and women was reduced by 44%. In other words, differences in household structure account for nearly half of the gender gap in economic well-being. And the major gender difference in household structure is that women are substantially more likely than men to be living with dependent children and no spouse present.

In summary, at the same time that increases in women's employment and earnings have improved the standard of living of childless women and married mothers, divorce is shifting large numbers of mothers into the ranks of the poor, thus undermining the movement toward gender equity. The high rate of marital disruption, therefore, is not only increasing the level of poverty in our society, but also subverting the progressive movement to achieve gender justice.

STRUCTURAL AND CULTURAL FACTORS

Women's Employment

As noted previously, married women and mothers have entered the labor force in increasingly large numbers during this century. Many observers have suggested that the increased labor force participation of women is an important factor—perhaps the most important factor—in explaining the rising rate of divorce (Cherlin, 1992; Furstenberg, 1994; Ruggles, 1997). According to this argument, women's economic independence decreases marital cohesion, lowers the gains associated with marriage, and makes it easier for wives to leave unhappy unions. A related argument is that the employment of wives and mothers increases the level of work-family conflict, as well as disagreements over the household division of labor, resulting in greater stress within marriage and a heightened risk of divorce.

Although women's labor force participation may have contributed to the rise in divorce, it is also plausible that the rise in divorce has contributed to the increase in women's labor force participation. In fact, the evidence for the proposition that women's economic independence is solely a cause (rather than a consequence) of marital instability is not as strong as many people think. Some studies show that wives' employment or income is positively associated with thoughts of seperation (Booth, White, Johnson, & Edwards, 1984) or divorce (Spitze & South, 1985). But it is difficult to establish the correct causal order between variables in most of these studies. In a recent longitudinal study, Rogers (1997) found that wives' perceptions of marital discord and thoughts of divorce *precede* their entry into the labor force. Another longitudinal study found that married women tend to increase their hours of employment *prior* to divorce (Johnson & Skinner, 1986). These studies suggest that many wives increase their labor force participation (and their economic independence) because they either fear or anticipate divorce. Indeed, to the extent that financial stress increases marital discord, wives' contributions to family income may strengthen, rather than undermine, marital quality and stability. Consistent with this notion, Greenstein (1990) found that wives' income was associated with a lowered risk of marital dissolution.

Additional support for the conclusion that women's employment and income do not undermine marriage comes from studies of the transition to marriage. In general, if economic independence increases wives' ability to leave unhappy marriages, then it should also slow down the rate at which they enter marriage in the first place. Because economically independent women do not need to marry, they can take more time to search for an appropriate spouse, or forgo marriage altogether if they wish. However, studies generally show that women's education, employment, and earnings *increase* their likelihood of marriage (Goldscheider & Waite, 1991; Lichter, McLaughlin, Kephart, & Landry, 1992; Oppenheimer, 1994). Given that the earnings of many men have declined since 1973, it is not surprising that women's ability to earn income increases their chances of marrying; it takes two incomes to attain a desirable standard of living these days, and many couples will not marry unless they feel financially secure. Curiously, the very factors that allow women to live independently of men also facilitate their transition to marriage.

Many reasons underlie women's long-term movement into the labor force, including increases in women's education, the growth of the service sector of the economy (which disproportionately employs women), and the influence of the feminist movement. Nevertheless, it is likely that many women enter, re-enter, or remain continuously in the labor force—and increase their potential for economic independence—because they are aware of the high rate of divorce. The spread of no-fault divorce, in which the process of marital dissolution can be initiated by one partner against the opposition of the other, may have exacerbated this trend (Parkman, 1995). Indeed, the continuous employment of women is increasingly necessary in a society in which women cannot count on the life-long economic support of husbands (Bumpass, 1990). Women have lower earnings than men largely because their employment histories have more stops and starts, with departures from the labor force occurring during the childbearing years, and returns to the labor force occurring when children reach school age (Spain & Bianchi, 1996). Although the number of mothers with infants who remain in the labor force has increased in recent years, about half of employed married women continue to exit the labor force for a period after the birth of their first child. Married mothers who quit their jobs lose seniority and their occupational skills deteriorate, resulting in declines in future income-earning potential. Consequently, dropping out of the paid labor force (or even decreasing one's hours of employment) requires a substantial degree of trust that one's husband will provide lifelong economic support. The high rate of divorce, the disappearance of alimony (except for short-term rehabilitative alimony) and the failure of many men to pay child support are sobering reality checks for women who are contemplating leaving the labor force after marriage or parenthood.

It is likely that the high rate of divorce is leading many women, especially those with children, to remain in the labor force against their wishes, or to work longer hours than they would prefer. Of course, most women work because they want to be employed. But about one sixth of employed wives would prefer not to be in the labor force at all (Bumpass, 1990). As long as the divorce rate remains high, however, it is in all married women's best interest to remain continuously in paid employment. This is true regardless of marital quality. A high rate of marital dissolution introduces an element of instability into all marriages; even happily married couples cannot assume that their spouses will be with them for a lifetime.

The realization that wives cannot count on the lifelong economic support of husbands may be strengthening the career orientations of young unmarried women. Increasing numbers of young women are rejecting the housewife role because they recognize that it is too risky. Girls growing up in divorced families learn this lesson firsthand. Following divorce, many daughters not only experience economic hardship, but also observe their mother's adoption of the sole breadwinner role. As a result, many daughters from divorced families plan careers to ensure that they will never be economically dependent on men. Consistent with this notion, Goldscheider and Waite (1991) found that growing up with a single mother is associated with a stronger employment orientation among young women, as well as fewer desired children.

The high rate of divorce, therefore, has worked to push women out of the homemaker role and into paid employment. In general, this movement has resulted in an increase in the status and power of women in U.S. society. Most people would view this as a positive outcome. But the effects of marital dissolution on women's status are paradoxical. Women who marry and remain married are most likely to benefit from the increase in women's employment and earnings, as they are able to pool incomes with their husbands and benefit from economies of scale. In contrast, women who experience divorce are disadvantaged economically, as are women who give birth to children outside of marriage. The high rates of divorce and single parenthood, therefore, have increased the degree of economic stratification among women, with the greatest cleavage occurring between married and single mothers.

Cultural Values

Although American culture has always stressed individualism, some observers claim that we have become even more individualistic in recent decades (Bellah, Madsen, Sullivan, Swidler, & Tipton, 1985). For example, Popenoe (1996, p. 46) argued that the individualism of earlier eras involved a balance between the pursuit of self-interest and responsiveness to the community, but today's unencumbered individualism is devoted to the pursuit of self-interest at the expense of the community. Some social scientists believe that this new individualism has undermined the stability of marriage. According to Norval Glenn (1996), the grown of hedonistic individualism has led people to adopt unrealistically high expectations about the degree of personal fulfillment they expect from a relationship. At the same time, a weak commitment to the norm of lifelong marriage has made people less willing to make the sacrifices and investments necessary to ensure marital success. The single-minded pursuit of happiness, therefore, results in people moving from one marriage to another in search of the perfect match—a goal that most people will never attain.

Consistent with the notion of greater individualism, attitude surveys reveal that the percentage of people who agree that personal happiness is more important than putting up with an unhappy marriage increased since the 1960s and now represents the majority view (Thornton, 1989). Earlier in our history, most people believed that marriage had intrinsic religious and social significance that transcended the needs of individuals. Consequently, maintaining a lifelong bond was of paramount importance, even if the couple was unhappy. In contrast, people today are less prepared to sacrifice personal happiness for the sake of continuing a marriage. Marriage is viable only to the extent that it promotes individual happiness; without happiness, the rationale for marriage disappears.

Whether this change in attitudes represents a new form of radical individualism is debatable. Nevertheless, it is reasonable to ask if this change has had an impact on marital quality and stability. Amato and Rogers (1997), in a longitudinal study, found that people who became more strongly committed to the norm of lifelong marriage (and less accepting of divorce) experienced increases in marital happiness and declines in marital conflict, whereas people who became less strongly committed to the norm of lifelong marriage (and more accepting of divorce) experienced declines in marital happiness and increases in marital conflict. This finding is consistent with Glenn's (1996) assumption that individualistic attitudes may, over time, undermine marital quality. In another longitudinal study, Amato (1996) found that married people who hold a strong commitment to the norm of lifelong marriage are less likely to divorce than are people with a weak commitment. Taken together, these findings suggest that shifts in the larger culture toward a more individualistic approach to marriage (and away from the belief that marital stability is more important than the happiness of individuals) may be increasing the overall level of marital discord and instability.

Cultural explanations always beg the question of the source of cultural change. Why are people these days less committed to the norm of lifelong marriage and more accepting of divorce? One possibility—and one not usually considered by cultural theorists—is that the increase in marital instability may be contributing to (as well as one of the results of) a growing culture of individualism. Two longitudinal studies show that individuals tend to adopt more liberal attitudes toward divorce *following* marital dissolution (Amato & Booth, 1991; Thornton, 1985). This finding is consistent with the social psychological principle that people often change their attitudes to make them congruent with their behavior. In addition, adults who experienced parental divorce as children tend to have relatively accepting attitudes toward divorce, presumably because they saw their own parents turn to divorce as a solution to an unhappy marriage (Amato & Booth, 1991). Even people who have not had direct experience with divorce (either their own or their parents') are likely to know of friends, relatives, or coworkers who have divorced. The constant exposure to divorce, inevitable in a society with a high divorce rate, is likely to reinforce the notion that most marriages no longer last a lifetime. Given the impermanence of most marriages, it makes sense for people to put their own needs before those of the relationship. These considerations suggest that the high level of marital instability may be a driving force behind the greater public acceptance of divorce, as well as a more individualistic orientation to marriage.

This argument does not necessarily contradict the thesis that changes in culture have contributed to the rise in divorce. As behavior previously defined as deviant becomes more common, public acceptance is likely to grow, and public acceptance, in turn, is likely to result in further increases in the behavior. Changes in culture and changes in behavior often reinforce one another. The employment of married mothers, for example, has probably followed a similar dynamic, with increases in employment resulting in a relaxation of public disapproval, and the relaxation of public disapproval, in turn, resulting in more employment.

The mutually reinforcing effects of individualism and marital instability can be demonstrated in relation to changes in gender roles within marriage. For example, wives are increasingly aware that dropping out of the labor force when they have children, or cutting back on their hours of employment, is risky if their husbands can initiate divorce at any time. Why should women sacrifice their income-earning potential without a guarantee of lifetime support from their husbands? To do so in a high divorce society would be irrational. At the same time, many wives' satisfaction would increase, and children would be better off, if more fathers took on an equal share of family work. But, in a high divorce society, men (like women) may be reluctant to cut back on their hours of employment and invest more time in their families. In other words, the high rate of marital instability may be creating a situation in which neither women nor men are willing to compromise their economic independence for the sake of the marriage. Thus, the high divorce rate has created a social trap. Marriage might become more stable if men increased their investment is marriage and family life, but men are unlikely to increase their investment as long as marriage is unstable (and hence, a risky venture). Knowing that they are unlikely to obtain custody following divorce, some fathers also may see their relationships with children as fragile and impermanent. Similarly, men and women may be reluctant to invest the time and energy in resolving marital disagreements if they know that divorce is an easy alternative.

Therefore, although some have argued that a culture of individualism promotes divorce, it is also true that a high rate of divorce promotes a culture of individualism. Once divorce becomes normative, as it is in our own society, it may well create the very culture that makes a high divorce rate self-perpetuating.

CONCLUSION

In this chapter, I have attempted to delineate some of the consequences of living in a high divorce rate society. Available evidence suggests that pervasive marital instability (and single parenthood) in the United States has lowered the age at which young people become sexually active, increased the frequency of nonmarital cohabitation (as well as the number of intimate relationships people have over a lifetime), weakened ties across generations (especially between fathers and children), broadened (but also diluted) people's kinship networks, increased the number of children living in poverty, undermined progress toward gender equality, strengthened women's labor force participation, and tilted our culture toward greater individualism. However, a systems perspective reminds us that most social trends are determined by multiple factors, so it would be a mistake to assume that divorce has been the single, monolithic force driving these transformations—a mistake often made by conservative critics who see divorce as the fundamental cause of all social problems.

A systems perspective also suggests that cause and effect relationships tend to be circular. In the present case, many of the outcomes of divorce—increases in poverty, women's growing economic independence, and greater public acceptance of marital dissolution—also have increased the rate of divorce. The list of factors that increase divorce can be extended to include early premarital sexual activity (Laumann, Ganong, Michael, & Michaels, 1994), fragile ties with parents in adulthood (Booth & Edwards, 1992), and weak kin support networks (Booth, Edwards, & Johnson, 1991). This is the manner in which a system operates, with feedback loops being common. Yet, most prior analyses have emphasized only half of the picture, viewing divorce as a phenomenon to be explained rather than as a factor that reciprocally determines other social processes.

Finally, a systems perspective suggests that periods of rapid change tend to be followed by a new equilibrium. Indeed, the trends described above represent the emergence of a new family pattern in American society—a pattern involving weaker ties between sex, childbearing, and marriage; a more vulnerable marriage bond; a more vulnerable father-child bond; a more individualistic orientation on the part of men and women; and greater relationship turnover.

Many of the effects of divorce noted above, such as an increase in the extent of family poverty and a weakening of intergenerational ties, are problematic. In contrast, most people value the freedom granted by current divorce laws to leave unhappy marriages and have a second chance at happiness—a freedom not available to previous generations. Similarly, the growing attachment of wives and mothers to the paid labor force has improved women's economic standing and given them greater power within marriage and the broader society—another positive outcome. One cannot say, therefore, that the increase in marital dissolution has been unequivocally bad.

The consequences of divorce, however, tend to look somewhat different depending on whether one adopts an adult-centered or a child-centered view. For example, consider the fact that most people these days have multiple intimate relationships, either through serial cohabitation, serial marriage, or a combination of the two. Perhaps this is a natural. Intimate relationships may be inherently fragile and unstable, and lifelong bonds may be common only when society forces couples to stay together. Indeed, the current pattern of serial monogamy may meet the needs of many adults better than one in which lifelong marriage is coerced. But it is unlikely that serial monogamy best meets the needs of most children. Virtually all available research shows that children develop best when reared by two biological parents who have a cooperative long-term relationship. Divorce may not be a major problem for children if divorces are conducted amicably, if children's ties with parents are not disrupted, and if children's postdivorce economic needs are met. Indeed, many of the policies described elsewhere in this volume (for example, policies regarding mediation, custody determination, and child support) are intended to make divorce a less disturbing ordeal for children. But regardless of how many protections are built into the legal system, as happy two-parent families become increasingly rare, many children will fall through the cracks and suffer.

Overall, many of the consequences of living in a high divorce rate society are serious enough that we should consider whether it is possible to shift the system back toward greater marital stability. In fact, a large number of states are considering legislation that is intended to decrease the number of divorces; many would achieve this through initiating a lengthy waiting period or returning to an exclusively fault-based system. But changing the legal system to make it more difficult for couples to dissolve their marriages is problematic for several reasons. First, creating barriers to divorce would trap more children in highly conflicted families, and research indicates that children are better off, in the long run, if they go through a divorce than if they are exposed to persistent, unresolved conflict (Amato & Booth, 1997). Returning to a fault-based system is especially problematic, as this would make the process of divorce even more acrimonious, with negative consequences for children. Second, restricting access to divorce will almost certainly increase the number of informal separations. And from a child's perspective, parental separation is little better than divorce. Indeed, some evidence indicates that separated mothers are more psychologically stressed and experience greater economic hardship than divorced mothers (Amato, in press)—outcomes that bode poorly for children's development. Finally, putting legal barriers in the way of divorce does little to address the underlying problem, that so many couples these days are unhappy with their marriages and want to terminate them. The ideal way to lower the divorce rate is to strengthen the institution of marriage to the point where fewer people want to divorce.

Therefore, although we need to think carefully about policies that minimize the potential damage of divorce, we also need to consider policies that provide greater resources to couples (especially those with children) whose marriages are at risk. Some marriages are unsalvageable, and expedited divorces are appropriate in these cases. But other marriages might be saved if sufficient supports were available. These supports include marriage counseling, work-place policies that decrease work-family conflict, affordable child care, and economic support. In relation to the last point, the Earned Income Tax Credit for working poor families is an example of a program that provides valuable economic assistance to couples. Expanding the Earned Income Tax Credit, as the Clinton administration recently did, has probably strengthened many at-risk marriages.

The goal of strengthening marriage is one that should appeal to the political left as well as the political right. Liberals tend to believe that divorce has increased people's freedom to have a second chance at happiness. Yet, many people are no happier the second time around, and second marriages are even more likely than first marriages to end in divorce. Feminists tend to see divorce as a positive reflection of women's rising status and ability to live independently of men. Yet, divorce has increased the extent of poverty among women and reduced fathers' involvement with their children—outcomes that are inconsistent with the feminist vision. Some divorces have happy endings, but many do not. Strengthening marriage does not have to mean a return to the patriarchal family of an earlier era—an idea promoted by conservative religious movements such as Promise Keepers. Indeed, greater marital stability will only come about when men are willing to share power, as well as housework and childcare, equally with women.

Furthermore, if we are serious about strengthening marriage, then we should extend the right to marry to *all* adults, including gay and lesbian couples. An unknown but large number of children are being raised in these types of families. Marriage would confer legitimacy and stability on these relationships, thus benefitting children as well as parents. Such a change in the law would also provide an important symbolic recognition of the fact that our society continues to value marriage as an institution within which children are raised. No child should be denied the right to reside with married parents because his or her parents are gay or lesbian.

In conclusion, the high level of marital instability in the U.S. has affected the lives of virtually every citizen. Furthermore, divorce is shaping personal, structural, and cultural conditions in the U.S. in ways that tend to make marital instability self-perpetuating. Consequently, any attempts to lower the rate of divorce, either through restricting access to divorce or strengthening marriage, are likely to have only a modest impact. Nevertheless, even small increases in marital quality and stability have the potential to benefit large numbers of children. And over the long haul, substantial change is possible. In the meantime, the long-term consequences of living in a postdivorce society will become clearer as new cohorts of children make the transition to adulthood.

REFERENCES

Acock, A. C., & Kiecolt, K. J. (1989). Is it family structure or socioeconomic status? Family structure during adolescence and adult adjustment. *Social Forces, 68,* 553-571.

Amato, P. R. (1987). *Children in Australian families: The growth of competence.* Sydney: Prentice Hall of Australia.

Amato, P. R. (1994a). Father-child relations, mother-child relations, and offspring psychological well-being in early adulthood. *Journal of Marriage and the Family, 56,* 1031-1042.

Amato, P. R. (1994b). The implications of research findings on children in stepfamilies. In A. Booth & J. Dunn (Eds.), *Stepfamilies: Who benefits? Who does not?* (pp. 81-87). Hillsdale, NJ: Lawrence Erlbaum.

Amato, P. R. (1996). Explaining the intergenerational transmission of divorce. *Journal of Marriage and the Family, 58,* 628-641.

Amato, P. R. (in press). Diversity among single-parent families. In D. H. Demo, K. R. Allen, & M. A. Fine (Eds.), *Handbook of family diversity.* New York: Oxford University Press.

Amato, P. R., & Booth, A. (1991). The consequences of divorce for attitudes toward divorce. *Journal of Family Issues, 12,* 306-322.

Amato, P. R., & Booth, A. (1997). *A generation at risk: Growing up in an era of family upheaval.* Cambridge, MA: Harvard University Press.

Amato, P. R., & Keith, B. (1991a). Consequences of parental divorce for children's well-being: A meta-analysis. *Psychological Bulletin, 110,* 26-46.

Amato, P. R., & Keith, B. (1991b). Parental divorce and adult well-being: A meta-analysis. *Journal of Marriage and the Family, 53,* 43-58.

Amato, P. R., Rezac, S. J., & Booth, A. (1995). Helping between parents and young adult offspring: The role of parental marital quality, divorce, and remarriage. *Journal of Marriage and the Family, 57,* 363-374.

Amato, P. R., & Rogers, S. J. (1997). *Do attitudes toward divorce affect marital quality?* Paper presented at the meeting of the American Sociological Association, Toronto.

Aquilino, W. S. (1991). Family structure and home-leaving: A further specification of the relationship. *Journal of Marriage and the Family, 53,* 999-1010.

Aquilino, W. S. (1994). Impact of childhood family disruption on young adults' relationships with parents. *Journal of Marriage and the Family, 56,* 295-313.

Axinn, W. G., & Barber, J. S. (1997). Living arrangements and family formation attitudes in early adulthood. *Journal of Marriage and the Family, 59,* 595-611.

Bellah, R. N., Madsen, R., Sullivan, W. M., Swidler, A., & Tipton, S. M. (1985). *Habits of the heart: Individualism and commitment in American life.* Berkeley, CA: University of California Press.

Betson, D. M., & Michael, R. T. (1997). Why so many children are poor. *Future of Children,7,* 25-39.

Bianchi, S. M. (1995). The changing demographic and socioeconomic characteristics of single-parent families. *Marriage and Family Review, 20,* 71-97.

Bogenschneider, K. (1997). Parental involvement in adolescent schooling: A proximal process with transcontextual validity. *Journal of Marriage and the Family, 59,* 718-734.

Booth, A., Brinkerhoff, D., & White, L. K. (1984). The impact of parental divorce on courtship. *Journal of Marriage and the Family, 46,* 85-94.

Booth, A., & Edwards, J. N. (1992). Starting over: Why remarriages are more unstable. *Journal of Family Issues, 13,* 179-194.

Booth, A., Edwards, J. N., & Johnson, D. (1991). Social integration and divorce. *Social Forces, 70,* 207-224.

Booth, A. & Johnson, D. R. (1988). Premarital cohibation and marital success. *Journal of Family Issues, 9,* 255-272.

Booth, A., Johnson, D. R., White, L., & Edwards, J. N. (1984). Women, outside employment, and marital instability. *American Journal of Sociology, 90,* 567-583.

Brooks-Gunn, J., & Duncan, G. J. (1997). The effects of poverty on children. *Future of Children, 7,* 55-71.

Buchanan, C. M., Maccoby, E. E., & Dornbusch, S. M. (1996). *Adolsecents after divorce.* Cambridge, MA: Harvard University Press.

Bumpass, L. L. (1984). Children and marital disruption: A replication and update. *Demography, 21,* 71-82.

Bumpass, L. L. (1990). What's happening to the family? Interactions between demographic and institutional change. *Demography, 27,* 483-498.

Bumpass, L. L., & Raley, R. K. (1995). Redefining single-parent families: Cohabitation and changing family reality. *Demography, 32,* 97-110.

Bumpass, L. L., & Sweet, J. A. (1989). National estimates of cohabitation: Cohort levels and union stability. *Demography, 25,* 615-625.

Castro, M. T., & Bumpass, L. L. (1989). Recent trends in marital disruption. *Demography, 26,* 37-51.

Cherlin, A. J. (1992). *Marriage, divorce, remarriage.* Cambridge, MA: Harvard University Press.

Cherlin, A. J., & Furstenberg, F. F., Jr. (1992). The new American grandparent: A place in the family, a life apart. Cambridge, MA: Harvard University Press.

Conger, R., Elder, G. H., Jr., Lorenz, F. O., Conger, K. J., Simons, R. L., Whitbeck, L. B., Huck, S., Melby, J. M. (1990). Linking economic hardship to marital quality and instability. *Journal of Marriage and the Family, 52,* 643-656.

Cooney, T. M. (1994). Young adults' relations with parents: The influence of recent parental divorce. *Journal of Marriage and the Family, 56,* 45-56.

Eggebeen, D. J., & Lichter, D. (1991). Family structure and changing poverty among American children. *American Sociological Review, 56,* 801-817.

Eggebeen, D. J., & Uhlenberg, P. (1985). Changes in the organization of men's lives. *Family Relations, 34,* 251-257.

Furstenberg, F. F., Jr. (1994). History and current status of divorce in the United States. *The Future of Children, 4,* 29-43.

Furstenberg, F. F., Jr., & Spanier, G. (1984). *Recycling the family: Remarriage after divorce.* Beverly Hills, CA: Sage.

Furstenberg, F. F., Jr. (1987). The new extended family: The experience of parents and children after remarriage. In K. Pasley & M. Ihinger-Tallman (eds.), *Remarriage and stepparenting: Current research and theory* (pp. 42-61). New York: Guilford Press.

Furstenberg, F. F., Jr., Nord, C. W., Peterson, J. L., & Zill, N. (1983). The life course of children of divorce. *American Sociological Review, 8,* 656-668.

Furstenberg, F. F. Jr., Hoffman, S. D., & Shrestha, L. (1995). The effect of divorce on intergenerational transfers: New evidence. *Demography, 32,* 319-333.

Glenn, N. (1996). Values, attitudes, and the state of American marriage. In D. Popenoe, J. B. Elshtain, & D. Blankenhorn (Eds.), *Promises to keep: Decline and renewal of marriage in America* (pp. 15-34). Lanham, Maryland: Rowman and Littlefield.

Glick, P. C. (1989). Remarried families, stepfamilies, and stepchildren: A brief demographic profile. *Family Relations, 38,* 24-27.

Goldscheider, F. K., & Goldscheider, C. (1991). The intergenerational flow of income: Family structure and the status of black Americans. *Journal of Marriage and the Family, 53,* 499- 508.

Goldscheider, F. K., & Waite, L. J. (1991). *New families, no families: The transformation of the American home.* Berkeley, CA: University of California Press.

Greenstein, T. N. (1990). Marital disruption and the employment of married women. *Journal of Marriage and the Family, 2,* 657-676.

Hetherington, E. M. (1972). Effects of father absence on personality development in adolescent daughters. *Developmental Psychology, 7,* 313-326.

Hetherington, E. M., & Clingempeel, W. G. (1992). *Coping with Marital Transitions.* Monographs of the Society for Research in Child Development, Vol. 57, No. 2-3. Chicago, IL: University of Chicago Press.

Hetherington, E. M., & Henderson, S. H. (1997). Fathers in stepfamilies. In M. E. Lamb (Ed.), *The role of the father in child development* (3rd ed., pp. 212-226). New York: Wiley.

Hetherington, E. M. & Jodl, K. M. (1994). Stepfamilies as settings for child development. In A. Booth and J. Dunn (Eds.), *Stepfamilies: Who benefits? Who does not?* (pp. 55-79). Hillsdale, NJ: Lawrence Erlbaum.

Hoffman, S. D., & Duncan, G. J. (1988). What are the economic consequences of divorce? *Demography, 25,* 641-645.

Holzer, H. J. (1996). *What employers want: Job prospects for less educated workers.* New York: Russell Sage Foundation.

Johnson, W. R., & Skinner, J. (1986). Labor supply and marital separation. *American Economic Review, 76,* 455-469.

Kiernan, K. (1992). The impact of family disruption in childhood on transitions made in young adult life. *Population Studies, 46,* 218-234.

Kitson, G. C. (1990). *Portrait of divorce: Adjustment to marital breakdown.* New York: Guilford.

Klerman, L. V. (1991). The health status of poor children: Problems and programs. In A. C. Huston (Ed.), *Children in Poverty: Child Development and Public Policy* (pp. 136-157). Cambridge, MA: Cambridge University Press.

Lamb, M. E. (1997). Fathers and child development: An introductory overview and guide. In M. E. Lamb (Ed.), *The role of the father in child development* (3rd ed. pp. 1-18). New York: John Wiley.

Laumann, E. O., Gagnon, J. H., Michael, R. T., & Michaels, S. (1994). *The social organization of sexuality.* Chicago, IL: University of Chicago Press.

Lichter, D. T., Mclaughlin, D. K., Kephart, G., & Landry, D. J. (1992). Race and the retreat from marriage: A shortage of marriageable men? *American Sociological Review, 57,* 781-799.

Mastekaasa, A. (1994). marital status, distress, and well-being: An international comparison. *Journal of Comparative Family Studies, 25,* 181-205.

McLanahan S. S., & Booth, K. (1989). Mother-only families: Problems, prospects, and politics. *Journal of Marriage and the Family, 51,* 557-80.

McLanahan, S. S., & Sandefur, G. (1994). *Growing up with a single parent: What hurts, what helps.* Cambridge, MA: Harvard University Press.

McLoyd, V. C., & Wilson, L. (1991). The strain of living poor: Parenting, social support, and child mental health. In A. C. Huston (Ed.), *Children in poverty: Child development and public policy* (pp. 105-135). Cambridge, MA: Cambridge University Press.

Mott, F. L., Fondell, M. M., Ju, P. N., Kowaleski-Jones, L., & Menaghan, E. G. (1996). The determinants of first sex by age 14 in a high-risk adolescent population. *Family Planning Perspectives, 28,* 13-18.

Oppenheimer, V. K. (1994). Women's rising employment and the future of the family in industrial societies. *Population and Development Review, 20,* 293-342.

Parkman, A. M. (1995). The deterioration of the family: A law and economics perspective. In G. B. Melton (Ed.), *The individual, the family, and social good: Personal fulfillment in times of change* (Nebraska Symposium on Motivation, Vol 42). Lincoln, NE: University of Nebraska Press.

Pleck, J. H. (1997). Paternal involvement: Levels, sources, and consequences. In M. E. Lamb (Ed.), *The role of the father in child development* (3rd ed. pp. 66-103). New York: John Wiley.

Popenoe, D. (1996). *Life without father.* New York: Free Press

Preston, S. H., & McDonald, J. (1979). The incidence of divorce within cohorts of American marriages contracted since the Civil War. *Demography, 16,* 1-26.

Rogers, S. J. (1997). *Women's income and marital quality: Are there reciprocal effects?* Unpublished manuscript, Department of Sociology, University of Nebraska-Lincoln.

Ross, C. E. (1995). Reconceptualizing marital status as a continuum of social attachment. *Journal of Marriage and the Family, 57,* 1129-1140.

Rossi, A. S., & Rossi, P. H. (1990). *Of human bonding: Parent-child relations across the life course.* Hawthorne, NY: Aldine de Gruyter.

Ruggles, S. (1997). The rise of divorce and separation in the United States, 1880-1990. *Demography, 34,* 455-466.

Seltzer, J. A, & Bianchi, S. M. (1988). Children's contact with absent parents. *Journal of Marriage and the Family, 50,* 663-677.

Snarey, J. (1993). *How fathers care for the next generation.* Cambridge, MA: Harvard University Press.

Spain, D., & Bianchi, S. M. (1996). *Balancing act: Motherhood, marriage, and employment among American women.* New York: Russell Sage.

Spitze, G., & South, S. J. (1985). Women's employment, time expenditure, and divorce. *Journal of Family Issues, 6,* 307-329.

Sweet, J., Bumpass, L. L., & Call, V. (1988). The design and content of the National Survey of Families and Households. Center for Demography and Ecology, University of Wisconsin, Madison.

Teachman, J. D., & Paasch, K. M. 1994. Financial impact of divorce on children and their families. *Future of Children, 4,* 63-83.

Thomson, E., McLanahan, S. S., & Curtin, R. B. (1992). Family structure, gender, and parental socialization. *Journal of Marriage and the Family, 54,* 368-378.

Thornton, A. (1985). Changing attitudes toward separation and divorce: Causes and consequences. *American Journal of Sociology, 90,* 856-872.

Thornton, A. (1989). Changing attitudes toward family issues in the United States. *Journal of Marriage and the Family, 51,* 873-894.

U.S. Bureau of the Census. (1992). *Current Population Reports. Households, families, and children: A 30-year perspective* (p. 23-181). Washington, DC: U.S. Government Printing Office.

U.S. Bureau of the Census. (1996). *Statistical Abstract of the United States* (116th ed.). Washington, DC: U.S. Government Printing Office.

Waite, L. J. (1995). Does marriage matter? *Demography, 32,* 483-507.

White, L. K. (1991). Determinants of divorce. In A. Booth (Ed.), *Contemporary families* (pp. 141-149). Minneapolis, MN: National Council on Family Relations.

White, L. K. (1994). Stepfamilies over the life course: Social support. In A. Booth & J. Dunn (Eds.), *Stepfamilies: Who benefits? Who does not?* (pp. 109-137). Hillsdale NJ: Lawrence Erlbaum.

White, L. K., & Booth, A. (1985). The quality and stability of remarriages: The role of stepchildren. *American Sociological Review, 50,* 689-698.

White, L. K., & Reidmann, A. (1992). When the Brady Bunch grows up: Step/half- and fullsibling relationships in adulthood. *Journal of Marriage and the Family, 54,* 197-208.

Widmer, E. D. (1997). Influence of older siblings on initiation of sexual intercourse. *Journal of Marriage and the Family, 59,* 928-938.

Chapter 8

Values, Policy, and Research on Divorce
Seeking Fairness for Children

Ross A. Thompson and Jennifer M. Wyatt

The postdivorce family is becoming a new American social institution. Divorce and single parenthood have, of course, long been part of domestic life, but the recent stabilization of divorce rates at historically high levels means that the postdivorce family has become an increasingly normative, and accepted, feature of American life. Nearly everyone has either first hand experience with divorce or knows others who have. Nearly everyone has observed the effects of divorce and considered its personal impact, whether actual or potential. As a consequence, adults approach marriage, and children experience family life, in ways that are meaningfully different than were true of past generations. The significance of this for individuals, families, and society is one of the more important topics of contemporary family scholarship, and the contributors to this volume explore this question from different orientations and viewpoints.

Recent public and scholarly attention to the postdivorce family derives not only from its prominence in domestic life. There is also concern about how best

AUTHORS' NOTE: We are grateful for thoughtful comments from Paul Amato on an earlier draft of this article, and also for provocative ideas from Gary Melton that inspired some of its themes.

to support family members when they make the transition to postdivorce life. This is a more challenging goal than may initially appear because the consequences of divorce are complex and multifaceted. Research on divorce outcomes, especially for children, shows that it is neither the straightforward panacea nor the disaster for family members that it has been portrayed in the past. Divorce offers parents and offspring escape from family conflict but entry into an uncertain and contingent future. That future is shaped by the efforts of family members to begin new lives in the context of the continuing obligations that survive divorce, as well as the support they experience from friends and relatives, and the formal and informal public policies that influence family life. The chapters of this volume reflect the challenges of applying research concerning divorce to the creation of supports and incentives that can potentially enable the postdivorce family to function well as an environment for nurturing offspring.

In this light, another reason for interest in the postdivorce family concerns its relevance to policy reform. Are contemporary families well-served by current laws and procedures governing divorce? What are the benefits and disadvantages of how custody, visitation, and child support guidelines are designed and implemented? How would proposed policy reforms contribute either to reducing the incidence of divorce (assuming this is a desirable goal), diminishing its detriments to children, or improving postdivorce family functioning? In the context of growing public concern about the effects of divorce on children and families, debate about policy reform reflects the importance of public policy in shaping family life (for good or ill), and the uncertainty of estimating its current and future effects.

In this final chapter of the volume, the dual themes of research and policy concerning postdivorce family life are reconsidered in light of the values underlying current public discourse about divorce and its outcomes, especially for children. Our goal is to examine the contemporary debate concerning the meaning and consequences of divorce, and the future of divorce policy, in light of broader public beliefs about the family. Much of this debate focuses on the values that are expressed or implied in contemporary American attitudes toward divorce, and whether these reflect the decline of marriage, the broadening of the family, or changing regard for family life. Thus, in the next section the relationship between divorce and values concerning the family is profiled in light of the conflicting, and sometimes complementary, views of conservative and liberal family scholarship. The new Louisiana Covenant Marriage Law is also discussed as one response of policymakers to this renewed concern about divorce and its outcomes, and what it reveals about values and the policymaking process. The interaction between values, policy, and research on divorce is then examined with respect to three questions that underlie the chapters of this volume concerning (1) how children are affected by divorce, (2) the allocation of parental care in postdivorce life, and (3) the role of fathers. The perspectives of the contributors to this volume, along with those of other researchers, are considered. Finally, several suggestions for a renewed scholarship of the post-divorce family are offered in a concluding comment.

Divorce and Contemporary Values

Divorce compels public attention because the process of divorce reflects social values concerning the family. In its approach to the end of marriage as well as its beginning, society enunciates its regard for family life. Thus incorporated into the formal policies and informal procedures governing divorce are assumptions concerning marital and parental roles and responsibilities, the nature of children and their needs, how to equitably divide the material and human capital that are merged in a marriage, and the role of the public sector in managing family relationships and resources when couples part, and providing incentives for them to remain together. Divorce practices and policies do not reflect enduring truths about the family so much as they reveal current social values about the family that form the basis for standards concerning marital dissolution, parental caregiving, and property.

This has been true throughout American history. From the colonial period to the present, divorce and custody standards have changed significantly over time to express prevailing cultural values concerning family roles and relationships (Mason, 1994). During the eighteenth century, for example, when legitimate offspring were encompassed within paternal property rights, custody of children was unquestioningly assumed by fathers. By contrast, a century later when children (especially during their young, "tender years") were widely regarded as requiring maternal nurturance, custody was equally unquestioningly awarded predominantly to mothers. Historically, standards governing the allocation of marital property, postdivorce economic support, and even the basis for divorce itself—requiring fault assignments or not, for example—have evolved considerably in accord with changing social values. Especially with regard to the family, the law has an expressive function that both reflects and institutionalizes prevalent values and beliefs.

As social conditions change and values evolve, public policies change accordingly. When these changes occur within a relatively short period, they can be controversial. Therefore, another reason for heightened recent attention to divorce is that the divorce rate has risen in concert with a constellation of changing social values concerning gender, marriage, and parenting that have also contributed to the reconceptualization of divorce. Concurrent with the escalation of divorce since the 1960s, for example, evolving values concerning the importance of mothering and fathering have fueled reconsideration of custody standards, legal versus physical custody, the benefits of joint custody, and visitation arrangements. At the same time, growing concern about the status of single mothers and their offspring has provoked new debate over child support guidelines, conceptualizations of property division, and renewed attention to transitional spousal support (traditionally conceived alimony) after divorce. As the postdivorce family has become normative, concerns about its stability underlie reform proposals concerning the process of divorce (encouraging mediation or detailed parenting plans) and its aftermath (including new ways of conceptualizing custody and visitation to emphasize shared parental responsibility to offspring). More broadly, values and assumptions about why people remain married and why couples divorce, and the incentives and disincentives offered by public policies, frame a broader debate about the deinstitutionalization of marriage and the effects of no-fault divorce on family stability. The current climate of public and scholarly discourse over divorce is one of significant social change, evolving public policies, and vigorous debate concerning social values relating to marriage, gender, and parental care. It is a combustible combination.

This is not restricted to the United States. It is a broader phenomenon, as divorce laws and practices in many countries are being revised to reflect changing social values and conditions. In many Western European countries, for example, divorce has not only become easier to obtain but the conditions of divorce have evolved as parents are increasingly encouraged to assume shared decision-making authority in postdivorce life, child support awards and their enforcement have been strengthened, and transitional spousal support is becoming less common (Fine & Fine, 1994; Glendon, 1989). These trends generally parallel those that have occurred in the United States. Perhaps the most dramatic change in divorce laws accompanying changing social conditions and values occured recently in the Republic of Ireland, where voters in 1995 narrowly approved a public referendum providing for civil divorce for the first time. A similar referendum had been resoundingly defeated less than 10 years earlier.

Its approval in 1995 reflected not only the diminished influence of the Catholic Church on public opinion on this issue but other influences, including increased urbanization, diminishing traditionalism concerning family matters, and an effort to modernize Irish domestic laws by bringing them closer to those of other countries in the European Union (Christopher, 1995). Although the political processes influencing divorce reform are local, the broader social changes instigating these reforms, and the evolving public values supporting them, are international.

The Meaning of Divorce

In the United States, where the divorce rate is highest among Western nations and where roughly half of first marriages end in divorce, attention has focused on the *meaning* of divorce for children, families, and society. Does divorce reflect the continuing plurality of family forms in the postmodern world, consistent with other social changes that have altered traditional views of gender, parental care, and marriage? Does divorce reveal stresses in the social and economic foundations of family life that diminish the incentives that keep marriage intact and increase its vulnerability? Does divorce indicate that adults have changed in some fundamental way in their commitment to relationships, families, and children? Given the breadth of these questions and their implications for divorce policy, it is unsurprising that there has been vigorous public and scholarly debate in the "national family wars" (Giele, 1996; Popenoe, 1993a).

Cultural Critique

According to one influential group of family scholars, divorce in America must be interpreted in the context of other cultural changes, especially the growth of nonmarital childbearing and cohabitation, that together reflect the deinstitutionalization of marriage in contemporary culture (Council on Families in America, 1995; Gallagher, 1996a, 1996b; Galston, 1996, 1997; Glenn, 1996; Mack, 1997; Popenoe, 1993b, 1996a, 1996b; Whitehead, 1996, 1997; see also Schneider, 1994, 1996). Marriage is threatened as a social institution, in this view, because of a preeminent emphasis on individual fulfillment in relationships that makes the maintenance of marriage contingent on current happiness rather than on a sense of responsibility and commitment to a partner and offspring. As a consequence, high rates of divorce and nonmarital childbearing "suggest a trend toward a 'postmarriage' society, marked by the decline of marriage as a childrearing institution and the rise of a more voluntary system of family relationships with easily dissoluble ties and more contingent and limited commitments" (Whitehead, 1996, p. 5). In other words, traditional values of community and responsibility to others have become supplanted by an emphasis on individual self-determination and fulfillment.

The deinstitutionalization of marriage has, in this conservative view, profound consequences for how adults experience marriage and how families function. Even if young adults enter marriage with no expectation of divorce (Baker & Emery, 1993), their observations of others' marriages and their knowledge of the demographics cannot but instill caution in their expectations for the future. Marital satisfaction suffers as adults anticipate more from marriage—expecting their partners to work toward their personal happiness and well-being—but do not anticipate that this will necessarily be a lifelong commitment (Glenn, 1996). Even if they do, their realization that divorce is a real possibility and observations of its consequences for others may cause spouses to make certain choices that they otherwise might not. Parkman (1995, 1998), for example, argues that one reason for escalating rates of dual-career families is the recognition by women that career assets provide a hedge against the economic detriments if divorce should occur (see Chapter 7 for research supporting this view). Parkman argues further that one reason why many men do not correspondingly increase their domestic and child-rearing involvement when their wives work is their implicit awareness that doing so does not comparably enhance their own marital and postdivorce assets. Although most couples do not enter marriage anticipating divorce, therefore, the "culture of divorce" is nevertheless likely to influence marital decisionmaking and partners' relative investment in their marriages, offspring, and careers.

Because children depend on the well-being of the family, these scholars argue that the deinstitutionalization of marriage is likely to have the most significant detriments for children. And indeed, it does. The poverty rate for children is now higher than for any other age group in the United States, and the increase in child poverty in recent decades is directly tied to the growth of single-parent households resulting from divorce and nonmarital childbearing (Betson & Michael, 1997; Eggebeen & Lichter, 1991; O'Neill, 1997). Children growing up with a single parent are hindered in other ways: they are more likely to drop out of high school and college, are more likely to become teen parents, and are more likely to be idle (without a job and out of school) in young adulthood compared with children growing up in two-parent families (McLanahan & Sandefur, 1994). Although many of the disadvantages of single parenthood are attributable to financial adversity, these outcomes underscore children's reliance on the economic and social support of a well-functioning family for healthy development and well-being. To family scholars concerned about the decline of marriage as a childrearing institution, the growth of divorce and the rise of nonmarital childbearing confirm that Dan Quayle was right (Whitehead, 1993): the two-parent family requires greater support.

The focus of this critique of cultural values is no-fault divorce, portrayed as unilateral divorce on demand by its detractors. By providing for less litigious divorce without fault assignment, no-fault divorce makes divorce easier and favors the spouse who seeks an escape from a difficult marriage over the partner who is being left. This causes divorce to occur when couples might otherwise strive to work out their problems, according to this analysis, and no-fault divorce also undermines the economic considerations in divorce (such as property division) that might otherwise compensate an abandoned spouse. Most importantly, no-fault divorce devalues marriage in a society "where it is legally easier and less risky to dump a wife than to fire an employee" (Gallagher, 1996b, p. 242).

Consequently, reform proposals emphasize changing the basis for legal divorce in several ways, especially for couples with minor children, to increase the disincentives to divorce, strengthen the position of partners who wish to remain married, and raise the moral stature of marriage. These include providing for no-fault divorce only by mutual consent (with fault-based divorce an alternative option when partners disagree about parting), imposing waiting periods of several years for contested no-fault divorces, and allowing couples to enter into marital covenants that restrict or eliminate altogether the grounds for divorce (see, for example, Gallagher, 1996a; Galston, 1997; Schneider, 1996). Other proposals include providing for no-fault divorce but using fault-based grounds for property allocation and determinations of spousal support, and mandatory mediation or counseling during the process of divorce with an emphasis on reconciliation and marital preservation rather than predivorce counseling.

Other reform proposals seek to revitalize and reinstitutionalize marriage as a stable and attractive avenue for couples (see especially Council on Families in America, 1995; Galston, 1996, 1997; Whitehead, 1997). Some advocates would institute premarital requirements, such as mandatory counseling or a waiting period, to promote better preparation and more thoughtful entry into marriage. Others emphasize strengthening the economic supports to families with children by increasing the child tax credit, reducing the marriage penalty in the tax system, raising the Earned Income Tax Credit, and other tax-based avenues. Other proposals include economic and social incentives to adolescents for completing high school as a buffer against early marriage and childbearing, and to increase their employment prospects after graduation.

A final set of reform proposals are significantly more far-reaching. The reinvigoration of fatherhood is viewed by some scholars as an essential part of reinstitutionalizing marriage and strengthening the two-parent family (Blankenhorn, 1995; Popenoe, 1996a, 1996b). A paternal recommitment to marriage and childrearing would reduce the escalation of nonmarital childbearing as well as curbing divorce, in this analysis, and help to ensure that children live with two (presumably married) adults who are each committed to their well-being. Fatherhood is important to society not only for its benefits to children, these scholars argue, but to men as well because fatherhood "domesticates masculinity" by reducing the propensity for male violence, deviance, and crime. Men who are committed to their wives and offspring are, in their view, less likely to engage in dangerous, deviant behavior than men who are not. In this analysis, however, the civilizing effect of fatherhood on men derives from their assumption of traditional marital gender roles in which "men prove their manhood by being good fathers" and loving husbands (Blankenhorn, 1995, p. 225). Consistent with the views recently advocated by groups like Promise Keepers, these scholars argue that traditional values of protecting the family, providing for its material needs, exerting leadership at home and instilling instrumentalism and toughness in offspring constitute the basis for a renewed ethic of masculine fatherhood necessary for the regeneration of a "marriage culture."

Emphasizing values of commitment and fidelity, this conservative analysis evaluates the meaning of divorce in terms of cultural critique and proposes reforms that strengthen two-parent families and traditional family roles. The focus is on preventing divorce before it occurs. But cultural critique is a tricky analysis. During the same period that Americans became increasingly accepting of divorce, cohabitation, and extramarital childbearing, they became less tolerant of extramarital sexuality and continued to value marriage and marital childbearing (Thornton, 1989, 1996). This suggests that the perceived importance of fidelity within relationships has been changing in more complex and nuanced ways than the conservative analysis suggests. Americans seem to value commitment within relationships while recognizing that sometimes relationships cannot—and perhaps should not—endure. More generally, an alternative group of family scholars argues that rather than reflecting a retreat from commitment, family change during the past several decades reveals plurality over decline in family functioning, and that traditional models of the family are an idealized fiction that provide no basis for cultural critique.

Socioeconomic Analysis

Divorce has different meaning within this liberal analysis (Coontz, 1992, 1997; Kain, 1990; Mahoney, 1995; Skolnick, 1991; Stacey, 1990, 1993, 1996). To some feminist scholars, divorce reflects positive changes in women's power and independence from men. To other liberal scholars, divorce arises from the impact of social and economic changes on family life. The rate of divorce has risen in concert with profound social changes that have affected the American family, including a revolution in reproductive technology, changes in gender (marital and childrearing) roles, a shift to a postindustrial service economy that has eroded the financial security of many families, and a significant increase in dual-earner families as a hedge against economic insecurity (Cherlin, 1992; Furstenberg, 1994; White, 1991). Taken together, these have contributed to marital instability as marital satisfaction has been threatened by economic uncertainty, changing marital expectations, and changing and conflicting gender-role expectations. These changes have been particularly important for women, who are more likely than men to initiate divorce (Goode, 1956; Gunter, 1977; Kitson, 1992; Spanier & Thompson, 1984). Women have returned to the workplace as wives and mothers, striving to balance childbearing and childrearing with domestic and career demands, and instituting changes in gender role expectations at home and the workplace. By contrast with their economic dependency on husbands of the previous generation, moreover, women today also have less reason to tolerate bad marriages and possess greater career assets to draw upon if divorce should occur, although they also suffer significant economic disadvantages when their marriages end.

The decline in marriage has, in other words, economic as well as cultural bases. The same is true of the rise in nonmarital childbearing which has coincided with the deteriorating employment status of poorly educated male workers in the new postindustrial economy. Young women are more likely to have children outside of marriage, these scholars argue, when the young men whom they might otherwise marry have little to offer in economic or social support because of their bleak prospects for consistent, well-paid employment (Williams, 1990; Wilson, 1987). The life circumstances of young women in socioeconomically disadvantaged conditions provide few incentives to wait either for marriage or parenthood. In this analysis, therefore, changes in family life begin with changes in the economic status of men and women.

As a consequence, the traditional two-parent family is no longer statistically normative in American life as dual-career families, single-parent families, stepfamilies, and nonmarital families have become more common. To some feminist scholars, this has resulted in laudable plurality in family forms that can accommodate greater diversity in gender roles, culture, and class, and diminished patriarchy in family life (Stacey, 1990, 1993, 1996). To most other liberal scholars, however, enthusiasm for the plurality of "family" is tempered by concern with its human consequences. Although women often initiate divorce, they typically enter postdivorce life with fewer career assets, enhanced childrearing responsibilities, and at a significant economic disadvantage compared with their former spouses (Weitzman, 1985; see also Hoffman & Duncan, 1988; Peterson, 1996; and Teachman & Paasch, 1994). Their offspring are also disadvantaged. Like the conservatives, liberal family scholars are worried about the material and developmental costs of divorce and nonmarital childbearing for children. They are also concerned about the diminishing investment of parental time and attention that accompanies life in a single-parent home or in a dual-earner family, where parents are often consumed by the demands of economic and domestic activity, leaving insufficient amounts even of "quality time" for offspring. The answer, argue these family scholars, is not the restigmatization of divorce and single parenthood and hearkening back to an idealized traditional family that is "the way we never were" (Coontz, 1992). Like the changes in gender roles, broadened reproductive decision making, and increased marital dual-earning that have accompanied them, they argue, changes in the family are unlikely to be reversed. Wise social policy will accommodate instead and provide support to those most vulnerable to harm.

Rather than preventing divorce from occurring, therefore, the focus of reform in the liberal analysis is on addressing its consequences, primarily through economic support for single mothers and their children. Linking the decline in the economic status of children to the "feminization of poverty" that has accompanied rising rates of divorce and nonmarital childbearing, these scholars argue that most of the difficulties that children face in single-parent homes derive from the economic stresses with which their mothers must cope. Buffer the economic problems of single mothers, according to this analysis, and it becomes easier for these families to function well as settings for child nurturance. Consistent with this analysis, therefore, considerable reform effort has been devoted to obtaining financial support from fathers in the establishment of higher, uniform child support guidelines and more rigorous enforcement procedures combined, in the case of nonmarital childbearing, with stronger efforts to establish paternity of offspring at birth (Roberts, 1994). These efforts culminated in the Family Support Act of 1988, which required states to establish uniform guidelines for judges to use in setting child support awards, institute routine withholding of child support obligations, and create computerized tracking and monitoring of compliance. A further proposed reform in child support is an assured benefit system in which the offspring of low-income parents are assisted by a government subsidy when the child support payments provided by the father fall below a guaranteed minimum level (Garfinkel, Meli, & Robertson, 1994).

Other proposed reforms in divorce policy are also oriented to its economic consequences for women and children (Carbone, 1994; Sugarman, 1990). They include proposals, such as those of Mary Ann Glendon (1981, 1986, 1989), that property allocation for divorces when children are involved adopt a "children-first principle" in which no property is divided between former spouses until allocations to address children's needs have been made (see also Fineman, 1991). They include revised concepts of marital property that encompass both the human as well as the material capital accumulated during marriage, and whose division includes consideration of nontangibles like career assets. They include reconsideration of traditional conceptualizations of alimony to provide for either temporary transitional spousal support after divorce or more enduring income-sharing based on marital partners' joint contributions to career development, as well as compensation for the career opportunities forsaken for child rearing. The overarching goal of these reforms is to ensure the well-being of children and to reward the parent (typically the mother) who invests more heavily in childrearing responsibilities during the marriage with financial benefits that reflect her contributions to her spouse and offspring.

Liberal family scholars also advocate noneconomic provisions related to divorce that are also intended to support women and children. Preeminent among these are more explicit standards for child custody to more clearly articulate the "best interests of the child" in a manner that protects children's needs and ensures support for postdivorce childrearing from both parents (see Chapters 3 and 4 in this volume; Scott, 1992). Consistent with this, the development of detailed parenting plans during divorce negotiations is also advocated as a basis for former spouses, but continuing parents, to agree concerning their ongoing responsibilities to offspring in postdivorce life.

More broadly, family scholars who emphasize the economic as well as the cultural sources of family decline also advocate reforms in public policy that would enable two-parent families to function more effectively (Coontz, 1997; Skolnick, 1991; Stacey, 1993). These include workplace policies that grant parents greater flexibility to attend to family needs (extending the provisions of the 1993 Family and Medical Leave Act), broadened assistance to ensure health care coverage to children and low-income families, enhanced job training and job creation programs to improve the employment prospects of underedu-cated young adults, and the development of a national system of high quality yet affordable child care. Not surprisingly, these proposals envision a consid-erable role for public policy in providing economic, as well as moral, assistance to the family.

Assessing Values and Assumptions

Although there are sharp differences between the cultural critique of conser-vative family scholars and the economic analysis of liberals, scholars from each group recognize the combination of social and the economic forces that have changed family life during the past four decades. Moreover, scholars from each group are preeminently concerned with the adverse effects of divorce and single parenthood on children, whose victimization by the consequences of divorce is least justifiable. Furthermore, it is important not to unduly polarize the views of advocates within each group. Many feminist scholars are, for example, also critical of no-fault divorce because it undermines the economic safeguards traditionally accorded women who are divorced after having devoted years to child-rearing and poses other risks to women (e.g., Brinig & Crafton, 1994; Fineman, 1991; Mason, 1988; see also Parkman, 1992). Meanwhile, some conservatives have thoughtfully analyzed the economic and sociodemographic conditions that have contributed to increases in divorce and nonmarital child-bearing (e.g., Galston, 1996, 1997).

Nevertheless, there are important differences in many features of the conser-vative and liberal analysis of the changing American family. Conservative and liberal family scholars differ in their assessment of why divorce has increased, the extent to which the rise in the divorce rate reflects public policy initiatives (particularly the advent of no-fault divorce) rather than broader socioeconomic conditions, whether (and how easily) current rates of divorce can be reversed, and whether necessary remedies are primarily hortatory or economic. They differ, sometimes sharply, in their portrayal of the extremity of the detriments of divorce and nonmarital childbearing for children, and the extent to which these harms are remediable through various kinds of family assistance. There are also important differences between scholars within these intellectual groups in their regard for the relative roles of mothers and fathers in advancing the well-being of offspring, and their perceptions of the weaknesses, and strengths, of single-parent families.

Perhaps most important, conservative and liberal family scholars differ in the values that guide their goals, risk preferences, and preferred avenues for enlisting public policy to advance family welfare. By contrast with many particulars in their analysis of family change, these value assumptions are not readily subject to empirical analysis. With respect to goals, the conservative emphasis on promoting fidelity to relational commitments (especially of adults to offspring) contrasts with the liberal emphasis on providing assistance to families in need (especially economically disadvantaged women and children). With respect to risk preferences, scholars from both groups exhibit an admirably preeminent concern for the welfare of children. However, there are significant differences in the risks incorporated into their proposed reforms that advocates from each group are willing to accept or tolerate. Conservatives who underscore reforms in no-fault divorce seem willing to accept the potential harms to children that may derive from living in conflicted, but nondivorced, families which may result from their proposed limits in the grounds for divorce. Liberals, by contrast, emphasize support for single parents but appear ready to tolerate the high divorce rate and the potential harms to children growing up in a postdivorce society and its influences on marital expectations, family functioning, and intimate relationships (see Chapter 7 in this volume). Family advocates from conservative and liberal groups differ sharply in their values concerning the risks that are tolerable for children in the context of their proposed remedies for family problems. Finally, conservatives and liberals also differ in their regard for the role of government activity in family life. The conservative analysis emphasizes the hortatory value of the incentives and disincentives arising from current (no-fault) and proposed divorce policy, while liberals underscore the importance of direct economic assistance and legal protections for vulnerable groups. Many of these differences in value orientation are, of course, consistent with the broader political philosophies of conservative and liberal advocates of the family.

There are other value assumptions that distinguish these alternative portrayals of family change. These include the relative emphasis of scholars in each group on ensuring individual self-determination in matters of marriage, childrearing, and other intimate relationships, and the desirability of ensuring plurality in family structure over normative prescriptions guided by child-oriented considerations. Taken together, it is clear that values assume a central role in shaping current scholarly and public discourse concerning the meaning of divorce, just as they have done so throughout American history. This is hardly surprising, because family life reflects fundamental beliefs about who we are as individuals and how we relate to others (and to the state) that have special meaning to citizens of this country. This helps to explain why fundamental differences in views of the family and of marital decline perhaps inevitably generate heated debate. But emphasizing the values underlying current scholarship and debate about the family highlights the uneasy relation between values and research in shaping public policy concerning divorce, and the realization that scholarship reflects both empirical realities and values assumptions.

There are some who believe that the "national family wars" are coming to a close as a centrist consensus of scholarship is pointing to some common conclusions concerning the causes of family change during the past 40 years, and potentially helpful responses that public policy reforms can offer (Galston, 1997). Although this may be true, public policy continues to be shaped by the polemics of recent years. Liberal analysis of the family has tended to guide divorce policy reform of the past decade, most notably in federal initiatives such as the Family Support Act of 1988 and the Family and Medical Leave Act of 1993, but also in a broad range of state-level reforms of child custody standards, child support guidelines, and rules for settling property division and other economic provisions of divorce. More recently, conservative voices have become preeminent influences in shaping new policies concerning the grounds for divorce itself, especially in restricting no-fault policies. The most visible of these was the Louisiana Covenant Marriage Law of 1997.

The Louisiana Covenant Marriage Law

Policy analysts, whether conservative or liberal, commonly argue that one of the benefits of the federalist system is that states can serve as laboratories of social policy. Innovations in welfare reform, education, neighborhood crime reduction, and other domestic policies can be explored in experimental initiatives on a state-by-state basis, the results of which are closely observed throughout the country to determine whether reform proposals merit implementation elsewhere, or should instead be abandoned or modified. Such a view is well-suited to proposed reforms in marital and divorce law which are, like other domestic policies, governed at the state rather than the federal level. As a consequence of local advocacy, for example, several states have revised divorce statutes in recent years to more explicitly incorporate domestic violence considerations into provisions for divorce and child custody, require the parents of minor children to participate in predivorce mediation, and incorporate provisions concerning joint custody into child custody guidelines.

In this spirit, on July 15, 1997, Governor Mike Foster quietly signed into state law a bill creating a two-tiered marriage system for the state of Louisiana with the words, "only time will tell if it's going to work" ("Foster Signs Law Setting Up Covenant Marriages in State," *Morning Advocate,* Baton Rouge, LA, July 16, 1997). Prior to its enactment on August 15, 1997, the Covenant Marriage Law commanded very little attention in the state and local media. Since that time, however, it has become representative of the broader national debate concerning the effects of no-fault divorce on family integrity and the reform proposals offered by conservative family advocates. The provisions of this legislation and the process by which it was passed are each instructive concerning the values and assumptions guiding the broader national debate, as well as the political process involved in divorce law reform.

The primary authors of the Covenant Marriage Law, Republican State Representative Tony Perkins and Louisiana State University law professor Katherine Shaw Spaht, envisioned a law intended to strengthen marriage by encouraging couples to consider their marital commitments more seriously and deliberately, and to reduce the divorce rate by providing for a form of marriage with restrictions on the grounds for divorce. Both were concerned about the impact of divorce on children and especially the association between divorce and child poverty, adolescent pregnancy, and juvenile delinquency. The evocative longitudinal research on children of divorce by Judith Wallerstein and her colleagues (Wallerstein & Blakeslee, 1989, 1995; Wallerstein & Kelly, 1980) was especially influential to Perkins and Spaht as documentation of the serious and longstanding harms suffered by children as a result of divorce ("Bound by Love," August 20, 1997; Spaht, 1997). Although the idea of a binding, yet voluntary, antenuptial agreement between couples intending marriage was a novel legislative approach to divorce reform, it was thoughtfully anticipated in an influential law review article by University of Virginia Professor Elizabeth Scott (1990), and legislators in a number of other states, including Michigan and Iowa, had also proposed reform initiatives constraining prevailing no-fault divorce statutes (Leland, 1996).

The Covenant Marriage Law requires couples intending to marry in Louisiana to choose between two types of marriage: a standard marriage or a covenant marriage. In order to obtain a covenant marriage, couples must first obtain premarital counseling that emphasizes the seriousness, lifelong commitment, and responsibilities of covenant marriage, and discusses the limited grounds for legally terminating a covenant marriage by divorce. They must also make a declaration of their understanding that covenant marriage is for life, and must assert their intent to "take all reasonable efforts" (including marital counseling) to preserve their marriage if difficulties later arise. Under the provisions of the Covenant Marriage Law, couples who have already been married under standard marital provisions may redesignate their marriages as covenant marriages after obtaining counseling and participating in a renewal of marital vows.

A divorce is more difficult to obtain in a covenant marriage. Under the law, only a non-offending spouse may obtain a divorce upon proof of the partner's adultery, felony imprisonment, abandonment (for a period of a year or longer), or physical or sexual abuse of the spouse or child. A divorce can also be granted if the couple has lived apart continuously for 2 years; if they become legally separated, this period is reduced to one year if the couple is childless, but is reduced only to 18 months if minor children are involved. A legal separation in a covenant marriage can occur on the basis of the conditions listed above, but may also be granted because of the "habitual intemperance" of the other spouse that makes living together "insupportable." By contrast, under conventional no-fault provisions of a standard marriage in Louisiana, a divorce may occur after a couple has lived apart for 180 days.

The covenant marriage thus emphasizes fault-based grounds for marital termination and, by permitting only the non-offending spouse to petition for divorce, fault considerations presumably also enter into child custody determinations, property settlement, visitation rights, child support, spousal support, and other divorce-related decisions. But the covenant marriage may also be terminated after a 2-year period of living apart, which is a surprising provision in light of the fact that this period (although longer than the 180 days for the termination of a standard marriage in Louisiana) is comparable to the waiting period required for obtaining a standard divorce in many other states. Interestingly, although much of the justification for an alternative covenantal marital agreement is because of the costs of divorce to children, relatively few provisions of the Covenant Marriage Law distinguish between marriages with children and those without. In sum, although couples entering into a covenant marriage make a commitment in which they "are sacrificing selfish interests in advance of a higher purpose" (Spaht, 1997, p. 26), divorce is neither impossible nor particularly difficult even when children are involved.

This may help to explain the relatively brief, and noncontroversial, legislative history of the Covenant Marriage Act. Introduced on March 31, 1997 by Representatives Perkins and Jim Donelon, the Act received little action until the last two months of the legislative session. It was reported from the House Committee on Civil Law and Procedure on May 7. In floor debate on May 28, Perkins amended the measure to broaden the grounds for divorce in a covenant marriage to include a spouse's felony imprisonment. The Act passed the House on the same day. In the Senate, the Committee on Judiciary A (which handles, among others, issues related to marriage and divorce) amended the Covenant Marriage Act in several ways. First, a notarized document was required from the premarital counselor that the required features of covenant marriage had been discussed in counseling, partly to limit the counselor's liability against a divorcing couple who subsequently wished to seek legal liability and damages from the counselor. Second, the Committee reduced the waiting time after a legal separation for a divorce in a covenant marriage from 18 months to 1 year in situations when child abuse was the basis for fault-based divorce. Third, "habitual intemperance" was incorporated into the grounds for divorce in a covenant marriage (this provision was later shifted to grounds for separation, not divorce). A final amendment required the production and distribution of an informational pamphlet explaining the terms of the covenant marriage, to be used in premarital counseling and other situations.

The amended Act was reported from the Senate Committee on June 10. Six days later, the measure was amended on the Senate floor to further expand the grounds for divorce in a covenant marriage to include the physical or sexual abuse of a spouse. Together with the amendments proposed by committee, the legislation was passed by a vote of 28-9 in the Senate the same day. On June 20, however, the House unanimously refused to concur with the Senate amendments, so the Act was sent to conference committee. On June 23, the final day of the legislative session, the conference committee reported a bill that retained most of the provisions of the Senate version, and this bill was adopted by both the House and the Senate with only one dissenting vote on the same day. Remarkably, the conference committee also included a further amendment in the Act requiring that couples seeking a covenant marriage recite the following statement (those seeking to redesignate an existing marriage as a covenant marriage were required to recite a slightly modified version):

A COVENANT MARRIAGE

We do solemnly declare that marriage is a covenant between a man and a woman who agree to live together as husband and wife for so long as they both may live. We have chosen each other carefully and disclosed to one another everything which could adversely affect the decision to enter into this marriage. We have received premarital counseling on the nature, purposes, and responsibilities of marriage. We have read the Covenant Marriage Act, and we understand that a Covenant Marriage is for life. If we experience marital difficulties, we commit ourselves to take all reasonable efforts to preserve our marriage, including marital counseling.

With full knowledge of what this commitment means, we do hereby declare that our marriage will be bound by Louisiana law on Covenant Marriages and we promise to love, honor, and care for one another as husband and wife for the rest of our lives.

Within 2 days, Governor Mike Foster (who is himself divorced and remarried) announced that he would sign the bill ("Churches Weighing 'Covenant Marriage,'" *Times-Picayune,* Baton Rouge, LA, June 25, 1997).

Despite disagreements between House and Senate versions of the bill, the swift passage of the Covenant Marriage Law with little legislative debate in Louisiana contrasts with the experience in the state of Washington when a similar bill restricting no-fault divorce was considered by the legislature in 1995 (Whitman, 1996). The Washington bill was similar to the Louisiana initiative in many ways: it would have given couples the option of signing an antenuptial agreement that would eliminate no-fault divorce, along with other provisions. Moreover, it appeared to enjoy public support as well as the sponsorship of the Republican leadership of the House of Representatives, who had a large legislative majority. Nevertheless, the bill was defeated in the House after floor debate raised concerns about the extent to which the process of fault-based divorce would heighten family conflict that could prove damaging to children, and the potential harm to women of remaining in conflictual marriages when specific grounds for fault-based divorce did not exist. In the end, moderate Republicans, especially women, crossed party lines to defeat the bill (Whitman, 1996).

Perhaps instructed by the Washington experience, the legislative history of the Louisiana Covenant Marriage Act shows that the grounds for fault-based divorce in covenant marriage were progressively expanded through amendments to provide protection to abused spouses and their offspring (as well as to provide for divorce in the event of a partner's felony imprisonment) to reduce some of the potential risks of fault-based divorce provisions. In the latter stages of the legislative process, moreover, the bill was also amended to incorporate provisions for divorce if the couple had merely lived apart for a 2-year period. Although the practical restrictions on divorce were progressively weakened, the hortatory significance of the law was strengthened, especially in the later addition of a pledge that all couples seeking a covenant marriage are required to recite. Thus the legislative process resulted in a bill with strong symbolic statements concerning marital integrity, but also with significantly broadened grounds for divorce. While important limitations in the provisions of the Act remain (most notably, in the failure to better differentiate marriages with offspring from those without), these compromises contributed significantly to the passage of the bill. As in Washington, the Louisiana Covenant Marriage Act received little media attention prior to its approval by the legislature, and this also may have resulted from a deliberate strategy to avoid publicity and controversy. According to John Crouch of Americans for Divorce Reform, proponents did not involve interest groups (either conservative or liberal), but instead worked with individual legislators to achieve a compromise bill that would achieve near-unanimous support (Crouch, personal communication, December 2, 1997).

The public debate that might have been anticipated over such a significant change in divorce law did not emerge until after the Louisiana Covenant Marriage Act had been signed into law by the governor. Considerable initial media attention focused on the response of church leaders, particularly of the Catholic Church (in this predominantly Catholic state), to the provisions of a bill that supported traditional religious values concerning marriage. In light of the requirements of premarital counseling and the commitment to marriage for life, which are consistent with the beliefs of many religious denominations, some proponents of the Act hoped that only covenant marriages would be recognized by the Catholic Church. Despite positive comments by some Catholic bishops prior to the passage of the bill, however, the first formal response of the Louisiana Catholic Conference in a pastoral statement on October 29, 1997 was disappointing to the supporters of covenant marriage. The statement declared that both standard and covenant marriages were acceptable to the church. More importantly, Catholic ministers were prohibited from providing the required premarital counseling for a covenant marriage since counselors were required by law to discuss the provisions for divorce, contrary to the Church's teaching. As a result, Catholics choosing covenant marriage would have to participate in premarital counseling in the church and also receive independent state-approved counseling prior to marriage. Leaders of other religious denominations, including United Methodist, Southern Baptist, and Episcopal churches, while affirming the sanctity of marriage, also expressed reservations about specific provisions of the Covenant Marriage Law ("Bishops Back Off Covenant Marriage," *Times-Picayune,* Baton Rouge, LA, October 30, 1997).

At the same time, national commentators have engaged in vigorous debate concerning the meaning and impact of covenant marriage in Louisiana. These include proponents such as leaders of the communitarian movement (Etzioni & Rubin, 1997; Galston, 1997), conservative Republicans and religious groups, and the Christian Coalition, and opponents which include representatives of feminist groups (Applewhite, 1997; Pollitt, 1997) and the ACLU (Carlson, 1997; Leland, 1996; Sack, 1997). Feminists have been divided on covenant marriage, with some opposed to the restrictions on divorce that can increase the emotional and financial costs of divorce and make divorce more difficult in cases of domestic violence, but others drawn to the fault-based provisions that might improve women's leverage in divorce negotiations concerning spousal support, property, and child support. In the meantime, legislators in other states, including Georgia, Idaho, Illinois, Iowa, Nebraska, Pennsylvania, and Virginia, have begun to prepare bills that curtail no-fault divorce with provisions that are similar to those of the Louisiana law (Leland, 1996).

What has been the impact of the Covenant Marriage Law on marriages in Louisiana? In the month after the law took effect on August 15, 1997, only 26 covenant marriage licenses had been issued out of a total of 3,000 licenses, according to Louisiana officials ("Covenant Marriages Slow-Going in State," *Times-Picayune,* Baton Rouge, LA, October 19, 1997). According to interviews with couples applying for marriage licenses, many young people felt that the designation of a covenant marriage would make little difference to the depth of commitment they felt toward each other, and those advising these couples were skeptical of the restrictions on divorce. In the words of one father of a bride-to-be, "If it doesn't work out, I want them to get a speedy divorce" ("Covenant Marriage Has No Takers on its First Day," *Times-Picayune,* Baton Rouge, LA, August 16, 1997).

The Louisiana Covenant Marriage Law illustrates how critical are the values and assumptions guiding assessments of family change in shaping the rhetoric and politics of marital and divorce reform. Consistent with the analysis of conservative family scholars, the perceived problem of divorce in Louisiana was addressed through a collection of provisions intended to encourage more thoughtful, deliberative entry into marriage and to promote longer-lasting marriages by restricting the grounds for fault-based divorce. Distinguishing between standard and covenant marriages (or "marriage lite" and "high-octane marriage" to wags) provided a basis for enlisting the moral voice of the community in couples' choices concerning marital commitment. Little attention was devoted to the economic circumstances of single-parent families after divorce occurs, however, and only in the later stages of legislative debate did attention focus on the special circumstances of women that may require a quick exit from a difficult or dangerous marriage. Interestingly, proponents who were galvanized by research reports concerning the experience of children of divorce crafted a measure that was intended to strengthen marriage and reduce the incidence of divorce, but with surprising little attention to the specific needs of marriages with minor children. The Act rarely differentiates between couples with dependent minors and couples who are childless.

The Covenant Marriage Act overwhelmingly passed legislative scrutiny when similar measures have failed in other states for at least two reasons. First, its proponents accepted amendments broadening the grounds for divorce in covenant marriage—even including a 2-year period of living apart, comparable to standard divorce provisions in other states—while strengthening the hortatory provisions of the law in a statement that couples entering covenant marriage must recite that resembles traditional marriage vows. Thus the law retained its rhetorical value while broadening the grounds for divorce to increase legislative support. Second, its proponents made the fault-based divorce requirements of covenant marriage an option, not a requirement, of marriage in Louisiana. In so doing, they respected the emphasis on self-determination and resistance to governmental restrictions on personal liberty that have long been paramount values to Americans, especially in the south.

As a laboratory in democracy, Louisiana's experiment with covenant marriage is being closely watched by legislators, family scholars, and policymakers in other states. Its provisions are, however, currently being incorporated into legal initiatives elsewhere long before it is possible to determine whether covenant marriage actually promotes marriage, and decreases divorce, as it was intended to do. Perhaps that is just as well. As an experiment, the Louisiana covenant marriage plan is flawed, of course, by the selection bias inherent in each couple's choice of either standard or covenant marriage. Although it is likely that future analysts will find that couples in covenant marriages tend to divorce less often than those with standard marital agreements, in other words, it will be impossible to know whether this is attributable to the marriage covenant itself or instead because these couples were already more committed to a lifelong union. It will thus be difficult to know from this experiment in marital law whether covenant marriages would be good for all couples who marry, not just those who choose it because of their preexisting beliefs and commitments.

VALUES, POLICY, AND THE
ROLE OF RESEARCH

In light of the preeminence of the values, beliefs, and risk preferences of policymakers, what is the role of research in shaping divorce policy? Do studies of child and family development and research on the impact of divorce have a meaningful contribution to guiding the future course of divorce reform? If so, what is the nature of that contribution?

It is arguable that contemporary research on family change has had a significant role in the current debate on marriage and divorce. Conservative and liberal family scholars have often cited important and well-publicized studies of the impact of single parenting on child development (Eggebeen & Lichter, 1991; Fuchs & Reklis, 1992; McLanahan & Sandefur, 1994), the economic detriments of divorce for women (Weitzman, 1985), the effects of child custody, visitation, and child support arrangements on children's well-being (Hetherington & Clingempeel, 1992; Hetherington, Cox, & Cox, 1982; Maccoby & Mnookin, 1992), and the declining role of fathers postdivorce (Furstenberg & Nord, 1985; Furstenberg, Nord, Peterson, & Zill, 1983) as reasons for greatly needed reforms in divorce policy. As a consequence of this research, nobody seriously argues anymore that children are unaffected by their parents' divorce, or that they reap unequivocal benefits from the end of an unhappy marriage. Prominent among these studies has been the longitudinal research on children of divorce by Judith Wallerstein and her colleagues that is often cited to document the enduring harms that children suffer from marital dissolution (Wallerstein & Blakeslee, 1989, 1995; Wallerstein & Kelly, 1980). Indeed, the focus of the chapters in this volume on the impact of divorce on children, the importance of custody, child support, and other divorce-related arrangements to their well-being, the postdivorce role of fathers, and related issues, reflects the importance of these research topics to divorce policy.

To be sure, the results of research are interpreted in terms of the values, assumptions about human behavior, expectations of the future, and risk preferences of the policy analyst. This is why conservative and liberal family scholars attach such different significance to studies revealing, for instance, the economic and psychosocial difficulties experienced by many children after divorce—with some arguing that discouragement of divorce should be the focus of policy reform, and others indicating that greater economic and social assistance to single parents should be the focus. As noted earlier, these values, expectations, and risk preferences assume an important role in the policy debate concerning divorce, but they also shape the interpretation—and thus the impact—of research findings. Research means different things from different values orientations. Moreover, divorce policy reform inevitably encompasses broader considerations, such as the budgetary impact of reform proposals, or their relevance to child care policies, welfare reform, tax incentives, or other issues that introduce complementary or competing priorities to the divorce policy debate. Sometimes the budgetary implications of reform proposals diminish their support; on other occasions the possibility of addressing multiple problems in reform measures enhances their appeal. One of the reasons, for example, for recent federal and state initiatives to strengthen child support enforcement was to enhance the economic resources of single mothers and, as an important consequence, to reduce their dependence on public assistance and shrink welfare expenditures (see Seltzer, McLanahan, & Hanson, in press). These additional considerations also have a legitimate role in policy debate, but they introduce influences that may compete with those arising from research. For these reasons, it is common to find research results enlisted into the rhetorical arsenal of policy advocates, even when the findings are dated or controversial among researchers, primarily because they support a particular viewpoint or policy position.[1] This tendency, although frustrating to researchers, merely highlights the multifaceted influences on public policymaking, not the unimportance of research on divorce.

Moreover, as Weiss (1978, 1987), Caplan (1979), and other students of research utilization by policymakers have noted, social research has considerable relevance to policy besides its direct applications to solving social problems (see also Thompson, 1993). Social research findings often frame the manner in which problems are conceptualized by influencing, for example, beliefs about children's needs, how the quality of marital relationships leads to family integrity or divorce, the contributions of mothers and fathers to child development, and others issues related to the family. For example, current concern about the failure of many fathers to remain involved in the lives of their offspring derives, in part, from research on the social and economic contributions of fathers to child well-being (see Lamb, this volume). Quite often, the assumptions implicitly adopted by policymakers derive from the "knowledge creep" by which social research findings become absorbed into the policymaking community through the mass media, presentation by advocacy groups, reports by expert commissions, and in other ways. In many circumstances, research can also sometimes be enlisted to question or challenge misleading assumptions concerning human behavior within the policymaking community. Social research is also important to the description of social problems, such that certain policy options become constrained and others more likely as the result of new knowledge concerning the conditions of the family. When researchers document the rising rate of childhood poverty and its links to single parenthood, when they illustrate through data how low child support awards and poor compliance in support payments exacerbates the economic difficulties of single mothers and their children, and when they describe the failure of many fathers to visit their offspring and pay child support, this information changes the debate concerning divorce reform in important ways.

Research is relevant to the policy debate on divorce in other indirect ways. Studies of the family commonly reveal that the social realities of family life are more complex than is commonly assumed (often to the frustration of media and policymaking communities), and these complexities are pertinent to evaluating the potential impact of proposed changes in family policy. This is important because the law is a very blunt instrument for regulating family relationships and managing family change, and therefore can have unintended as well as intended consequences (Thompson, 1994; Thompson, Scalora, Castrianno, & Limber, 1992). As a result, changes in marital and divorce policy intended to remedy certain problems may create new problems at the same time, and these unexpected problems can sometimes be anticipated in contemporary research on the family. Significant broadening of the grounds for divorce in Louisiana's Covenant Marriage Law occurred, for example, when legislators were alerted to circumstances (such as spousal or child abuse) when, as research shows, a quick and nonnegotiated exit from a potentially dangerous family environment is necessary.

In short, contemporary research on divorce and the family has multifaceted applications to the national debate on divorce reform, but many of these contributions are indirect, relevant to the conceptualization, description, and assumptions underlying the analysis of family change rather than providing compelling new avenues for policy redirection. Quite often, research applications involve raising new questions rather than resolving old ones which is (despite the obstacles this creates to quick legislative reforms) an important contribution to policy analysis. To illustrate these contributions, we consider some of the research perspectives offered by the authors of the chapters of this volume, and other researchers, as they address three questions that are at the heart of contemporary discourse concerning divorce and children. The questions are: (1) How are children affected by the experience of divorce? (2) What are children's "best interests," especially with respect to parental care after divorce? and (3) What is the role of fathers in postdivorce life?

How Are Children Affected by Divorce?

Critical to contemporary debate concerning divorce are concerns about its impact on children. Evocative portrayals of the plight of children growing up in poverty with their overstressed mothers, together with predictions of their academic underachievement and proneness to juvenile delinquency and adolescent parenting, characterize much of the discussion of divorce and its aftermath of liberal as well as conservative family scholars. In these views, it seems, children are predisposed to psychosocial dysfunction as a result of their experience of divorce.

It is important to seriously consider the harms that children may suffer from divorce, and the research described by the contributors to this volume portrays these outcomes as *contingent,* not necessarily inevitable. The process of divorce creates stress for children and their parents, and for some children there is an increased risk of mental health problems. But as Robert Emery in Chapter 1 notes, the normative response of children to divorce is resiliency, not dysfunction (see also Emery, 1994, 1998). In the context of the distress and life upheaval that divorce typically brings for children, the conclusion of research on divorce outcomes is that most children show no signs of psychosocial dysfunction, although many experience lingering pain. As Emery notes elsewhere, "It is empirically inaccurate and socially unjust to conclude that divorce does substantial damage to children's mental health. It is equally inaccurate and personally insensitive to ignore the practical and emotional struggles that children face as a result of divorce" (Emery, 1994, p. 200). Children experience psychological pain as a consequence of divorce, but the large majority adjust well.

If one answer to the question "How are children affected by divorce?" is "It depends"—then on what does it depend? In Chapter 1, Emery argues that individual differences in how well children cope with divorce are based on several features of postdivorce life, including (1) the quality of the child's relationship with the residential parent (which is affected by the quality of the adult's social and emotional functioning after divorce), (2) the extent and extremity of conflict between the child's parents, and how it is expressed, (3) the economic circumstances of the child and her family after divorce, and (4) the nature of the child's relationship with the nonresidential parent. Alan Booth, in Chapter 2, adds several other considerations. Children's postdivorce adjustment is influenced, he argues, by the quality of family relationships prior to the divorce, with children from low-conflict and high-conflict homes experiencing marital dissolution much differently and exhibiting different long-term outcomes (see also Amato & Booth, 1997). Children's adjustment is also influenced by the number of family transitions they experience in the postdivorce years, such as parents divorcing, remarrying, cohabiting, and sometimes divorcing again. Research findings reported by Emery and Booth suggest that with respect to children, divorce should be viewed both as an outcome (reflecting poor prior family functioning which can itself have long-term effects on children) and as a cause of further life transitions that influence children's well-being in complex ways.

The conclusions of these contributors are consistent with those of other researchers. Cherlin, Chase-Lansdale, and their colleagues, reporting findings from a large-scale longitudinal British study of children born in 1958, compared the later life experiences of children whose parents divorced after the age of 7 with those whose parents remained together (Chase-Lansdale, Cherlin, & Kiernan, 1995; Cherlin, Chase-Lansdale, & McRae, in press; Cherlin, Furstenberg, Chase-Lansdale, Kiernan, Robins, Morrison, & Teitler, 1991; Cherlin, Kiernan, & Chase-Lansdale, 1995). They found that (1) children whose parents divorced had already exhibited emotional and behavioral problems by age 7, suggesting that preexisting family problems (perhaps leading to divorce) had already had a mental health impact; these preexisting difficulties also accounted for children's initial postdivorce problems that appeared by age 11, (2) children of divorce showed escalating mental health risks as they reached adolescence and young adulthood that could not be explained by predivorce family functioning, but derived from features of postdivorce life, and (3) the vast majority of children showed healthy outcomes by age 33, although an important minority remained at psychosocial risk. Comprehensive reviews of other research on children's divorce outcomes likewise indicate that children in divorced families experience, on average, more psychosocial difficulty and diminished well-being by comparison with children in continuously intact homes but that these differences are small (Amato, 1994; Amato & Keith, 1991). Greater understanding of divorce outcomes is achieved by examining the factors that mediate individual differences in children's adjustment. A consensus statement written by leading family scholars[2] summarized the research in this manner:

Despite the significant and troubling risks of maladjustment among children whose parents divorce, the majority of children in these circumstances appear, in the long run, to be developing within the normal range—without identifiable psychosocial scars or other adverse consequences—even when the process of marital dissolution was painful for them. (Lamb, Sternberg, & Thompson, 1997, p. 396)

What are the public policy implications of this research? They are not as transparent as they might first seem to be, although they suggest some general directions. All other things being equal, for example, it would seem worthwhile to improve the conditions contributing to children's well-being, such as the economic circumstances of postdivorce family life, the coping capacities of the residential parent, the maintenance of a positive relationship between children and the nonresidential parent, and the ability of both parents to cooperate on the child's behalf. There is greater uncertainty in the manner in which these broad goals are to be advanced (public education? economic incentives? mediation, parenting plans, and other divorce-related measures?), how to resolve conflict between these goals (e.g., when a residential parent must move from the area with her child for a better job, but contact with the nonresidential parent will thus become more difficult), and possible disincentives to their accomplishment (such as in cases of domestic violence). These remain difficult problems for policymakers (see Chapter 4 in this volume, and recommendations of the U.S. Commission on Child and Family Welfare [1996] for some relevant proposals). Furthermore, as Booth suggests, if many of the difficulties that children experience in postdivorce life are attributable to family problems antedating divorce, addressing the adjustment problems of children may be more challenging because of their early origins, and Booth outlines some of the research and policy directions suggested by this problem.

The research on divorce outcomes for children also supports the view that a wise society will seek to reduce the incidence of divorce, even though most children are not undermined by its consequences (in a manner similar to how society wisely seeks to reduce cigarette smoking, although most smokers do not contract lung cancer; see Galston, 1997). However, a number of questions might be raised about proposed policies to strengthen marriage and reduce divorce. To what extent are children likely to benefit from the maintenance of a troubled marriage when parents are discouraged from divorce by long waiting periods, fault-based litigation (and its financial and emotional costs), or the prohibition of divorce altogether (such as in antenuptial agreements)? What factors predict whether children are likely to benefit or be harmed by such circumstances? When divorce must occur, how much will fault assessments heighten parental acrimony during divorce litigation, and will this continue into their postdivorce life? How will children be affected by these and other transaction costs of fault-based divorce? When access to divorce is restricted, to what extent will couples choose simply to live apart rather than divorce when their marriages are troubled? How could children be affected by such arrangements (e.g., potentially without legal provisions of child support, property distribution, and other forms of economic assistance)? If greater restrictions on divorce delay or inhibit remarriage, is this good or bad for children?

Taken together, research on the consequences of divorce poses challenging questions concerning the potentially unanticipated consequences for children of reforms intended to curb the divorce rate, while raising new queries concerning the origins of children's postdivorce adjustment problems and their remediation. These questions constitute, in part, an agenda for future research on families and divorce (with some researchers, such as Amato & Booth [1997] having already begun this task), especially as more states incorporate restrictions into their divorce laws and state-by-state comparisons of the effects of these changes in divorce policy can be conducted.

Parental Care After Divorce

The interests of children are justifiably preeminent (although not exclusive) in divorce because children are least responsible for—and most vulnerable to—the significant changes in family life that occur when parents part. As a consequence, provisions for child custody and visitation, child support, and even property settlement are oriented toward protecting children's current and future well-being. The "best interests of the child" has particular legal significance with respect to decisions concerning parental care after divorce, which are foundational to children's postdivorce adjustment and which have traditionally been guided by gender-based presumptions that have awarded children either to their fathers or, more recently, to mothers (Mason, 1994).

Chapters 3 and 4 by Eleanor Maccoby and Katharine Bartlett illustrate the "knowledge creep" by which new ways of conceptualizing children's needs and family functioning from social research have become part of the working knowledge of policymakers. Each contributor underscores the value of moving away from traditional "winner takes all" approaches to postdivorce child care in which one parent assumes "custody" of offspring and the other assumes a "visitation" relationship (terms which are, in some ways, vestiges of traditional portrayals of children as parental property). This is because of a growing recognition of how mothers and fathers each contribute meaningfully to the well-being of offspring, even though their caregiving roles usually differ, and the value to children of maintaining positive relationships with each parent after divorce. Legal reforms in recent years have moved in this direction by increasingly distinguishing legal custody (which both parents commonly share) from physical custody, providing the option of joint physical custody and parenting plans that enable greater sharing of caregiving responsibility for offspring, and in other ways increasingly emphasizing that although marriages may end, the parenting responsibilities of both adults do not. Consistent with this theme, both Maccoby and Bartlett recognize the importance of acknowledging the continuing caregiving contributions of each parent in the allocation of residential responsibility and decision-making authority for offspring after divorce. Maccoby illustrates these contributions with evocative illustrations from the Stanford Custody Study, an important empirical examination of custody and its outcomes for children (Buchanan, Maccoby, & Dornbusch, 1996; Maccoby & Mnookin, 1992).

Drawing on developmental research as well as legal analysis, Maccoby and Bartlett each look to the relative contribution of each parent in the day-to-day care of children prior to divorce as the basis for determining postdivorce responsibilities (see also Scott, 1992). Such an approach is more objective, predictable, and reliable than are judicial efforts to determine a child's "best interests" in custody (Mnookin, 1975), but it is also likely to represent, with some degree of accuracy, the depth of each parent's commitment to the child and the nature of the parent-child relationship. Both Maccoby and Bartlett recognize, however, that with respect to assessing predivorce parenting involvement, the devil is in the details. What behaviors define parental care? The task is relatively easier with respect to infants and young children, for whom the most important features of parental care involve continuous attention related to feeding, dressing and bathing, sleep and waking routines, social play, behavior management, distress relief, medical attention, transportation, and arranging substitute care (see, for example, Neely, 1984). Because these features of parental care can be more clearly defined and assessed, and figure more prominently in the establishment and maintenance of a secure parent-child relationship, Maccoby and others (see Chambers, 1984; Thompson, 1983) have argued for a preference for primary caretakers in custody decisions. That is, custody should be awarded to the parent who has most often performed these tasks in the child's day-to-day life. Each has argued, however, that the primary caretaker preference should be strongest with younger children (reviving the traditional "tender years" doctrine), but considerably weaker the older the child is.

But what about older children? In applying the "approximation standard" by which the extent of postdivorce residential responsibility is based on each parent's predivorce parenting, Bartlett broadens the criteria of parental care to include discipline, education, recreational play, even taking the child to a soccer game. Less clear is whether activities related to the child but not directly interacting with the child are also encompassed in these criteria of parental care, such as purchasing and cleaning the child's clothes, food shopping, toy purchases and repairs, general housekeeping and yard work. Indeed, there is inconsistency in the evaluation of these features of parenting by other scholars who have proposed similar custody guidelines (e.g., Neely, 1984; Scott, 1992; Thompson, 1983). The uncertainty of how to comprehensively define parental care is not necessarily an obstacle to enlisting the approximation standard into custody decisions, as Bartlett notes, because general estimates of proportionate parental contributions to caregiving are all that are needed (see also Scott, 1992). But this uncertainty raises the risk that in defining criteria for assessing predivorce parental care, policymakers will be prone to do what judges who seek to interpret children's "best interests" do: esteeming certain kinds of parental care over other kinds based on values concerning parental nurturance. To researchers, this means that considerably more knowledge of how children of various ages perceive the value and meaning of parenting, and its most important behavioral constituents, is needed.

More research is also needed on an issue raised by Maccoby. She comments that we know little about how well the predivorce caregiving roles of parents predict the quality of each parent's relationship with children after divorce. Although there are reasons for expecting that parents who are more involved and committed to offspring during marriage will maintain strong bonds to their children after divorce, other circumstances may weaken the continuity of the parent-child relationship. Parents typically go through considerable emotional turmoil accompanying divorce in ways that can significantly alter their relationships with offspring, who are themselves also distressed and confused (Hetherington, Cox, & Cox, 1982; Wallerstein & Kelly, 1980). Other obligations may also change these relationships. During marriage, the time devoted to child care by parents is based on many factors, including their relative earning power and employment obligations, other domestic and extrafamilial responsibilities, as well as their commitment to nurturing offspring. After divorce, competing obligations increase as parents move into independent residences, increase their work and domestic responsibilities, and take on other commitments that may compete with children for attention. Perhaps unsurprisingly, some researchers have found that the quality of predivorce parenting is a poor predictor of postdivorce father involvement with children (Hetherington, Stanley-Hagan, & Anderson, 1989; Wallerstein & Kelly, 1980). Greater study of continuity and change in parent-offspring relationships throughout the transition of divorce may be important to understanding which features of predivorce parental care are most predictive of the depth and warmth of caregiving relationships after divorce. Although there is particular value, as Bartlett notes, to maintaining continuity in parental care for offspring in the midst of all that otherwise changes in the process of divorce, such research would be helpful in conceptualizing the nature of parental care before and after this transition, and how (and if) they are related.

What Is the Role of Fathers in Postdivorce Life?

These considerations lead to a third question concerning the role of fathers. Conservative and liberal family scholars differ strikingly in their portrayal of the importance of fathers to children's well-being, and the nature of his contribution. While some conservatives emphasize the need for a paternal recommitment to traditional roles in marriage and childrearing, in the liberal analysis the role of fathers is primarily devoted to providing economic support for the family and contributing to child care. Neither approach provides the basis for a very useful understanding of fathers in postdivorce life.

In Chapters 5 and 6, Michael Lamb and Daniel Meyer each seek to understand the perplexities of fatherhood after marriages end. Their research suggests that the end of marriage seems to be accompanied by a decline in paternal commitment to offspring. Fathers who may initially remain in touch with their children progressively visit less frequently with the passage of time; at the same time, the fidelity of their child support payments may also decline. To be sure, there is evidence that this discouraging portrayal of postdivorce paternity has been changing in recent years. By contrast with widely-cited earlier estimates (i.e., Furstenberg & Nord, 1985; Furstenberg et al., 1983), for example, paternal visitation rates have recently increased meaningfully (Kelly, 1994; Maccoby, Buchanan, Mnookin, & Dornbusch, 1993; Maccoby & Mnookin, 1992; Seltzer, 1991; Seltzer & Brandreth, 1994; Zill & Nord, 1996). And as Meyer notes, greater enforcement of child support obligations by state agencies in recent years (particularly in the mandatory withholding of support payments from paychecks) has yielded greater fidelity by fathers to their support responsibilities. Even so, one has to wonder whether the problems with visitation and child support reflect, as some have suggested (Furstenberg, 1988), a deeper and more disconcerting problem that nonresidential fathers are only weakly attached to their offspring after divorce. Outside of the context of marriage, in other words, paternal ties tend to erode.

The contributors to this volume argue, however, that the reality is far more complex. According to Lamb, typical visitation arrangements offer little opportunity to create a meaningful postdivorce parenting role for most fathers and, indeed, often seem not designed to do so. Divorced from the routines, settings, and everyday activities of the child's usual life, a visiting relationship with the nonresidential parent quickly becomes constrained and artificial, making it easier for fathers and their children to drift apart as their lives become increasingly independent. According to Meyer, child support is not only a matter of a father's willingness to pay but also capacity to pay, and poor compliance with child support orders is predicted not only by the father's low income but also by the proportionate share of income (or "burden") encompassed by his child support obligations. While both contributors note that some fathers are capable of paying and do not, or fail to visit because of disinclination, each describes the problems of visitation and child support as having more complex origins than cultural portrayals of the decline in fatherhood typically provide.

What are the public policy implications of this research? Neither a society-wide rejuvenation of traditional fatherhood (and masculinity) nor the relegation of fathers to economic providers alone are satisfactory alternatives. Instead, greater understanding of the dynamics of postdivorce paternity is needed in the context of the changes that have occurred in marital and gender roles during the past three decades. One way of doing so is to broaden an appreciation of the ways that fathers can potentially contribute to the well-being of offspring after divorce. For years, researchers have focused exclusively on the benefits to children of visitation and child support, finding that the father's fidelity to his economic support obligations enhances his children's well-being but also discovering, perhaps paradoxically, that regular visitation does not necessarily do so (see, e.g., Amato, 1993, 1994; Furstenberg & Cherlin, 1991; McLanahan & Sandefur, 1994; Thompson, 1994). But a focus on visitation and economic child support may provide only a truncated view of postdivorce paternity. In a recent meta-analytic review of this research, Amato and Gilbreth (in press) replicated the results of earlier researchers but also identified two other features of postdivorce paternity that had previously been neglected: *active parenting* (reflected in activities such as helping with homework, participating in projects with the child, using noncoercive discipline to deal with misbehavior, listening to children's problems and giving advice, and related behaviors) and *emotional bonding* (indexing the strength of the emotional ties between father and child, including affection, mutual respect, and identification). Amato and Gilbreth found that the strength of the emotional bond between fathers and children, and the extent to which fathers engage in active parenting, are each consistently and significantly predictive of children's well-being. With respect to active parenting, its influence is stronger even than economic support. It is important, in other words, that fathers are capable of functioning like real parents in their encounters with offspring as well as maintaining fidelity to their economic child support obligations. Both active parenting and emotional bonding may—or may not—occur in the context of conventional visitation arrangements.

Such a conclusion is consistent with the views of Seltzer and her colleagues that responsibilities like child support must be viewed in the context of the other responsibilities and privileges of postdivorce paternity: fathers are more likely to provide reliable child support when they have assumed other meaningful roles in the child's life (Seltzer, 1991; Seltzer, Schaeffer, & Charng, 1989). In a recent longitudinal study, Seltzer and her colleagues (in press) report that fathers who pay child support (owing, in part, to stricter enforcement procedures) are also more likely to visit with their children, see their children more frequently, and have greater influence with them over time. As Seltzer and her colleagues note, the increase in contact associated with child support payments can derive from complex motives (fathers may seek to monitor, for example, how their support money is spent) and may be associated with the child's exposure to greater interparental conflict. These concerns are consistent with those of Maccoby (this volume) concerning the connection recently established between visitation and child support in California and the advent of "born again dads." These concerns suggest that considerably greater research into the dynamics of postdivorce paternity are needed, especially in the context of more rigorous child support enforcement procedures and policy reforms (like those in California) explicitly linking support with visitation frequency.

In a society that is deeply concerned about the abandonment of children by their fathers after divorce, however, these research findings offer hopeful new glimpses into the incentives that may exist to connect fathers better with their offspring as nonresidential parents. In the context of evidence that patterns of visitation, child support, and other aspects of nonresidential parenting seem to become established during the first year or two after marital dissolution (Thompson & Laible, in press), it appears that the initial postdivorce period is best-suited to establishing constructive patterns of postdivorce family functioning that will contribute to children's enduring well-being.

CONCLUSION

Divorce policy derives from the intersection of public values with the assumptions, risk preferences, and beliefs of the policymaking community and the knowledge derived from research into the family. In a complex and, at times, frustrating elusive fashion, these direct influences combine with a multitude of indirect factors (including the media, competing priorities presented by other policy problems, and specific actors and agencies) to shape contemporary policies concerning divorce. Because family policy expresses many fundamental American values, it is not surprising that these issues command broad public attention and, at times, heated controversy.

There is another value assumption associated with divorce that contemporary discourse concerning marital dissolution also questions. It is the assumption that adults can make a "clean break" of each other after divorce. As the final termination to an unhappy marriage, divorce is intended to permit former spouses to inaugurate new relationships with other partners and begin new lives apart. But with the growing recognition that marriages (especially long-term marriages) entail the merging of human as well as material capital that is not easily divided upon separation, family scholars from a variety of viewpoints are questioning how easily partners can part after they have been married, or whether efforts to do so disadvantage one partner over the other. Some scholars seek, for example, to encompass within marital property the career assets achieved by a spouse with the support of the other, and to provide for the division of career assets in the form of postdivorce financial support for the partner who has contributed to the other's professional growth and advancement. In this manner, and in others, proposed divorce policy reforms increasingly question whether two people who have shared their lives, especially for an enduring period of time together, can easily go their separate ways after divorce.

When children are involved, there are even more reasons to question whether adults can justifiably make a "clean break" of each other following divorce. When they seek to do so, they seem to be divorcing offspring as well as a spouse. Responsible postdivorce parenting requires that adults do several things together. They must coordinate their lives to enable children to maintain satisfying relationships with each parent, negotiate child support arrangements that inevitably involve accommodations to the changing needs of children and other family members, communicate concerning decisions that affect children's well-being, and occasionally meet congenially on special occasions (like graduations, weddings, and other special events) for the benefit of their children. The realization of these responsibilities surprises many divorcing parents with the discovery that although they seek to end a marital relationship with a spouse, they must nevertheless maintain a future relationship with the parent of their children. The title of this volume—*The Postdivorce Family*—underscores that although divorce ends marriage, it does not end the family.

Seeking fairness for children, wise public policy might be oriented toward disabusing adults of the fiction that they can make a "clean break" of each other when children are involved. As some family scholars advocate, this might involve policies that encourage adults to take more seriously the obligations of marriage *and of parenting* so these become more thoughtful, intentional decisions. They might involve restrictions on the ease of divorce for couples with children, provided that these are combined with support and incentives to restore healthy family functioning rather than enduring in an unhappy marriage. When divorce must occur, wise public policies oriented toward fairness for children ensure that adults enter postdivorce life with a realization of the continuing obligations they experience as parents, and with appropriate incentives to remain committed to offspring regardless of the subsequent changes in their living circumstances. More broadly, wise public policy might also be oriented toward family support throughout marriage so that parents need not reach the crisis of divorce or other family trauma before help is available (Melton & Thompson, in press).

Researchers have an important contribution to offer in the evolution of divorce policy because of the knowledge they provide. To the extent that they do so with an ear toward the family values that underlie the contemporary debate about marriage and divorce, they become more cognizant of the hidden value assumptions that may be incorporated into the interpretation of their research, and they can also ask new questions for future study that reflect the concerns Americans have about the status of the family. In doing so, researchers contribute more "usable knowledge" (Lindblom & Cohen, 1979) to policymakers, and advance the interests of children.

NOTES

1. For example, the continuing reassessment of the findings of Weitzman's (1985) important study documenting the economic disadvantages suffered by women after divorce have not diminished some advocates' citations of her estimate that mothers undergo a 73% decline in their income folowing divorce while fathers experience a 42% increase, despite the failure of subsequent researchers to replicate these extreme estimates (see Hoffman & Duncan, 1988, Peterson, 1996, and Teachman & Paasch, 1994). Although all agree that women are financially disadvantaged by divorce while men usually benefit economically, the extent of the disparity and the manner in which it is estimated continues to be debated by family researchers. Likewise, although the research by Wallerstein and her colleagues (Wallerstein & Blakeslee, 1989, 1995; Wallerstein & Kelly, 1980) on the impact on children of divorce was designed in a manner that may exaggerate its portrayal of the harms suffered by children (e.g., families participated in the study as an accompaniment to divorce counseling and thus presumably entered the project because they were already having difficulties; children were not observed prior to divorce so it is impossible to distinguish preexisting from divorce-related difficulties; the sample was small, especially when children were studied years after divorce, and there was no appropriate comparison group of nondivorced families), it is frequently cited by family scholars both because of its uniquely longitudinal perspective on the unfolding consequences of divorce, and also because it offers an evocative portrayal of the detriments of marital dissolution to children, consistent with current concerns among family advocates.

2. Contributors to the statement included psychologists E. Mark Cummings, Robert Emery, Phillip W. Esplin, Kathleen Gilbride, E. Mavis Hetherington, Joan B. Kelly, and Nicholas Zill, sociologists Paul Amato, Janet Johnston, Guillermina Jasso, and Sarah McLanahan, social welfare scholar Irwin Garfinkel, legal scholars David L. Chambers and Judge Gary Crippen, and Joyce Thomas.

REFERENCES

Amato, P. R. (1993). Children's adjustment to divorce: Theories, hypotheses, and empirical support. *Journal of Marriage and the Family, 55,* 23-38.

Amato, P. R. (1994). Life-span adjustment of children to their parents' divorce. *The Future of Children, 4,* 143-164.

Amato, P., & Booth, A. (1997). *A generation at risk: Growing up in an era of family upheaval.* Cambridge, MA: Harvard University Press.

Amato, P. R., & Keith, B. (1991). Parental divorce and the well-being of children: A meta-analysis. *Psychological Bulletin, 100,* 26-46.

Amato, P. R., & Gilbreth, J. (in press). Nonresident fathers and children's well-being: A meta-analysis. *Journal of Marriage and the Family.*

Applewhite, A. (1997). Q: Would Louisiana's "covenant marriage" be a good idea for America? No: It won't lower the divorce rate and will raise the human and economic cost of divorce. *Insight,* October 6-13, 1997.

Baker, L. A., & Emery, R. E. (1993). When every relationship is above average: Perceptions and expectations of divorce at the time of marriage. *Law and Human Behavior, 17,* 439-450.

Betson, D. M., & Michael, R. T. (1997). Why so many children are poor. *The Future of Children, 7,* 25-39.

Blankenhorn, D. (1995). *Fatherless America.* New York: Basic.

"Bound by Love," from *The Newshour with Jim Lehrer,* Public Broadcasting Service, August 20, 1997 (transcript available through the PBS website, www.pbs.org/newshour/bb/law/july-dec97/marriage_8-20.html)

Brinig, M. F., & Crafton, S. M. (1994). Marriage and opportunism. *Journal of Legal Studies, 23,* 869-894.

Buchanan, C. M., Maccoby, E. E., & Dornbusch, S. M. (1996). *Adolescents after divorce.* Cambridge, MA: Harvard University Press.

Caplan, N. (1979). The two-communities theory and knowledge utilization. *American Behavioral Scientist, 22,* 459-470.

Carbone, J. (1994). A feminist perspective on divorce. *The Future of Children, 4,* 183-209.

Carlson, M. (1997). Till depositions do us part. *Time, 150,* 21 (July 7, 1997).

Chambers, D. L. (1984). Rethinking the substantive rules for custody disputes in divorce. *Michigan Law Review, 83,* 477-569.

Chase-Lansdale, P. L., Cherlin, A. J., & Kiernan, K. E. (1995). The long-term effects of parental divorce on the mental health of young adults: A developmental perspective. *Child Development, 66,* 1614-1634.

Cherlin, A. J. (1992). *Marriage, divorce, remarriage* (Rev. Ed.). Cambridge, MA: Harvard University Press.

Cherlin, A. J., Chase-Lansdale, P. L., & McRae, C. (in press). Effects of divorce on mental health through the life course. *American Sociological Review,* in press.

Cherlin, A. J., Furstenberg, F. F., Jr., Chase-Lansdale, P. L., Kiernan, K. E., Robins, P. K., Morrison, D. R., & Teitler, J. O. (1991). Longitudinal studies of effects of divorce on children in Great Britain and the United States. *Science, 252,* 1386-1389.

Cherlin, A. J., Kiernan, K. E., & Chase-Lansdale, P. L. (1985). Parental divorce in childhood and demographic outcomes in young adulthood. *Demography, 32,* 299-318.

Christopher, A. J. (1997). The Irish Divorce Referendum of 1995. *Geography, 82,* 79-90.

Coontz, S. (1992). *The way we never were: American families and the nostalgia trap.* New York: Basic.

Coontz, S. (1997). *The way we really are: Coming to terms with America's changing families.* New York: Basic.

Council on Families in America (1995). *Marriage in America: A report to the nation.* New York: Instiute for American Values.

Eggebeen, D. J., & Lichter, D. (1991). Race, family structure, and changing poverty among American children. *American Sociological Review, 56,* 801-817.

Emery, R. E. (1994). *Renegotiating family relationships: Divorce, child custody, and mediation.* New York: Guilford.

Emery, R. E. (1998). *Marriage, divorce, and children's adjustment* (Rev. ed.). Beverly Hills, CA: Sage.

Etzioni, A. & Rubin, P. (1997). Opportuning virtue: Covenant marriages, the Louisiana experience, and beyond. In A. Etzioni & P. Rubin (Eds.), *Opportuning virtue: Lessons of the Louisiana Covenant Marriage Law* (pp. 1-4). Washington, DC: The Communitarian Network.

Fine, M. A., & Fine, D. R. (1994). An examination and evaluation of recent changes in divorce laws in five Western countries: The critical role of values. *Journal of Marriage and the Family, 56,* 249-263.

Fineman, M. A. (1991). *The illusion of equality: Rhetoric and the reality of divorce reform.* Chicago: University of Chicago Press.

Fuchs, V. R., & Reklis, D. M. (1992). America's children: Economic perspectives and policy options. *Science, 255,* 41-46.

Furstenberg, F. F., Jr. (1988). Good dads—bad dads: Two faces of fatherhood. In A. J. Cherlin (Ed.), *The changing American family and public policy* (pp. 193-218). Washington, DC: The Urban Institute Press.

Furstenberg, F. F., Jr. (1994). History and current status of divorce in the United States. *The Future of Children, 4,* 29-43.

Furstenberg, F. F., Jr., & Cherlin, A. J. (1991). *Divided families: What happens to children when parents part.* Cambridge, MA: Harvard University Press.

Furstenberg, F. F., Jr., & Nord, C. W. (1985). Parenting apart: Patterns of childrearing after marital disruption. *Journal of Marriage and the Family, 47,* 893-904.

Furstenberg, F. F., Jr., Nord, C. W., Peterson, J. L., & Zill, N. (1983). The life course of children of divorce: Marital disruption and parental contact. *American Sociological Review, 48,* 656-668.

Gallagher, M. (1996a). *The abolition of marriage: How we destroy lasting love.* Washington, DC: Regnery.

Gallagher, M. (1996b). Re-creating marriage. In D. Popenoe, J. B. Elshtain, & D. Blankenhorn (Eds.), *Promises to keep: Decline and renewal of marriage in America* (pp. 3-14). Lanham, MD: Rowan & Littlefield.

Galston, W. A. (1996). The reinstitutionalization of marriage: Politial theory and public practice. In D. Popenoe, J. B. Elshtain, & D. Blankenhorn (Eds.), *Promises to keep: Decline and renewal of marriage in America* (pp. 271-290). Lanham, MD: Rowan & Littlefield.

Galston, W. A. (1997, November). *A progressive family policy for the twenty-first century*. Plenary address to a conference, "The Future of the Family." Center on Children, Families, and the Law, University of Virginia, Charlottesville.

Garfinkel, I., Melli, M. S., & Robertson, J. G. (1994). Child support orders: A perspective on reform. *The Future of Children, 4,* 84-100.

Giele, J. Z. (1996). Decline of the family: Conservative, liberal, and feminist views. In D. Popenoe, J. B. Elshtain, & D. Blankenhorn (Eds.), *Promises to keep: Decline and renewal of marriage in America* (pp. 89-115). Lanham, MD: Rowan & Littlefield.

Glenn, N. D. (1996). Values, attitudes, and the state of American marriage. In D. Popenoe, J. B. Elshtain, & D. Blankenhorn (Eds.), *Promises to keep: Decline and renewal of marriage in America* (pp. 233-246). Lanham, MD: Rowan & Littlefield.

Glendon, M. A. (1981). *The new family and the new property.* Toronto: Butterworth.

Glendon, M. A. (1986). Fixed rules and discretion in contemporary family law and succession law. *Tulane Law Review, 60,* 1165-1205.

Glendon, M. A. (1989). *The transformation of family law: State, law, and family in the United States and Western Europe.* Chicago: University of Chicago Press.

Goode, W. J. (1956). *After divorce.* Glencoe, IL: Free Press.

Gunter, B. G. (1977). Notes on divorce filing as role behavior. *Journal of Marriage and the Family, 39,* 95-98.

Hetherington, E. M., & Clingempeel, W. G. (1992). *Coping with marital transitions: A family systems perspective. Monographs of the Society for Research in Child Development, 57* (Serial no. 227).

Hetherington, E. M., Cox, M., & Cox, R. (1982). Effects of divorce on parents and children. In M. E. Lamb (Ed.), *Nontraditional families* (pp. 223-288). Hillsdale, NJ: Erlbaum.

Hetherington, E. M., Stanley-Hagan, M., & Anderson, E. R. (1989). Marital transitions: A child's perspective. *American Psychologist, 44,* 303-312.

Hoffman, S. D., & Duncan, G. J. (1988). What are the economic consequences of divorce? *Demography, 25,* 641-645.

Kain, E. L. (1990). *The myth of family decline.* Lexington, MA: Lexington.

Kelly, J. B. (1994). The determination of child custody. *The Future of Children, 4,* 121-142.

Kitson, G. C. (1992). *Portrait of divorce: Adjustment to marital breakdown.* New York: Guilford.

Leland, J. (1996). Tightening the knot: Convinced that single-parent families are bad for everyone, some lawmakers want to end no-fault divorce. *Newsweek, 127,* 72 (February 19, 1996).

Lindblom, C. E., & Cohen, D. K. (1979). *Usable knowledge: Social science and social problem solving.* New Haven, CT: Yale University Press.

Maccoby, E. E., Buchanan, C. M., Mnookin, R. H., & Dornbusch, S. M. (1993). postdivorce roles of mothers and fathers in the lives of their children. *Journal of Family Psychology, 7,* 24-38.

Maccoby, E. E., & Mnookin, R. H. (1992). *Dividing the child: Social and legal dilemmas of custody.* Cambridge, MA: Harvard University Press.

Mack, D. (1997). *The assault on parenthood: How our culture undermines the family.* New York: Simon & Schuster.

Mahoney, R. (1995). *Kidding ourselves: Breadwinning, babies, and bargaining power.* New York: Basic.

Mason, M. A. (1988). *The equality trap.* New York: Simon & Schuster.

Mason, M. A. (1994). *From father's property to children's rights: The history of child custody in the United States.* New York: Columbia University Press.

McLanahan, S., & Sandefur, G. (1994). *Growing up with a single parent.* Cambridge, MA: Harvard University Press.

Melton, G. B., & Thompson, R. A. (in press). *Toward a child-centered, neighborhood-based child protection system.* Lincoln, NE: University of Nebraska Press.

Mnookin, R. H., (1975). Child-custody adjudication: Judicial functions in the face of indeterminacy. *Law and Contemporary Problems, 39,* 226-293.

Neely, R. (1984). The primary caretaker parent rule: Child custody and the dynamics of greed. *Yale Law and Policy Review, 3,* 168-186.

O'Neill, J. (1997, November). *Families, poverty, and welfare reform.* Address to a conference, "The Future of the Family." Center on Children, Families, and the Law, University of Virginia, Charlottesville.

Parkman, A. M. (1992). *No-fault divorce: What went wrong?* Boulder, CO: Westview.

Parkman, A. M. (1995). The deterioration of the family: A law and economics perspective. In G. B. Melton (Ed.), *The individual, the family, and social good: Personal fulfillment in times of change. Nebraska Symposium on Motivation,* Vol. 42. Lincoln: University of Nebraska Press.

Parkman, A. M. (1998). Why are married women working so hard? *International Review of Law and Economics, 18,* 41-49.

Peterson, R. R. (1996). A re-evaluation of the economic consequences of divorce. *American Sociological Review, 61,* 528-536.

Pollitt, K. (1997). What's right about divorce. *New York Times,* June 27, 1997.

Popenoe, D. (1993a). The national family wars. *Journal of Marriage and the Family, 55,* 553-555.

Popenoe, D. (1993b). American family decline, 1960-1990: A review and appraisal. *Journal of Marriage and the Family, 55,* 527-555.

Popenoe, D. (1996a). *Life without father.* New York: Free Press.

Popenoe, D. (1996b). Modern marriage: Revising the cultural script. In D. Popenoe, J. B. Elshtain, & D. Blankenhorn (Eds.), *Promises to keep: Decline and renewal of marriage in America* (pp. 247-270). Lanham, MD: Rowan & Littlefield.

Roberts, P. G. (1994). Child support orders: Problems with enforcement. *The Future of Children, 4,* 101-120.

Sack, K. (1997). Louisiana approves measure to tighten marriage bonds. *New York Times,* June 24, 1997.

Schneider, C. E. (1994). Marriage, morals, and the law: No-fault divorce and moral discourse. *Utah Law Review, 1994,* 503-585.

Schneider, C. E. (1996). The law and the stability of marriage: The family as a social institution. In D. Popenoe, J. B. Elshtain, & D. Blankenhorn (Eds.), *Promises to keep:*

Decline and renewal of marriage in America (pp. 187-213). Lanham, MD: Rowan & Littlefield.

Scott, E. S. (1990). Rational decisionmaking about marriage and divorce. *Virginia Law Review, 76,* 9-94.

Scott, E. S. (1992). Pluralism, parental preference, and child custody. *California Law Review, 80,* 615-672.

Seltzer, J. A. (1991). Relationships between fathers and children who live apart: The father's role after separation. *Journal of Marriage and the Family, 53,* 79-101.

Seltzer, J. A., & Brandreth, Y. (1994). What fathers say about involvement with children after separation. *Journal of Family Issues, 15,* 49-77.

Seltzer, J. A., McLanahan, S., & Hanson, T. L. (in press). Will child suport enforcement increase father-child contact and parental conflict after separation? In I. Garfinkel, S. McLanahan, S. Seltzer, & D. R. Meyer (Eds.), *Fathers under fire.* New York: Russell Sage Foundation.

Seltzer, J. A., Schaeffer, N. C., & Charng, H. (1989). Family ties after divorce: The relationship between visiting and paying child support. *Journal of Marriage and the Family, 51,* 1013-1032.

Skolnick, A. (1991). *Embattled paradise: The American family in an age of uncertainty.* New York: Basic.

Spaht, K. S. (1997). Q: Would Louisiana's "covenant marriage" be a good idea for America? Yes: Stop sacrificing America's children on the cold altar of convenience for divorcing spouses. *Insight,* October 6-13, 1997.

Spanier, G. B., & Thompson, L. (1984). *Parting: The aftermath of separation and divorce.* Beverly Hills, CA: Sage.

Stacey, J. (1990). *Brave new families: Stories of domestic upheaval in late 20th century America.* New York: Basic.

Stacey, J. (1993). Good riddance to "the family": A response to David Popenoe. *Journal of Marriage and the Family, 55,* 545-547.

Stacey, J. (1996). *In the name of the family: Rethinking family values in the postmodern age.* Boston: Beacon Press.

Sugarman, S. D. (1990). Dividing financial interests on divorce. In S. D. Sugarman & H. H. Kay (Eds.), *Divorce reform at the crossroads* (pp. 130-165). New Haven, CT: Yale University Press.

Teachman, J. D., & Paasch, K. M. (1994). Financial impact of divorce on children and their families. *The Future of Children, 4,* 63-83.

Thompson, R. A. (1983). The father's case in child custody disputes. In M. E. Lamb & A. Sagi (Eds.), *Fatherhood and family policy* (pp. 53-100). Hillsdale, NJ: Erlbaum.

Thompson, R. A. (1993). Developmental research and legal policy: Toward a two-way street. In D. Cicchetti & S. L. Toth (Eds.), *Child abuse, child development, and social policy. Advances in Applied Developmental Psychology,* Vol. 8 (pp. 75-115). Norwood, NJ: Ablex.

Thompson, R. A. (1994). Fathers and divorce. *The Future of Children, 4,* 210-235.

Thompson, R. A., & Laible, D. J. (in press). Noncustodial parents. In M. E. Lamb (Ed.), *Nontraditional families.* Hillsdale, NJ: Erlbaum.

Thompson, R. A., Scalora, M. J., Castrianno, L., & Limber, S. (1992). Grandparent visitation rights: Emergent psychological and psycholegal issues. In D. K. Kagehiro & W. S. Laufer (Eds.), *Handbook of psychology and law* (pp. 292-317). New York: Springer-Verlag.

Thornton, A. (1989). Changing attitudes toward family issues in the United States. *Journal of Marriage and the Family, 51,* 873-894.

Thornton, A. (1996). Comparative and historical perspectives on marriage, divorce, and family life. In D. Popenoe, J. B. Elshtain, & D. Blankenhorn (Eds.), *Promises to keep: Decline and renewal of marriage in America* (pp. 69-87). Lanham, MD: Rowan & Littlefield.

U.S. Commission on Child and Family Welfare (1996). *Parenting our children: In the best interest of the nation.* Washington, DC: U.S. Government Printing Office.

Wallerstein, J. S., & Kelly, J. B. (1980). *Surviving the breakup: How hcildren and parents cope with divorce.* New York: Basic.

Wallerstein, J. S., & Blakeslee, S. (1989). *Second chances: Men, women, and children a decade after divorce.* New York: Ticknor and Fields.

Wallerstein, J. S., & Blakeslee, S. (1995). *The good marriage.* Boston, MA: Houghton Mifflin.

Weiss, C. H. (1978). Improving the linkage between social research and public policy. In L. E. Lynn, Jr. (Ed.), *Knowledge and policy: The uncertain connection* (pp. 23-81). Washington, DC: National Academy of Sciences.

Weiss, C. H. (1987). The diffusion of social science research to policymakers: An overview. In G. B. Melton (Ed.), *Reforming the law: Impact of child development research* (pp. 63-85). New York: Guilford.

Weitzman, L. J. (1985). *The divorce revolution.* New York: Free Press.

White, L. K. (1991). Determinants of divorce. In A. Booth (Ed.). *Contemporary families* (pp. 141-149). Minneapolis, MN: National Council on Family Relations.

Whitehead, B. D. (1993). Dan Quayle was right. *Atlantic Monthly,* April, 47-84.

Whitehead, B. D. (1996). The decline of marriage as the social basis of childrearing. In D. Popenoe, J. B. Elshtain, & D. Blankenhorn (Eds.), *Promises to keep: Decline and renewal of marriage in America* (pp. 3-14). Lanham, MD: Rowan & Littlefield.

Whitehead, B. D. (1997). *The divorce culture.* New York: Knopf.

Whitman, D. (1996). The divorce dilemma: Most people want getting a divorce to be tougher, except when the failing marriage is their own. *U.S. News and World Report, 121,* 58 (Sept. 30, 1996).

Williams, C. W. (1990). *Black teenage mothers: Pregnancy and child rearing from their perspective.* Lexington, MA: Lexington.

Wilson, W. J. (1987). *The truly disadvantaged: The inner city, the under class, and public policy.* Chicago: University of Chicago Press.

Zill, N., & Nord, C. W. (1996). *Causes and consequences of involvement by non-custodial parents in their children's lives: Evidence from a national longitudinal study.* Unpublished manuscript, Westat, Rockville, MD.

Index

233

About the Editors

Paul R. Amato is Professor of Sociology at the University of Nebraska. He has written extensively on divorce and its effects on children, stepfamilies, parent-child relationships, and families and social support, as well as studying cross-cultural family issues. His most recent book, *A Generation at Risk: Growing Up in an Era of Family Upheaval,* was coauthored with Alan Booth. He has been a 1992 Fulbright scholar in India and a Research Fellow at the Australian Institute of Family Studies. In 1994 he won the Reuben Hill Award from the National Council on Family Relations for the best article of the year combining research and theory on the family. Together with Ross Thompson, he convened the symposium on which this volume is based.

Ross A. Thompson is Professor of Psychology at the University of Nebraska. He works at the intersection of developmental psychology and public policy, and consequently he has written on issues ranging from parent-infant attachment and early emotional growth to the effects of divorce on children, child maltreatment, and research ethics. His most recent books include *Preventing Child Maltreatment Through Social Support: A Critical Analysis* (1995) and *Early Brain Development and Public Policy* (in press). He has received the Myer Elkin Award for the best essay contributed to *Family and Conciliation Courts Review,* and has been a Senior NIMH Fellow in Law and Psychology at Stanford University as well as a former Associate Editor of *Child Development.*

About the Contributors

Katharine T. Bartlett is Professor of Law at Duke University, where she teaches family law, gender and law, and contracts. She has lectured and published extensively on topics in family law, children, gender theory, and legal education, with important contributions to the reconsideration of parenthood within divorce law. Since 1994, Bartlett has been a Reporter with the American Law Institute's Principles of the Law for Family Dissolution, for which she is responsible for the provisions relating to custodial responsibility for children. Her chapter reflects the most current draft, although it has not yet been approved by the ALI membership.

Alan Booth is Professor of Sociology and Human Development at the Pennsylvania State University. His research interests focus on the origins and consequences of marital instability. Since 1980, he has directed a national longitudinal study of marital instability over the life course which provides the basis for much of the research reported in his chapter, and he has authored more than 100 articles and books concerning the family. Booth has also served as editor of *Journal of Marriage and the Family,* and coauthored with Paul Amato *A Generation at Risk: Growing Up in an Era of Family Upheaval* (1997).

Robert E. Emery is Professor of Psychology and Director of Clinical Training at the University of Virginia, where he is an associate faculty member in the Institute of Law, Psychiatry, and Public Policy. He also serves as the Director of the Center for the Study of Children, Families, and the Law. His research focuses on family relationships and children's mental health, including parental conflict, divorce, child custody, family violence, and associated legal and policy issues. He is author of *Marriage, Divorce, and Children's Adjustment* (Rev. ed., 1998) and *Renegotiating Family Relationships: Divorce, Child Custody, and Mediation* (1994). He is also engaged in limited practice as a clinical psychologist and divorce mediator.

Michael E. Lamb is Head of the Section on Social and Emotional Development of the National Institute of Child Health and Human Development. As a developmental psychologist who studies the effects of rearing conditions on child development, Lamb is a nationally-recognized authority on fatherhood, nontraditional families, the effects of nontraditional child care, sibling influences, parent-child attachment, and other topics. He has also studied applied problems such as the evaluation of children's accounts of sexual abuse and the effects of domestic violence on children's development. Among his recent books are *The Role of the Father in Child Development* (3rd ed., 1997), *Investigative Interviews of Children* (1998), and *Parenting and Development in "Non-Traditional" Families* (1999).

Eleanor E. Maccoby is Professor of Psychology (Emeritas) at Stanford University. As a developmental psychologist, she has made significant contributions to knowledge about parent-child relationships, gender differentiation in childhood and adolescence, and the effects of alternative custody arrangements on children of divorce. In her chapter, she draws extensively from the findings of the Stanford Custody Study, a uniquely large, longitudinal examination of the outcomes of divorce and custody decisions for children in California. Other conclusions from this study can be found in *Dividing the Child: Social and Legal Dilemmas of Custody* (with Mnookin; 1992) and *Adolescents After Divorce* (with Buchanan and Dornbusch; 1996).

Daniel R. Meyer is Associate Professor of the School of Social Work and Affiliate of the Institute for Research on Poverty at the University of Wisconsin at Madison. He has contributed extensively to the research literature on the effects of child support orders on children, mothers, and fathers, as well as the economic consequences of changes in welfare policies. He has collaborated in *Fathers Under Fire* (with Garfinkel, McLanahan, and Seltzer; 1998) and written many other articles and chapters on these topics. He has also worked as an economist and policy analyst for the U.S. Department of Health and Human Services, and prior to receiving his Ph.D. he was a social worker and caseworker for the Missouri Department of Family Services.

Jennifer M. Wyatt is a doctoral student at the University of Nebraska–Lincoln. Her interests are focused in areas of applied developmental psychology, including divorce, child maltreatment, emotional and behavioral disorders in children, and adolescent risk behaviors.

DATE DUE